The Future of Law Enforcement

Technology, Policy, and Reform

snova
New York

Law, Crime and Law Enforcement Series

Justice-Home Affairs Diplomacy: The Palermo Treaty System in the New Era
Anis H. Bajrektarevic, PhD
Carlos López-Veraza Pérez
ISBN: 979-8-89530-656-7
eBook ISBN: 979-8-89530-809-7

Deviance in Business: Seriousness of Harmful Occupational and Corporate Convenience
Petter Gottschalk
ISBN: 979-8-89530-459-4
eBook ISBN: 979-8-89530-524-9

Hypocrisy in International Criminal Justice
Farhad Malekian
ISBN: 979-8-89530-205-7
eBook ISBN: 979-8-89530-311-5

Critical Women's Issues
Gary I. Lilienthal, PhD
ISBN: 979-8-89530-002-2
eBook ISBN: 979-8-89530-126-5

Evaluating the Use of Force: Policies and Practices in Law Enforcement
Robert J. Welch (Editor)
ISBN: 979-8-89530-731-1
eBook ISBN: 979-8-89530-923-0

Corporate Manslaughter by Unsafe Food: An Australasian Perspective
S. M. Solaiman
ISBN: 979-8-89113-776-9
eBook ISBN: 979-8-89113-851-3

Understanding the Fentanyl Crisis
Michael K. Reyes (Editor)
ISBN: 979-8-89113-830-8
eBook ISBN: 979-8-89113-869-8

Conundrums of Paternalism in International Criminal Justice
Farhad Malekian
ISBN: 979-8-89113-284-9
eBook ISBN: 979-8-89113-743-1

More information about this series can be found at
https://novapublishers.com/product-category/series/law-crime-and-law-enforcement/

Mohamed Swift
Editor

The Future of Law Enforcement

Technology, Policy, and Reform

snova
New York

Library of Congress Cataloging-in-Publication Data

ISBN: 979-8-89530-863-9 (Hardcover)
ISBN: 979-8-89530-964-3 (eBook)

Published by Nova Science Publishers, Inc. † New York

Contents

Preface vii

Chapter 1 **Law Enforcement and Technology: Use of Automated License Plate Readers** 1
Kristin Finklea

Chapter 2 **Law Enforcement and Technology: Use of Unmanned Aircraft Systems** 17
Kristin Finklea

Chapter 3 **Law Enforcement and Technology: Using Social Media** 33
Kristin Finklea

Chapter 4 **Law Enforcement and Technology: The "Lawful Access" Debate** 49
Kristin Finklea

Chapter 5 **Law Enforcement Use of Artificial Intelligence and Directives in the 2023 Executive Order** 55
Kristin Finklea

Chapter 6 **Federal Support for Law Enforcement: Selected Department of Justice Programs** 59
Karma Ester

Chapter 7 **Standing Strong on the Thin Blue Line: How Congress Can Support State and Local Law Enforcement** 81
Committee on Homeland Security

Chapter 8 **The Community Oriented Policing Services (COPS) Program: Potential Issues for Reauthorization** 101
Nathan James

Chapter 9 **Community Oriented Policing Services (COPS) Program** 141
Nathan James

Chapter 10 **Issues in Law Enforcement Reform: Responding to Mental Health Crises** 147
Nathan James, Johnathan H. Duff, Jill C. Gallagher and Isobel Sorenson

Chapter 11 **Congress and Law Enforcement Reform: Constitutional Authority** 195
Whitney K. Novak

Chapter 12 **Congress and Police Reform: Recent Proposals** 201
Joanna R. Lampe

Chapter 13 **Congress and Police Reform: Current Law** 209
Joanna R. Lampe

Chapter 14 **Regulating Federal Law Enforcement: Considerations for Congress** 217
Whitney K. Novak

Index 225

Preface

Law enforcement encompasses agencies and personnel responsible for enforcing laws, maintaining public order, and managing public safety. The primary functions of law enforcement include the investigation, apprehension, and detention of individuals suspected of committing crimes. Some law enforcement agencies, particularly sheriffs' offices, also play an important role in the incarceration of persons convicted of criminal offenses.

Chapters 1–5 explore the integration of technology in law enforcement operations. Chapter 6 provides brief descriptions of Department of Justice grant programs, summary information on eligibility, purpose areas, matching requirements, links to program information, and grant program solicitations. Chapters 7-9 emphasize initiatives supporting community policing efforts nationwide.

Chapter 1

Law Enforcement and Technology: Use of Automated License Plate Readers*

Kristin Finklea

Summary

Over the past couple of decades, law enforcement use of automated license plate readers (ALPRs; also referred to as LPRs) has increased. These tools are now relatively commonplace in policing. According to the Bureau of Justice Statistics' 2020 Law Enforcement Management and Administrative Statistics Survey, larger law enforcement offices were more likely to use ALPR technology than smaller offices; nearly 90% of sheriffs' offices with 500 or more sworn deputies reported using the technology, and of police departments serving over 1 million residents, 100% used ALPRs.

ALPRs are camera systems that capture the license plate data of passing vehicles, along with related information. They are generally available in fixed and mobile formats. Fixed ALPR systems are mounted in specific locations, often using existing infrastructure such as light poles, traffic lights, buildings, or bridges. Mobile ALPR systems are frequently mounted on police vehicles or privately contracted vehicles. ALPRs automatically capture images or videos of passing vehicles. An algorithm then detects the license plates within the photo/video and reads the numbers. (ALPR technology can also detect additional, related information, including vehicle type and color, global positioning system [GPS] location data, and date and time.) After they capture and catalog license plate information, ALPR systems can compare these data against

* This is an edited, reformatted and augmented version of Congressional Research Service Publication No. R48160, dated August 19, 2024.

In: The Future of Law Enforcement
Editor: Mohamed Swift
ISBN: 979-8-89530-863-9

various databases, including what are known as *hot lists*, which contain license plates linked to vehicles of interest. If there is a match to a hot list license plate, the ALPR system can alert a police officer in real time.

Law enforcement agencies may use ALPRs for a variety of proactive and reactive policing purposes, including gathering intelligence and evidence, helping identify potential suspects, and facilitating crime scene analysis. There does not appear to be publicly available data on the frequency and extent to which ALPR technology is used for various purpose areas, and there are no data on its use at various phases of the criminal justice system—from generating investigative leads and helping establish probable cause for an arrest or indictment to serving as evidence in courtrooms.

Generally, federal law does not direct or prohibit specific tools and technologies—such as ALPRs—used by federal law enforcement agencies to aid investigations. However, there are policies that influence their use. For instance, the U.S. Department of Justice (DOJ) provides *Guidance for Federal Law Enforcement Agencies Regarding the Use of Race, Ethnicity, Gender, National Origin, Religion, Sexual Orientation, or Gender Identity*, which specifies what type of information may or may not be used in law enforcement and intelligence activities, even when law enforcement activities involve automated systems or artificial intelligence (AI). As such, while this DOJ guidance isn't specific to use of ALPRs, it broadly applies to law enforcement use of technologies such as ALPRs that may involve AI systems. In addition, the Federal Bureau of Investigation (FBI) maintains a *Criminal Justice Information Services (CJIS) Security Policy*, which provides guidance to all partners who may have access to CJIS information—including license plate data in CJIS.

No specific federal legislative framework exists that governs federal law enforcement use of ALPRs, though there are federal laws and policies broadly governing law enforcement investigations and intelligence gathering. Some observers argue that ALPR use can enhance law enforcement operations—including using them as tools to help locate missing persons or stolen vehicles. Others have raised concerns that law enforcement use of ALPRs could infringe upon individuals' privacy rights if law enforcement agencies' collection and retention of data on vehicle locations are used to track law abiding citizens. Policymakers may debate these trade-offs as they conduct oversight and deliberate on legislation that may influence federal, state, local, and tribal law enforcement use of ALPR technology.

Over the past couple of decades, law enforcement use of automated license plate readers (ALPRs; also referred to as LPRs) has increased.[1] These tools are now relatively commonplace in policing. According to the Bureau of Justice Statistics' (BJS') 2020 Law Enforcement Management and Administrative Statistics Survey, larger law enforcement offices were more likely to use ALPR technology than smaller offices; nearly 90% of sheriffs' offices with 500 or more sworn deputies reported using the technology, and of police departments serving over 1 million residents, 100% used ALPRs.[2] These readers are one of many tools law enforcement agencies have in their toolkits to help investigate crime. Initially, ALPRs were thought of as a tool to help combat automobile theft, but their use has expanded. Agencies use ALPRs for a variety of purposes, including gathering intelligence and evidence, helping identify or apprehend potential suspects in a range of criminal investigations, locating missing or kidnapped individuals, and facilitating crime scene analysis.[3]

Law enforcement use of ALPRs raises a range of questions for policymakers and the public. For instance, some may examine what policies and procedures agencies have in place to govern ALPR use and how police and policymakers conduct oversight for this technology. Some may also question how ALPR use may simultaneously enhance law enforcement agencies' work and potentially infringe upon individuals' privacy and civil liberties. These considerations have reportedly led to some states passing laws governing the use of ALPRs and the retention of data collected by these tools.[4]

---

[1] In the late 1990s, ALPRs were first used by the U.S. Border Patrol, and the technology started to be used more by police departments in the 2000s. See Tom Simonite, "AI License Plate Readers Are Cheaper—So Drive Carefully," *Wired*, January 27, 2020; Keith Gierlack et al., *License Plate Readers for Law Enforcement: Opportunities and Obstacles*, RAND Corporation, 2014; and Cynthia Lum et al., "The Rapid Diffusion of License Plate Readers in US Law Enforcement Agencies," *Policing: An International Journal*, vol. 42, no. 3 (2019). This report uses the acronyms ALPR and LPR interchangeably.

[2] Connor Brooks, *Sheriffs' Offices, Procedures, Policies, and Technology, 2020 – Statistical Tables*, U.S. Department of Justice, Office of Justice Programs, Bureau of Justice Statistics, NCJ307234, November 2023; and Sean E. Goodison, *Local Police Departments, Procedures, Policies, and Technology, 2020 – Statistical Tables,* U.S. Department of Justice, Office of Justice Programs, Bureau of Justice Statistics, NCJ307405, November 2023.

[3] Assistant Police Chief Travis Martinez, *Innovative Uses of Automated License Plate Readers to Enhance Criminal Investigations*, National Police Foundation, National Resource and Technical Assistance Center for Improving Law Enforcement Investigations, June 2019.

[4] National Conference of State Legislatures, *Automated License Plate Readers: State Statutes*, February 3, 2022.

This report focuses on the use of ALPRs specifically for law enforcement purposes. It provides an overview of how they work and federal law enforcement agencies' use of them—with an emphasis on U.S. Department of Justice (DOJ) agencies. The report also presents considerations for policymakers debating whether or how to affect federal, state, local, and tribal law enforcement agencies' use of ALPRs.

ALPRs and How They Work

Automated license plate readers are camera systems that capture the license plate data of passing vehicles, along with related information. They are generally available in fixed and mobile formats. Fixed ALPR systems are mounted in a specific location, often using existing infrastructure such as light poles, traffic lights, buildings, or bridges. Mobile ALPR systems are frequently mounted on police vehicles or can be installed on private vehicles contracted by companies that may share ALPR data with law enforcement.

ALPR systems work by automatically capturing images or videos of passing vehicles. An algorithm then detects the license plates within the photo/video and reads their numbers. ALPR technology can also detect additional, related information, including vehicle type and color, global positioning system (GPS) location data, and date and time. These tools also have the potential to identify individuals in the photos/videos through the use of facial recognition technology (FRT).[5] ALPR systems catalogue and store information, particularly license plate number, GPS data, and date and time. This data retention can help law enforcement track where vehicles have been over time.

After they catalog the license plate information, ALPR systems can compare these data against various databases, including what are known as hot lists, which contain a list of license plates linked to vehicles of interest. If there is a match to a hot list license plate, the ALPR system can alert a law enforcement officer in real time.[6]

---

[5] For information on law enforcement use of facial recognition technology, see CRS Report R46586, *Federal Law Enforcement Use of Facial Recognition Technology*.

[6] Axon Enterprise, Inc., *Second Report of the Axon AI & Policing Technology Ethics Board: Automated License Plate Readers*, October 2019. There are both local and national hot lists. The national list is maintained by the Federal Bureau of Investigation and is discussed elsewhere in this report.

As law enforcement use of ALPRs has become more commonplace, some observers have noted that one factor contributing to this expansion is that the price to use this technology has dropped substantially. And, while acquiring a new ALPR camera system can be costly, evolving technology now allows ALPR software to be used on existing security camera systems— including police vehicle dashboard cameras—for a fraction of the price of acquiring a new ALPR camera system.[7] For example, some estimates put the cost of a new ALPR device at $15,000-$20,000, while software installed on existing cameras to read license plates can reportedly cost as little as $50 per camera.[8]

How LPRs May Be Used by Law Enforcement Agencies

Law enforcement agencies—including federal law enforcement—may use LPRs for a variety of proactive and reactive policing purposes. The International Association of Chiefs of Police (IACP) has identified four broad categories of LPR uses:[9]

- Community caretaking. LPRs may help locate missing individuals, including those who may be kidnapped or otherwise endangered. They may also be used to provide additional context to suspicious or unexplained situations to help determine whether a crime has been committed.
- Investigations. In the course of investigations, LPRs can be used to collect evidence, including evidence that helps identify or apprehend suspects or locate and recover stolen vehicles. Police can also analyze stored LPR data to help identify patterns of suspicious or criminal activity.
- Crime prevention. While it may be difficult to measure when something doesn't happen (i.e., when a crime is prevented), some have noted that the presence of LPRs may deter individuals from engaging in unlawful activity. LPRs may also help provide investigative leads so police can intervene in suspicious situations before criminal or harmful activity occurs.

---

[7] Tom Simonite, "AI License Plate Readers Are Cheaper—So Drive Carefully," Wired, January 27, 2020.

[8] Ibid.

[9] International Association of Chiefs of Police, License Plate Reader (LPR) Systems: Use Cases, 2024.

- Traffic compliance. LPRs may be used in cities' traffic systems that automate toll payment as well as citations or fines for traffic violations and infractions. Some have suggested that the presence of LPRs may help deter certain risky driving behaviors like speeding or violating traffic signals.

U.S. Department of Justice Use of LPRs

LPRs are used by a range of federal law enforcement agencies and their partners. This section highlights law enforcement entities within DOJ that use LPR technology or data, including data collected by their partners. While some information is available on agencies' use of the technology, there do not appear to be publicly available agency documents with comprehensive details on its use. This is not a phenomenon unique to LPRs. Agencies do not necessarily provide public documentation detailing use data for each of the tools they may employ in investigations. This may help protect sensitive law enforcement information and case details. As illustrated in the examples below, while agencies may use LPR technology themselves, they may also rely on LPR data that were collected by other law enforcement and partner entities.

- *Federal Bureau of Investigation (FBI).* FBI press releases indicate that the bureau and its investigative partners have used LPR technology for purposes including to help identify potential suspects in criminal investigations.[10] The FBI also runs an LPR Program—detailed below—that shares LPR information with law enforcement partners.
- *Drug Enforcement Administration (DEA).* The DEA administers a National License Plate Reader Program, to facilitate investigations related to drug trafficking criminal networks. The DEA notes that this program involves a "network of LPR equipment owned by DEA, other federal agencies, and state, local, and tribal police departments. All law enforcement agencies involved have Memorandums of

[10] See, for instance, DOJ, "License Plate Reader Helped Identify Robbery Suspect," press release, October 17, 2018; and FBI, "Alleged Armed Robber of Three Manhattan Banks Arrested and Charged in Manhattan Federal Court," press release, July 14, 2015.

Understanding with DEA detailing the parameters for use and sharing of the LPR information."[11]

- *Bureau of Alcohol, Tobacco, Firearms, and Explosives (ATF).* ATF press releases indicate that the ATF and its investigative partners have relied on LPR technology for facilitating investigations, including to gather information on the location of suspects' vehicles.[12]
- *U.S. Marshals Service.* The USMS has relied on partners' use of LPRs to help locate wanted persons.[13]

DOJ does not appear to publish publicly available data on the frequency and extent to which LPR technology is used for each of the purpose areas described above. Similarly, there are no data on its use at various phases of the criminal justice system—from generating investigative leads and helping establish probable cause for an arrest or indictment, to serving as evidence in courtrooms.

FBI's LPR Program

The FBI runs a License Plate Reader program to facilitate LPR information sharing with and between its law enforcement partners.[14] Specifically, through the National Crime Information Center (NCIC), the FBI maintains a hot list of vehicle data against which law enforcement agencies can compare their LPR data. The NCIC is operated by the FBI's Criminal Justice Information Services (CJIS) Division and serves as a clearinghouse of "records contributed by and accessible to criminal justice agencies nationwide. Its purpose is to enhance officer and public safety, and it has been called the lifeline of law enforcement."[15] The NCIC has 22 broad files, collectively containing over 18

---

[11] DEA, *Privacy Impact Assessment for the National License Plate Reader Program (NLPRP)*, April 19, 2019, p. 2.

[12] See, for instance, DOJ, "Pittsburgh Felon Charged with Possession of a Destructive Device After Throwing a Homemade Explosive from a Moving Vehicle in Pittsburgh's Lawrenceville Neighborhood," press release, January 6, 2021.

[13] Mt. Juliet Police Department, "An Escapee, Wanted by the U.S. Marshals, was Apprehended After Attempted Traffic Stop, License Plate Reader Alerts, and K9 Track," press release, December 20, 2023.

[14] This program was approved by the FBI's Criminal Justice Information Services Advisory Policy Board in 2004. FBI, *License Plate Reader Technology Enhances the Identification, Recovery of Stolen Vehicles*, November 1, 2011.

[15] For more information, see FBI, National Crime Information Center (NCIC), https://le.fbi.gov/informational-tools/ ncic. The FBI notes that authorized users may only

million records. There are 15 persons files and 7 property files. The FBI notes that persons files generally may contain a range of information about individuals, including their associated license plate numbers.[16] Similarly, property files generally may contain a range of information about property, including vehicles and associated license plate numbers.

One of the property files in NCIC is the License Plate File. The FBI notes that

> The License Plate File contains records of stolen license plates. Information in the License Plate File includes the license plate number, the state in which the license plate was issued, the year the license plate was issued, and the type of license plate (e.g., passenger automobile, motorcycle, trailer, truck, aircraft, antique automobile, bus, commercial vehicle, dune buggy, farm vehicle). Only law enforcement/criminal justice agencies can enter records into the License Plate File.[17]

Similarly, another relevant property file in NCIC is the Vehicle File. The FBI notes that

> The Vehicle File contains records of stolen vehicles, vehicles used in the commission of a felony, or vehicles that a law enforcement agency seizes based upon a federally issued court order. Information in the Vehicle File includes the vehicle identification number, vehicle make, vehicle model, vehicle style, vehicle color, vehicle year, owner applied number (if applicable), and license plate number. Only law enforcement/criminal justice agencies can enter records into the Vehicle File.

Authorized criminal justice users may query NCIC with LPR data for authorized purposes, which range from solving crimes, apprehending fugitives, and combating terrorism to locating missing persons and stolen property and enhancing law enforcement officer safety. The NCIC supplies

---

access data in NCIC for specified purposes, which are "apprehending fugitives, solving crimes, combating acts of terrorism, locating missing persons, locating and returning stolen property, protecting individuals during declared emergency situations, protecting victims of domestic violence, monitoring registered sex offenders, performing background checks for firearms, explosives, and weapon-related permits, and enhancing the safety of law enforcement officers"; FBI, Privacy Impact Assessment for the National Crime Information Center, November 7, 2022, p. 17.

[16] FBI, Privacy Impact Assessment for the National Crime Information Center, November 7, 2022.

[17] Ibid., p. 7.

license plate data to authorized criminal justice users for use with LPRs. It extracts these data from various persons and property files; these data are refreshed twice daily and pushed out to authorized law enforcement agencies.[18] LPR systems allow law enforcement users to import data directly from NCIC to establish a hot list.[19] If officers query NCIC data with a license plate number and receive a positive match to their hot list or a record in the system, this match alone is not sufficient for an officer to establish probable cause and make an arrest; they must first confirm the information is accurate and up to date.[20]

ALPR Law and Policy Guidance for Law Enforcement

Generally, federal law does not direct or prohibit specific tools and technologies—such as ALPRs—used by law enforcement agencies to aid investigations. However, there are policies that influence their use.

While DOJ does not appear to have a publicly available policy specifically guiding federal law enforcement use of ALPRs,[21] other DOJ policies affect its use by federal law enforcement agencies. For instance, DOJ's *Guidance for Federal Law Enforcement Agencies Regarding the Use of Race, Ethnicity, Gender, National Origin, Religion, Sexual Orientation, or Gender Identity* specifies that "federal law enforcement personnel may not consider race, ethnicity, gender, national origin, religion, sexual orientation, gender identity, or disability in law enforcement or intelligence activities" with the exception of instances where specific details provide assurance that the information is reliable and linked to a specific "criminal incident, scheme, or organization; a threat to national or homeland security; a violation of Federal immigration or customs law; or an authorized intelligence activity" and that the law

---

[18] FBI, License Plate Reader Technology Enhances the Identification, Recovery of Stolen Vehicles, November 1, 2011.

[19] According to the Major Cities Chiefs Association, this is the most common method of creating hot lists. Major Cities Chiefs Association, *Automated License Plate Reader Technology in Law Enforcement: Recommendations and Considerations*, 2023, https://majorcitieschiefs.com/wp-content/uploads/2023/02/MCCA-Automated-License-Plate- Reader-Technology-in-Law-Enforcement.pdf.

[20] FBI, Privacy Impact Assessment for the National Crime Information Center, November 7, 2022.

[21] The American Civil Liberties Union (ACLU) obtained documents indicating DOJ may have an LPR policy, but if one has been developed, CRS has not been able to obtain a copy. See Bennett Stein, ACLU, Internal Documents Show FBI Was 'Wrestling' With License Plate Scanner Privacy Issues, May 15, 2015.

enforcement activity is merited given the totality of circumstances.[22] These standards apply even when law enforcement activities involve automated systems or artificial intelligence (AI). These automated systems can capture images of individuals—images that may contain information on an individual's race, ethnicity, gender, national origin, religion, sexual orientation, gender identity, or disability. As such, while this DOJ guidance isn't specific to law enforcement use of ALPRs, it broadly applies to law enforcement use of technologies such as ALPRs that may involve AI systems, as ALPRs collect photos that may include, among other things, images of individuals in vehicles. For instance, law enforcement may not use photos captured by an ALPR and decide to take action against an individual based on the race of the driver, unless a situation meets the specified exceptions.

There is also federal guidance that applies broadly to the security of criminal justice information (CJI), including license plate data. For instance, the FBI maintains a *Criminal Justice Information Services (CJIS) Security Policy*, which provides guidance to all partners who may have access to CJIS information, including license plate data in CJIS. While this does not direct policies about the operations of partners' LPR programs, it guides "the creation, viewing, modification, transmission, dissemination, storage, and destruction of CJI" held in CJIS, which would include LPR data.[23]

Additionally, there has been LPR-related research and guidance from DOJ agencies directed toward law enforcement at various levels of the criminal justice system. For example, DOJ's Bureau of Justice Assistance (BJA), in collaboration with the U.S. Department of Homeland Security (DHS), supported the development of a *License Plate Reader Policy Development Template for Use in Intelligence and Investigative Activities*. This guidance notes that while law enforcement and related justice entities are increasingly using LPR technology, "individual privacy, civil rights, and civil liberties must also be vigorously protected."[24] It suggests that developing an LPR policy should be one of many steps taken in establishing an LPR program, and notes that the program should include the following:

---

[22] DOJ, Guidance for Federal Law Enforcement Agencies Regarding the Use of Race, Ethnicity, Gender, National Origin, Religion, Sexual Orientation, or Gender Identity, May 2023.

[23] FBI, Criminal Justice Information Services (CJIS) Security Policy: Version 5.9.4, December 20, 2023, p. i.

[24] DOJ/BJA and DHS, License Plate Reader Policy Development Template for Use in Intelligence and Investigative Activities, February 2017.

- educating and raising awareness on the importance of privacy, civil rights, and civil liberties protections;
- assessing agency privacy, civil rights, and civil liberties risks by evaluating the process of collecting, receiving, accessing, using, disseminating, retaining, and purging LPR information;
- developing an LPR policy on how the agency handles LPR information;
- evaluating whether the LPR policy will address current law, standards, and privacy protection recommendations;
- implementing the LPR policy and training LPR users on the rules and procedures;
- reviewing and updating the LPR policy in response to factors including experience, oversight, law, technology, and public expectations; and
- auditing the processes outlined in the LPR policy.[25]

Policy Considerations Concerning Law Enforcement Use of ALPRs

No specific federal legislative framework exists that governs federal law enforcement use of ALPRs; rather, there are federal laws and policies broadly governing law enforcement investigations and intelligence gathering. Some states have ALPR-specific laws, contributing to a patchwork of laws and polices across the country.[26] Some observers argue that ALPR use can enhance law enforcement operations—including using them as tools to help locate missing persons or stolen vehicles. Others have raised concerns that law enforcement use of ALPRs could infringe upon individuals' privacy rights if, for example, law enforcement agencies' collection and retention of data on vehicle locations are used to track law abiding citizens. Policymakers may debate these trade-offs as they conduct oversight and deliberate on legislation that may influence federal, state, local, and tribal law enforcement use of ALPR technology.

---

[25] Ibid.

[26] National Conference of State Legislatures, *Automated License Plate Readers: State Statutes*, February 3, 2022, https://www.ncsl.org/technology-and-communication/automated-license-plate-readers-state-statutes.

Oversight of LPR Use

If Congress debates law enforcement use of specific technologies such as LPRs, it may consider how any boundaries might apply. For example, while many tools and technologies used by law enforcement agencies to aid investigations have not been specifically permitted or prohibited by law, Congress has legislated on and conducted oversight of certain technologies that could affect individual privacy. With electronic surveillance, for instance, investigators must generally obtain a warrant to conduct wiretaps;[27] however, exceptions exist for emergency situations that may involve death or serious injury, threaten national security, or involve conspiracies of organized crime.[28]

Policymakers may also examine whether federal law enforcement agencies have developed and maintained an LPR program—including an LPR policy—as recommended in the joint DOJ/DHS License Plate Reader Policy Development Template for Use in Intelligence and Investigative Activities. Congress may consider these issues as they conduct oversight of federal law enforcement use of LPRs. They may do this through a variety of mechanisms, including hearings and directives to oversight entities such as the Government Accountability Office (GAO) or various department Inspectors General.

Influencing Law Enforcement Use of LPRs

Policymakers can legislate directly on federal law enforcement agencies' ability to utilize certain technologies such as LPRs, as well as specify under which circumstances federal law enforcement may use these tools. They can also direct federal departments and agencies to develop or rely on established guidelines surrounding the technologies, require them to use technology that meets specified standards, and conduct broad oversight of federal law enforcement agencies' use of technology such as LPRs.

Congress can also influence state, local, and tribal law enforcement agencies' use of LPRs through the provision or withholding of grant funding. Programs such as the Edward Byrne Memorial Justice Assistance Grant (JAG)

---

[27] 18 U.S.C. §§2510 et seq. See also DOJ, *Justice Manual*, Title 9, 9.7000: Electronic Surveillance.

[28] 18 U.S.C. §2518.

program[29] and the Community Oriented Policing Services (COPS) program[30] are regularly used to incentivize certain activities by state and local law enforcement and could similarly be leveraged to support or restrict agencies' use of LPRs. Indeed, both JAG and COPS funds have been used to support law enforcement agencies' LPR programs around the country.[31] If policymakers wanted to provide additional guidance on the use of grant funds, Congress could further specify when, and under what circumstances, grant programs may be used to support law enforcement use of LPRs. And, federal grant administering agencies can require that grantees adhere to certain requirements with respect to LPR use. For instance, DHS requires all fusion centers that are supported under the Homeland Security Grant Program and use LPR data or tools for investigative, analytic, or intelligence purposes to "maintain an approved LPR policy" that adheres to the joint DOJ/DHS *License Plate Reader Policy Development Template for Use in Intelligence and Investigative Activities*.[32] Policymakers may examine whether a similar requirement regarding LPR policies may be appropriate for other federal grantees.

LPR Technology and Police-Community Relations

In the current discourse about police-community relations,[33] there have been questions about whether law enforcement use of LPRs could contribute to tensions between the police and the communities they serve. The joint DOJ/DHS *License Plate Reader Policy Development Template for Use in Intelligence and Investigative Activities* notes that "a comprehensive LPR policy that is developed in a transparent manner and properly enforced fosters

---

[29] For more information, see CRS In Focus IF10691, The Edward Byrne Memorial Justice Assistance Grant (JAG) Program.

[30] For more information, see CRS In Focus IF10922, Community Oriented Policing Services (COPS) Program.

[31] DOJ, BJA, Expansion of Flock Automated License Plate Reader (ALPR) Safety Camera Program, https://bja.ojp.gov/funding/awards/15pbja-23-gg-03112-jagx; DOJ, Office of Community Oriented Policing Services, FY24 COPS Technology and Equipment Program Invitational Solicitation, https://cops.usdoj.gov/pdf/ 2024ProgramDocs/tep/solicitation.pdf.

[32] For more information, see DHS, Homeland Security Grant Program, https://www.dhs.gov/ homeland-security-grant- program-hsgp; see also DOJ/BJA and DHS, License Plate Reader Policy Development Template for Use in Intelligence and Investigative Activities, February 2017.

[33] For more information, see CRS Report R43904, Public Trust and Law Enforcement—A Discussion for Policymakers.

trust—not only within and between justice partners but also by the public, whose LPR information may be collected and utilized."[34] Some local police complaint review boards have also recommended enhanced transparency of information on law enforcement use of LPRs. For instance, in Washington, DC, the Police Complaints Board released a report on LPRs recommending, among other things, that the Metropolitan Police Department be transparent with the public about data collected with LPRs to help improve community relations and enhance public trust.[35] Policymakers could opt to examine not only the availability and transparency of federal law enforcement LPR policies but also those of state, local, and tribal law enforcement who may be recipients of federal grant funding.

LPR Accuracy and Data Security

The accuracy of LPR technology has come under scrutiny, particularly instances wherein individuals have claimed that LPRs—particularly the algorithms that detect license plates within the photo/video and read the numbers from the license plates—have made errors resulting in the wrong vehicle/individual coming under scrutiny of law enforcement. Some observers have noted that while the accuracy of LPR technology has been improving, as of 2019 at least one estimate had put the accuracy of LPRs at around 90%.[36] And, this less than perfect accuracy has led some to question possible implications of law enforcement taking actions based on imperfect technology. For instance, there is a concern that innocent individuals may become, even temporarily, the subject of law enforcement attention or investigation if their license plate matches what is an incorrect or incomplete read by an LPR system.

The security of data collected and held by federal agencies and their contractors—through a variety of technologies, including LPRs—is of ongoing interest to Congress. For instance, in June 2019 U.S. Customs and Border Protection (CBP) revealed that images of faces and license plates were

---

[34] DOJ/BJA and DHS, License Plate Reader Policy Development Template for Use in Intelligence and Investigative Activities, February 2017, p. 2.

[35] District of Columbia, Office of Police Complaints, Police Complaints Board Releases Report on Automated License Plate Readers, September 25, 2020.

[36] Justin Klawans, "The Pros and Cons of License-Plate Reader Technology," The Week, December 17, 2023. This estimate is just that: an estimate provided by an observer, rather than the result of a formal scientific study.

compromised in a cyberattack on one of its subcontractors that provides LPR technology to the agency.[37] This breach reportedly exposed confidential agreements, hardware schematics, and other records related to border security.[38] Breaches like this highlight the vulnerability of data, including LPR data captured and held by governmental agencies. In evaluating the security of federal law enforcement data systems, policymakers may pay particular attention to the security of LPR data and other CJI.

Federal law enforcement agencies are required to provide information to the public on their data collection systems through Privacy Impact Assessments (PIAs) and System of Records Notices (SORNs).[39] Policymakers could question whether these are sufficient measures to notify the public about federal law enforcement agencies use of LPRs to search against databases in which individuals' personal data are held. In addition, they could opt to conduct oversight over the timeliness with which federal law enforcement agencies publish and update relevant PIAs and SORNs.

---

[37] For more information, see CRS Insight IN11143, Exposed Data Highlights Law Enforcement Use of Selected Technologies.

[38] Drew Harwell, "Surveillance Contractor That Violated Rules by Copying Traveler Images, License Plates Can Continue to Work with CBP," Washington Post, October 10, 2019.

[39] This requirement is not specific to federal law enforcement. Federal agencies are subject to requirements under Section 208 of the E-Government Act of 2002 (P.L. 107-347) regarding the protection of personal information collected, maintained, or disseminated using information technology. For more information, see Office of Management and Budget, OMB Guidance for Implementing the Privacy Provisions of the E-Government Act of 2002, M-03-22, September 26, 2003. In this guidance, a PIA is defined as "an analysis of how information is handled: (i) to ensure handling conforms to applicable legal, regulatory, and policy requirements regarding privacy, (ii) to determine the risks and effects of collecting, maintaining and disseminating information in identifiable form in an electronic information system, and (iii) to examine and evaluate protections and alternative processes for handling information to mitigate potential privacy risks." In addition, SORNs are required to be published for any newly created or revised system of records.

Chapter 2

Law Enforcement and Technology: Use of Unmanned Aircraft Systems*

Kristin Finklea

Summary

Alongside growth in the use of unmanned aircraft systems (UAS), commonly referred to as *drones*, for both commercial and recreational purposes, law enforcement agencies' use of this technology has been increasing as well. Drones are one of many technologies that agencies are increasingly employing, and these devices are used for a variety of purposes from gathering intelligence and evidence to providing for remote communication and operational support.

There is no specific legislative framework that governs federal law enforcement use of drones. Generally, federal law does not direct or prohibit specific tools and technologies—such as UAS—used by federal law enforcement agencies to aid investigations. Rather, there are laws and policies broadly governing law enforcement investigations and intelligence gathering. Additionally, there are a number of policies directing the use of drones by federal agencies, including law enforcement, and pertinent guidance resources including the following:

- A 2015 presidential memorandum, Promoting Economic Competitiveness While Safeguarding Privacy, Civil Rights, and Civil Liberties in Domestic Use of Unmanned Aircraft Systems, placed certain requirements on executive departments and agencies—including law enforcement agencies—that use UAS. Its requirements

* This is an edited, reformatted and augmented version of Congressional Research Service Publication No. R47660, dated August 22, 2023.

In: The Future of Law Enforcement
Editor: Mohamed Swift
ISBN: 979-8-89530-863-9

include protecting privacy, civil rights, and civil liberties; ensuring accountability of agencies using UAS; and promoting transparency of UAS programs.

- The Department of Justice (DOJ) maintains the Department of Justice Policy on the Use of Unmanned Aircraft Systems, which guides the department's use of this technology. DOJ also has a UAS Working Group, which is a forum to discuss and coordinate UAS-related matters.
  - DOJ's UAS programs are not centralized at the department level; rather, they are managed by each agency employing a UAS program. DOJ notes that each of its five law enforcement components (Federal Bureau of Investigation; Drug Enforcement Administration; Bureau of Alcohol, Tobacco, Firearms, and Explosives; U.S. Marshals Service; Bureau of Prisons) uses UAS in support of its law enforcement and national security missions.
- The Department of Homeland Security (DHS) does not have a department-wide policy on its agencies' use of UAS, though it has developed Best Practices for Protecting Privacy, Civil Rights & Civil Liberties in Unmanned Aircraft Systems Programs to support its component agencies' and law enforcement partners' use of the technology.
  - Like DOJ, DHS activities involving UAS are managed at the agency level. Both U.S. Customs and Border Protection and U.S. Immigration and Customs Enforcement, Homeland Security Investigation use UAS in support of law enforcement activities.

Some observers have raised concerns that law enforcement use of drones could infringe upon individuals' privacy or could chill free speech—such as in situations where law enforcement may fly drones over First Amendment-protected activities. Others argue that drone use can greatly enhance public safety and national security—including using them as first responders. Policymakers may debate the tradeoffs as they conduct oversight or legislate on law enforcement use of UAS. For example, in conducting oversight of federal law enforcement use of UAS, key considerations policymakers may examine include the extent to which agencies adhere to the 2015 presidential memorandum on UAS or to their department- or agency-specific policy guidance. With respect to legislating on law enforcement use of UAS, while Congress can legislate directly on federal law enforcement agencies' use of the technology, policymakers may seek to influence the use of UAS at the state, local, and tribal law enforcement levels through means such as the provision or withholding of federal grant funding.

Alongside growth in the use of unmanned aircraft systems (UAS), commonly referred to as drones, for both commercial and recreational purposes, law enforcement agencies' use of this technology has been increasing as well.[1] One estimate from 2020 indicates that more than 1,500 state and local public safety agencies (over 70% of which work in law enforcement) had acquired drones at that time—an increase of more than 500 agencies from the estimated number in 2018.[2] Drones are one of many technologies that agencies are increasingly employing, and these devices are used for a variety of purposes, from gathering intelligence and evidence to providing for remote communication and operational support.

The use of drones by law enforcement agencies raises questions across a range of topics. Some observers may question the scope and effectiveness of laws and policies governing law enforcement agencies' use of this technology. Others may examine how drone use may simultaneously enhance law enforcement agencies' work and potentially infringe upon individuals' privacy and civil liberties. Some concerns about drone use have manifested in state-level actions to prohibit or bound law enforcement agencies' use of UAS.[3]

This report focuses on the uses of UAS specifically for law enforcement purposes.[4] It provides an overview of federal law enforcement agencies' policies and use of this technology. It also discusses considerations for policymakers debating whether or how to affect federal, state, and local law enforcement agencies' use of UAS.

---

[1] Federal Aviation Administration (FAA) data on drones registered in the United States are available at https://www.faa.gov/node/54496. This report uses the terms *UAS* and *drone* interchangeably.

[2] Dan Gettinger, *Public Safety Drones, 3rd Edition*, Center for the Study of the Drone at Bard College, March 2020. For the purpose of this study, public safety agencies include law enforcement (police, sheriff's offices, campus police), emergency management, and fire and rescue entities.

[3] For instance, in June 2023 Illinois enacted HB3902, the Drones as First Responders Act, which, among other things, places restrictions on law enforcement agencies' retention of data gathered with drones and on equipping drones with facial recognition technology or weapons. For more information on state laws involving UAS, see National Conference of State Legislatures, *Current Unmanned Aircraft State Law Landscape*, March 27, 2023.

[4] A discussion of additional official uses of UAS, including those by the military, and efforts by law enforcement agencies to counter the unlawful use of UAS is beyond the scope of this report.

Conceptualizing Unmanned Aircraft Systems[5]

An unmanned aircraft is defined in U.S. Code as an aircraft that is operated without the possibility of direct human intervention from within or on the aircraft.[6] An unmanned aircraft system (UAS), or drone, generally refers to the entire drone system, including both the unmanned aircraft and ground control unit.[7] As such, an unmanned aircraft is generally considered a subpart of a UAS rather than a synonym because it only refers to the aircraft, not the entire system.

How UAS May Be Used by Federal Law Enforcement Agencies

Law enforcement agencies—including federal law enforcement—may use UAS for a variety of purposes.[8] For instance, they may use drones to gather intelligence prior to conducting an operation. This can reportedly help with identifying where a suspect may be hiding or with visualizing the layout of a building before officers enter. Drones can also be used to support an operation that is underway; for example, by live streaming an operation to monitor where a suspect exited a building or to illuminate where a suspect might have discarded evidence when officers cannot see all the possibilities from the ground. Drones can also be used to collect photo evidence in instances where access may be hindered or dangerous. They can aid in reconstructing certain scenes such as those involving traffic accidents, fires or explosives, or crime scenes where an aerial view can provide an additional perspective. Drones can

---

[5] For an overview of UAS, see CRS Report R44352, Unmanned Aircraft Operations in Domestic Airspace: U.S. Policy Perspectives and the Regulatory Landscape.

[6] 49 U.S.C. §44801(11).

[7] 49 U.S.C. §44801(12). See also Department of Justice (DOJ), Community Oriented Policing Services (COPS) and Police Executive Research Forum (PERF), Drones: A Report on the Use of Drones by Public Safety Agencies—and a Wake-Up Call about the Threat of Malicious Drone Attacks, 2020, https://portal.cops.usdoj.gov/resourcecenter/RIC/Publications/cops-w0894-pub.pdf. At times, other terms such as small unmanned aircraft system (sUAS) or unmanned aerial vehicle (UAV) have been used to refer to UAS.

[8] The uses of drones discussed in this section are outlined in sources including Charles Werner, "11 Ways Police Departments Are Using Drones," Police1, January 7, 2023; DOJ, COPS and PERF, Drones: A Report on the Use of Drones by Public Safety Agencies—and a Wake-Up Call about the Threat of Malicious Drone Attacks, 2020, https://portal.cops.usdoj.gov/resourcecenter/RIC/Publications/cops-w0894-pub.pdf; and DOJ, Department of Justice Summary of Unmanned Aircraft Systems (UAS) Operations During Fiscal Year 2022, December 1, 2022.

serve as a force multiplier by helping officers search for suspects or missing persons, because UAS can survey more ground at a faster pace than officers.

Some observers note that drones can help enhance officer safety in a number of ways, such as by providing visuals on dangerous suspects or collecting evidence from hazardous crime scenes (e.g., those involving explosives). They can also provide for remote communication—such as with a hidden suspect or one who has taken hostages—and distance may provide a valuable safety buffer to officers, potential victims, and others nearby.

Generally, federal law does not direct or prohibit specific tools and technologies—such as UAS— used by law enforcement agencies to aid investigations. However, there are a number of policies that govern their use, as discussed below.

Federal Aviation Administration (FAA) Policies on Law Enforcement Drone Use

The FAA offers law enforcement agencies two options for operating UAS under 55 pounds:

- Operating under the small UAS rule. This rule, also called the Part 107 rule (named after 14 C.F.R. part 107) allows entities, including law enforcement agencies, to operate UAS at or below 400 feet above ground level in operations that have "visual line of sight" of the aircraft.[9]
- Receiving a certificate of authorization (COA) to function as a public aircraft operator.[10] Law enforcement agencies that receive the COA are able to self-certify drone pilots to carry out official law enforcement operations.

The FAA can also issue emergency authorizations to entities operating under the Part 107 rule or with a COA, allowing them to carry out specified law enforcement operations under certain conditions.[11] An emergency authorization can include a tactical beyond visual line of sight waiver; while drone operators are normally required to have a visual line

[9] 14 C.F.R. §107.

[10] 49 U.S.C. §§40102(a) and 40125.

[11] FAA, *Unmanned Aircraft Systems (UAS), Advanced Operations, Emergency Situations*, https://www.faa.gov/uas/ advanced_operations/emergency_situations.

of sight of the aircraft, the FAA can grant an authority for law enforcement officers to operate outside of these parameters in emergency situations.[12]

Presidential Memorandum on UAS

A 2015 presidential memorandum, Promoting Economic Competitiveness While Safeguarding Privacy, Civil Rights, and Civil Liberties in Domestic Use of Unmanned Aircraft Systems (hereinafter, "2015 presidential memorandum on UAS"), placed certain requirements on executive branch departments and agencies that use UAS. It notes that "as with information collected by the Federal Government using any technology, where UAS is the platform for collection, information must be collected, used, retained, and disseminated consistent with the Constitution, Federal law, and other applicable regulations and policies."[13] While this directive is not specific to federal law enforcement, it encompasses federal law enforcement agencies using UAS. The directives in the memorandum include the following:[14]

- *Protecting privacy.* Before deploying new UAS technology, and every three years thereafter, agencies shall examine their policies and procedures with respect to the collection, use, retention, and dissemination of information obtained from UAS to ensure the protection of privacy, civil rights, and civil liberties.
- *Protecting civil rights and civil liberties.* Agencies shall ensure UAS activities are conducted in accordance with the Constitution, applicable laws, executive orders, and presidential directives, and that there are processes in place to address complaints with respect to privacy, civil rights, and civil liberties. Agencies shall ensure their data collection using UAS technology does not violate the First Amendment or antidiscrimination laws.

---

[12] FAA, *First Responder Tactical Beyond Visual Line of Sight (TBVLOS) 91.113 Waiver Guide*, https://www.faa.gov/ sites/faa.gov/files/uas/public_safety_gov/public_safety_toolkit/TBVLOS_Waiver_Final.pdf.

[13] The White House, *Promoting Economic Competitiveness While Safeguarding Privacy, Civil Rights, and Civil Liberties in Domestic Use of Unmanned Aircraft Systems*, presidential memorandum, February 15, 2015.

[14] Ibid.

- *Ensuring accountability.* Agencies shall have UAS oversight policies and procedures consistent with agency policies and regulations. They shall have rules of conduct and training for individuals working on UAS programs and have policies for oversight of individuals with access to sensitive information collected with UAS. They shall also confirm that UAS data sharing policies conform to laws, policies, and regulations. Agencies shall ensure they have policies to authorize UAS use in response to support requests from federal, state, local, tribal, or territorial government operations. They shall also ensure that any recipients of grant funding to purchase or use UAS have policies to safeguard privacy, civil rights, and civil liberties.
- *Promoting transparency.* Without compromising law enforcement or national security, agencies shall provide public notice about the location of their authorized UAS operations; provide public information about their UAS operations and how they are safeguarding privacy, civil rights, and civil liberties; and provide an annual summary report of their UAS operations, including information on UAS mission types and assistance provided to other agencies or federal, state, local, tribal, or territorial governments.

Selected Federal Law Enforcement Policies on Using UAS

Federal law enforcement agencies across a number of departments may rely on UAS technology to aid in carrying out their law enforcement duties. This section provides examples from the Department of Justice (DOJ) and Department of Homeland Security (DHS) of policies directing law enforcement use of UAS. These examples highlight the scope of existing policies that guide law enforcement activities involving drones.

Department of Justice (DOJ) Use of UAS

A number of DOJ's components (Federal Bureau of Investigation [FBI]; Drug Enforcement Administration [DEA]; Bureau of Alcohol, Tobacco, Firearms, and Explosives [ATF]; U.S. Marshals Service [USMS]; and Bureau of Prisons [BOP]) use UAS in support of its law enforcement and national security missions.[15] DOJ issued the Department of Justice Policy on the Use of

---

[15] DOJ, Department of Justice Summary of Unmanned Aircraft Systems (UAS) Operations During Fiscal Year 2022, December 1, 2022.

Unmanned Aircraft Systems, which guides the department's use of this technology.[16] The policy requires DOJ components to adhere to certain requirements when using UAS, including the following:

- *Legal compliance.* DOJ use of UAS must comply with constitutional provisions and federal law and regulations, including antidiscrimination laws and policies.
- *Scope.* UAS may only be used in connection with "properly authorized investigations and activities," which are defined by statutory authorities; rules and regulations; and Attorney General Guidelines, policies, and guidance.
- *Approval.* DOJ components must ensure UAS operations are approved at an "appropriate level," based on particular operational and tactical needs of that component, and these approval levels must in turn be approved by the Deputy Attorney General.
- *Airspace access.* UAS operations must comply with FAA regulations, and DOJ components must work with the FAA to develop plans to provide necessary support for air traffic and airspace management.
- *Training.* The Deputy Attorney General is responsible for approving minimum UAS training standards, including relevant legal and policy requirements, and DOJ components may implement additional requirements tailored to their needs. DOJ employees operating UAS must be certified as having completed the training requirements.
- *Reporting.* The Deputy Attorney General is responsible for issuing requirements for department components to track and report information on UAS operations, including operations in which DOJ components are providing UAS support to other federal, state, local, tribal, or territorial agencies as well as operations in which DOJ components receive such support from other agencies. Annual minimum reporting requirements include descriptions of mission categories involving UAS, data on component support provided to or received from other agencies (and information on its purpose), and the privacy review conducted for the components' UAS activities.
- *Stakeholder engagement.* DOJ components may engage with stakeholders, including law enforcement and other community

[16] DOJ, *Justice Manual, Title 9: Criminal, 9-95.100 Department of Justice Policy on the Use of Unmanned Aircraft Systems,* https://www.justice.gov/jm/9-95000-unmanned-aircraft-systems-uas. DOJ notes that this 2019 policy supersedes earlier guidance issued in 2015.

stakeholders, and in doing so must ensure the protection of law enforcement, national security, and other protected information.

- *Privacy and civil liberties protections.* DOJ components are responsible for assessing potential intrusiveness and effects on privacy and civil liberties before determining whether or how to use cameras and other sensors associated with UAS. Privacy officials are responsible for making these assessments prior to their use. Components are also responsible for addressing privacy and civil liberties omplaints.
- *Data retention.* Information collected using UAS that may contain personally identifiable information may not be retained for longer than 180 days unless it is necessary for an authorized purpose or is maintained in a system of records pursuant to the Privacy Act.[17] Any retained data must be protected in compliance with federal laws, regulations, and policies.
- *Procurement.* Any procurement of information technology associated with UAS constituent parts must comply with relevant laws, policies, and regulations. Additionally, department components providing grants to state, local, tribal, or territorial agencies to purchase or use UAS must verify that grant recipients have procedures in place to safeguard privacy and civil liberties and mitigate cybersecurity risks.
- *Implementation.* DOJ components seeking to use UAS must implement DOJ's standards and requirements with respect to the technology and must issue component-specific UAS policies consistent with the Department of Justice Policy on the Use of Unmanned Aircraft Systems.

This policy only applies to DOJ components and not other federal, state, local, tribal, or territorial law enforcement agencies that may be using drones. However, if DOJ components are working with other agencies on joint investigations or task forces, the DOJ components—and possibly by extension, their partners—would need to adhere to the DOJ policies.

[17] For more information, see U.S. General Services Administration, *Systems of Records – Privacy Act*, https://www.gsa.gov/reference/gsa-privacy-program/systems-of-records-privacy-act.

UAS Working Group

DOJ has a UAS Working Group,[18] which is a forum to discuss and coordinate UAS-related matters. It is chaired by the Office of Legal Policy (OLP). OLP consults with the working group on a number of activities, including advising the Deputy Attorney General on UAS training standards, UAS tracking and reporting requirements, and recommended changes or improvements to the department's UAS policy. In supporting DOJ's UAS policy, OLP also reviews DOJ components' proposals with respect to the approval level at which UAS operations are approved within a component as well as components' implementation of DOJ's UAS policy. Further, OLP supports DOJ annual reporting on UAS operations as well as reporting on UAS procurement and training. It also shares best practices on UAS use across the department and with law enforcement partners.

DOJ UAS Activities

DOJ's UAS programs are not centralized at the department level; rather, they are managed by each component employing a UAS program. For instance, the FBI's UAS program is managed by its Critical Incident Response Group, which is responsible for, among other things, managing the FBI's mobile and aviation surveillance programs (which encompasses its UAS program).[19]

DOJ publishes an annual report on its UAS activities that outlines how it complies with the requirements of the 2015 presidential memorandum on UAS.[20] In its most recent report, on FY2022 UAS activities, DOJ notes that five components (FBI, DEA, ATF, USMS, and BOP) use UAS to carry out their law enforcement and national security missions. Specifically, in FY2022 these agencies conducted 1,447 *UAS deployments*[21] for purposes including

---

[18] This working group "includes representatives from the Federal Bureau of Investigation, the Drug Enforcement Administration, the United States Marshals Service, the Bureau of Alcohol, Tobacco, Firearms and Explosives, the Bureau of Prisons, the Office of the Deputy Attorney General, the Office of Legal Policy, the National Security Division, the Criminal Division, the Executive Office for United States Attorneys, the Office of Justice Programs, the Office of Community Oriented Policing, the Office of Privacy and Civil Liberties, the Office of the Chief Information Officer, and the Office of Legislative Affairs." See DOJ, *Justice Manual, Title 9: Criminal, 9-95.100 Department of Justice Policy on the Use of Unmanned Aircraft Systems*, https://www.justice.gov/jm/9-95000-unmanned-aircraft-systems-uas.

[19] DOJ, FBI, FY20204 President's Budget Request, February 2023.

[20] Annual reports are available at https://www.justice.gov/olp/unmanned-aircraft-systems.

[21] DOJ notes that these deployments refer to the sending and/or tasking of a UAS and one or more operators in support of an official duty and that any given deployment might involve more than one UAS flight, often due to UAS battery life.

"fire and explosive scene investigation; pre-warrant surveillance; photography; officer safety; execution of search warrants; communications tower inspections; criminal investigations; counterterrorism; counterintelligence; counter weapons of mass destruction; fugitive apprehension; and judicial security."[22]

Department of Homeland Security (DHS) Use of UAS

Like DOJ, DHS activities involving UAS are managed at the agency level rather than being centralized at the department level. DHS does not have a department-wide policy on law enforcement use of UAS, though it has developed best practices for protecting privacy, civil rights, and civil liberties in UAS programs.[23] These best practices were developed by the DHS Unmanned Aircraft Systems Privacy, Civil Rights and Civil Liberties Working Group to inform DHS and its federal, state, and local government partners and grantees about UAS program policies respecting privacy, civil rights, and civil liberties.[24] And, like other executive branch components, DHS is subject to the directives outlined in the 2015 presidential memorandum on UAS.

DHS UAS Activities

U.S. Immigration and Customs Enforcement (ICE) Homeland Security Investigations (HSI) uses Small Unmanned Aircraft Systems, or small drones, among its suite of surveillance technologies to support its investigations.[25] DHS notes that it complies with FAA regulations that apply to commercial and recreational small UAS users. DHS further notes that any video recordings collected through the use of its small drones are to be used only for official purposes in compliance with Homeland Security Investigations Directive 19-01, and not in violation of the First Amendment or in a manner that targets individuals based on race, color, religion, sex, sexual orientation, gender

---

[22] DOJ, Department of Justice Summary of Unmanned Aircraft Systems (UAS) Operations During Fiscal Year 2022, December 1, 2022.

[23] DHS, Best Practices for Protecting Privacy, Civil Rights & Civil Liberties in Unmanned Aircraft Systems Programs, December 18, 2015. These best practices are consistent with the 2015 presidential memorandum on UAS.

[24] Ibid.

[25] Other surveillance technologies include body wires, location tracking technologies, cell-site simulators, license plate readers, and video surveillance technology. See DHS, Privacy Impact Assessment for the Homeland Security Investigation (HSI) Surveillance Technologies, January 24, 2022.

identity, or national origin.[26] Any use of video recordings collected by these small drones must also be approved by an HSI supervisor in coordination with ICE counsel.[27]

U.S. Customs and Border Protection (CBP) uses a variety of aircraft, including small and large UAS, for border surveillance and law enforcement purposes. CBP notes that they may be equipped with video, radar, and sensor technologies.[28] Specifically, when CBP uses UAS for law enforcement purposes, they support operations conducted by other DHS components such as ICE and other federal law enforcement agencies such as the FBI or DEA. In these cases, requests for UAS support are reviewed by "the respective [U.S. Border Patrol] sector Chief Patrol Agent responsible for the geographic area in which operations are to be conducted for authorization."[29]

Policy Considerations Surrounding Law Enforcement Use of UAS

There is no specific federal legislative framework that governs federal law enforcement use of drones. Rather, there are laws and policies broadly governing law enforcement investigations and intelligence gathering; and, there are laws and policies broadly governing drone operations. In addition, there are policies, but not laws, governing the specific use of drones by federal law enforcement.

Some observers argue that drone use can greatly enhance public safety and national security— including using them as first responders.[30] Others have raised concerns that law enforcement use of drones could infringe upon individuals' privacy or could chill free speech—such as in situations where law enforcement flies drones over First Amendment-protected activities.[31] Policymakers may debate the tradeoffs. If Congress debates law enforcement

---

[26] Homeland Security Investigations Directive 19-01, Use of Small Unmanned Aircraft Systems, issued April 3, 2019, outlines ICE HSI policies and procedures for the use and operation of UAS.

[27] DHS, Privacy Impact Assessment for the Homeland Security Investigation (HSI) Surveillance Technologies, January 24, 2022.

[28] DHS, Privacy Impact Assessment Update for the Aircraft Systems, April 6, 2018.

[29] Ibid. Similarly, state and local law enforcement may also request UAS support from CBP.

[30] Wayne Parham, "10 Tips for Starting a Drone as First Responder Program," Police Magazine, March 17, 2023.

[31] Matthew Guariglia, How are Police Using Drones?, Electronic Frontier Foundation, January 6, 2022.

use of specific technologies such as UAS, it may consider how any boundaries might apply. For example, while many tools and technologies used by law enforcement agencies to aid investigations have not been specifically permitted or prohibited by law, Congress has legislated on and conducted oversight of certain technologies that could affect individual privacy. With electronic surveillance, for instance, investigators must generally obtain a warrant to conduct wiretaps;[32] however, exceptions exist for emergency situations that may involve death or serious injury, threaten national security, or involve conspiracies of organized crime.[33] Policymakers may consider these issues as they conduct oversight or debate legislation on law enforcement use of drones.

Oversight of Law Enforcement Use of Drones

Congress could consider oversight of federal law enforcement use of UAS through a variety of mechanisms, including hearings and directives to oversight entities such as the Government Accountability Office (GAO) or various department and agency Inspectors General. Among the issues that could receive attention, policymakers might opt to examine agency adherence to the 2015 presidential memorandum on UAS or to their department or agency-specific policy guidance, such as the Department of Justice Policy on the Use of Unmanned Aircraft Systems.[34]

Policymakers might also opt to explore how law enforcement use of drones intersects with other technologies, such as facial recognition technology (FRT). Questions have been raised about the extent to which drones may be able to support FRT systems onboard as well as which videos and images captured by UAS may be used in law enforcement agencies' FRT programs.[35] Some of the concerns raised about law enforcement use of drones,

---

[32] 18 U.S.C. §2510, et seq. See also Department of Justice, Justice Manual, Title 9, 9.7000: Electronic Surveillance.

[33] 18 U.S.C. §2518.

[34] Some entities have conducted oversight at various points. For instance, DOJ's Office of the Inspector General (OIG) issued a 2015 *Audit of the Department of Justice's Use and Support of Unmanned Aircraft Systems*, available at https://oig.justice.gov/reports/2015/a1511.pdf. Since then, DOJ has developed the *Department of Justice Policy on the Use of Unmanned Aircraft Systems*, which provides for guidelines and record-keeping requirements that did not exist when the DOJ OIG issued its 2015 report.

[35] Drew Harwell, "FBI, Pentagon Helped Research Facial Recognition for Street Cameras, Drones," *Washington Post*, March 7, 2023.

including privacy risks, have also been raised about law enforcement use of other technologies such as FRT.[36] Some jurisdictions have responded to these concerns by placing restrictions on drones being equipped with FRT.[37]

Influencing Law Enforcement Use of Drones

Policymakers can legislate directly on federal law enforcement agencies' ability to utilize certain technologies such as drones, as well as specify under which circumstances federal law enforcement may use these tools. They can also direct federal departments and agencies to develop or rely on established guidelines surrounding the technologies, require them to use technology that meets specified standards, and conduct broad oversight of law enforcement agencies' use of UAS.

Congress can also influence state, local, and tribal law enforcement agencies' use of UAS technologies through the provision or withholding of grant funding. Programs such as the Edward Byrne Memorial Justice Assistance Grant (JAG) program[38] and the Community Oriented Policing Services (COPS) program[39] have been used to incentivize certain activities by state and local law enforcement and could similarly be leveraged to support or restrict agencies' use of UAS. Congress could also further specify when, and under what circumstances, grant programs may be used to support law enforcement use of UAS. However, even when supporting a drone program may be considered as generally falling under the umbrella of a statutorily allowable use of funds, federal agencies may prohibit the use of funds for UAS in some cases. For instance, DOJ's Bureau of Justice Assistance (BJA)—which administers the JAG program (a program which allows grant recipients to use funds for equipment and supplies, among other purpose areas)—notes that currently, "the use of BJA grant funds for unmanned aircraft systems

---

[36] A discussion of other technologies used by law enforcement is outside the scope of this report. For information on law enforcement use of FRT, see CRS Report R46586, *Federal Law Enforcement Use of Facial Recognition Technology*.

[37] For instance, in June 2023 Illinois enacted HB3902, the Drones as First Responders Act, which, among other things, places restrictions on law enforcement agencies equipping drones with FRT. It is permissible in certain situations involving a credible terrorist threat, imminent harm to life, or imminent escape of a suspect or destruction of evidence.

[38] For more information, see CRS In Focus IF10691, *The Edward Byrne Memorial Justice Assistance Grant (JAG) Program*.

[39] For more information, see CRS In Focus IF10922, *Community Oriented Policing Services (COPS) Program*.

(UAS), including unmanned aircraft vehicles (UAV), and all accompanying accessories to support UAS or UAV is unallowable."[40]

In addition to providing grants for state and local law enforcement use of UAS, grantmaking entities have provided guidance to agencies implementing these programs. For instance, DOJ's COPS Office, along with the Police Executive Research Forum and the UAS Working Group, developed a roadmap for state, local, tribal, and territorial law enforcement implementing an effective UAS program, as well as strategies for these agencies on community engagement and education on their UAS programs. Among other things, they recommend strategies for the planning, implementation, and operational phases to address concerns about privacy and the purpose and details of drone use.[41] Policymakers could consider the federal role in providing guidance to state and local entities, and whether any adjustments are warranted.

[40] DOJ, BJA, *Funding & Awards*, https://bja.ojp.gov/funding.

[41] Community Oriented Policing Services and Police Executive Research Forum, *Community Engagement Strategies for State, Local, Tribal, and Territorial Law Enforcement Unmanned Aircraft System Programs*, 2022.

Chapter 3

Law Enforcement and Technology: Using Social Media*

Kristin Finklea

Summary

As the ways in which individuals interact continue to evolve, social media has had an increasing role in facilitating communication and the sharing of content online—including moderated and unmoderated, user-generated content. Over 70% of U.S. adults are estimated to have used social media in 2021. Law enforcement has also turned to social media to help in its operations.

Broadly, law enforcement relies on social media as a tool for information sharing as well as for gathering information to assist in investigations.

Social Media as a Communications Tool. Social media is one of many tools law enforcement can use to connect with the community. They may use it, for instance, to push out bulletins on wanted persons and establish tip lines to crowdsource potential investigative leads. It provides degrees of speed and reach unmatched by many other forms of communication law enforcement can use to connect with the public. Officials and researchers have highlighted social media as a tool that, if used properly, can enhance community policing.

Social Media and Investigations. Social media is one tool in agencies' investigative toolkits to help establish investigative leads and assemble evidence on potential suspects. There are no federal laws that *specifically* govern law enforcement agencies' use of information obtained from social media sites, but their ability to obtain or use certain information

* This is an edited, reformatted and augmented version of Congressional Research Service Publication No. R47008, dated January 11, 2022.

In: The Future of Law Enforcement
Editor: Mohamed Swift
ISBN: 979-8-89530-863-9

may be influenced by social media companies' policies as well as law enforcement agencies' own social media policies and the rules of criminal procedure. When individuals post content on social media platforms without audience restrictions, anyone— including law enforcement—can access this content without court authorization. However, some information that individuals post on social media may be restricted—by user choice or platform policies—in the scope of audience that may access it. In the instances where law enforcement does not have public access to information, they may rely on a number of tools and techniques, such as informants or undercover operations, to gain access to it. Law enforcement may also require social media platforms to provide access to certain restricted information through a warrant, subpoena, or other court order.

Social Media and Intelligence Gathering. The use of social media to gather intelligence has generated particular interest from policymakers, analysts, and the public. Social media companies have weighed in on the issue of social media monitoring by law enforcement, and some platforms have modified their policies to expressly prohibit their user data from being used by law enforcement to monitor social media. Law enforcement agencies themselves have reportedly grappled with the extent to which they should gather and rely on information and intelligence gleaned from social media. For instance, some observers have suggested that agencies may be reluctant to regularly analyze public social media posts because that could be viewed as spying on the American public and could subsequently chill free speech protected under the First Amendment.

At the federal level, there is no specific legislative framework that governs law enforcement use of social media. Rather, there are laws and policies governing law enforcement investigations and intelligence gathering broadly. Some observers, however, have questioned whether the nature of social media may place it in a qualitatively different category than law enforcement's use of other investigative tools and have suggested that there should be enhanced boundaries with respect to law enforcement operations in these online spaces. For instance, some have suggested that law enforcement agencies should have written, publicly available policies on their use of social media; they should obtain local government approval before using these online spaces; they should obtain judicial approval for conducting undercover operations using social media; there should be restrictions on law enforcement contacting minors via social media; and law enforcement's use of social media should be audited. Policymakers may consider these issues as they conduct oversight or debate legislation on law enforcement use of social media.

As the ways in which individuals interact continue to evolve, social media[1] has had an increasing role in facilitating communication and the sharing of content online—including moderated and unmoderated, user-generated content. Law enforcement has also turned to social media to help in its operations. Broadly, law enforcement relies on social media as a tool for information sharing as well as for gathering information to assist in investigations.

Over 70% of U.S. adults are estimated to have used social media in 2021, a substantial increase over the 5% of adults who were believed to use some form of social media in 2005.[2] Similarly, according to a 2016 survey of law enforcement agencies by the Urban Institute (Urban) and the International Association of Chiefs of Police (IACP) on their use of social media, it "is becoming an increasingly popular tool that law enforcement agencies use."[3] Law enforcement agencies use this tool for purposes including engaging with the public and gathering evidence pursuant to investigations. In the Urban and IACP survey, respondents indicated that they use social media for a variety of purposes, the most common being to notify the community of public safety concerns (91%). They also reported using social media for community outreach and citizen engagement (89%), public relations and notifying the community of noncrime issues (86%), soliciting crime tips (76%), monitoring public sentiment (72%), intelligence gathering for investigations (70%), and recruitment and applicant vetting (58%).[4] In addition, 60% of agency respondents indicated that they had reached out to a social media company to request information to use as evidence.[5]

---

[1] For purposes of this report, social media is conceptualized as an internet-based platform that allows users to create individual and group profiles, generate content, and connect with other individuals and groups. These platforms include Facebook, YouTube, Instagram, Twitter, Pinterest, LinkedIn, Snapchat, WhatsApp, TikTok, Reddit, Nextdoor, and Parler among others. For more information on conceptualizing social media, see Jonathan Obar and Steve Wildman, "Social Media Definition and the Governance Challenge: An Introduction to the Special Issue," *Telecommunications Policy*, vol. 39, no. 9 (2015), pp. 745-750.

[2] Pew Research Center, *Social Media Fact Sheet*, April 7, 2021. The most widely used platforms are YouTube (81% of adults report having ever used) and Facebook (69%). Pew began its survey on this topic in 2005.

[3] Urban Institute and International Association of Chiefs of Police, *2016 Law Enforcement Use of Social Media Survey*, February 2017, p. 13.

[4] Ibid., p. 3. A total of 539 law enforcement agencies across the country participated in the survey.

[5] Ibid., pp. 4-5. An additional 9% indicated that they were uncertain whether or not their agency had reached out to a social media company to request evidence.

There has been increased attention—particularly following high-profile incidents such as the January 6, 2021, attack on the U.S. Capitol[6]—on how law enforcement might access and use certain information shared on social media platforms to help prevent and investigate criminal activity. This report provides an overview of how law enforcement may leverage social media to communicate with the public and to aid in gathering information and evidence as part of its investigative duties. It also discusses information sharing between social media companies and law enforcement and raises issues that policymakers may consider as they examine the broader issue of how law enforcement may use social media.[7]

Social Media as a Law Enforcement Communication Tool

Social media is one of many tools law enforcement can use to connect with the community. Law enforcement agencies, even without the use of social media, engage with the public to share and request information via newspaper, radio, television, and other media; push out bulletins on wanted persons; and establish tip lines to crowdsource potential investigative leads. However, social media provides degrees of speed and reach unmatched by many other forms of communication law enforcement uses to connect with the community.

Officials and researchers have highlighted social media as a tool that law enforcement agencies can use to improve public relations and enhance community policing.[8] For instance, the President's Task Force on 21st Century Policing—a Department of Justice (DOJ) task force established to identify best practices and offer recommendations on how law enforcement agencies can both promote crime reduction and build public trust—specifically cited technology and social media as tools that law enforcement agencies can

---

6 Some planning of the incident reportedly occurred with the aid of social media. In addition, some participants and witnesses reportedly shared information on social media during and after the incident.

7 For more information about social media, including issues involving misinformation and content moderation, see CRS Report R46662, *Social Media: Misinformation and Content Moderation Issues for Congress*.

8 For more information on community policing, see CRS Report R43904, *Public Trust and Law Enforcement—A Discussion for Policymakers*. There are different conceptualizations of community policing, but there are common elements of what many argue may constitute it. These include emphasizing partnerships, promoting citizen input, focusing on prevention and problem solving, rethinking officer assignments and organizational structures, fostering positive interactions, and sharing information.

leverage to build community engagement and trust.[9] The task force, in its 2015 report, noted that information shared on social media must be current and accurate so as not to harm trust and legitimacy.

Many observers have pointed to the Boston Police Department's use of Twitter during its evolving investigation of the Boston Marathon bombing in April 2013 as a social media use success story; reportedly, the Boston Police

> used Twitter to keep the public informed about the status of the investigation, to calm nerves and request assistance, to correct mistaken information reported by the press, and to ask for public restraint in the tweeting of information from police scanners. This demonstrated the level of trust and interaction that a department and a community can attain online.[10]

Federal law enforcement agencies have turned to a variety of social media platforms, including Facebook, Instagram, Twitter, YouTube, LinkedIn, and others to share information.[11] Some departments and agencies have designed policies specifically governing the use of social media to communicate with the public.[12]

Social Media and Investigations

Just as social media is one of many communication platforms used by law enforcement, it is also one tool among many others in agencies' investigative toolkits. There are a variety of means to help establish investigative leads and assemble evidence on potential suspects—including gathering information from social media sites. There are no federal laws that specifically govern law enforcement agencies' use of information obtained from social media sites,

---

[9] President's Task Force on 21st Century Policing, Final Report of the President's Task Force on 21st Century Policing, May 2015.

[10] Ibid., p. 33. See also Edward F. Davis III, Alejandro A. Alves, and David Alan Sklansky, "Social Media and Police Leadership: Lessons from Boston," New Perspectives in Policing (Washington, DC: National Institute of Justice, March 2014).

[11] For a directory of social media accounts of the component agencies of the Department of Justice, see https://www.justice.gov/social.

[12] See, for example, Department of Justice, *DOJ Policy Statement: Use of Social Media to Communicate with the Public*, January 10, 2018. DOJ has also developed a Privacy Impact Assessment for its use of social media; see Department of Justice, *Adapted Privacy Impact Assessment for Use of Third-Party Social Media Tools to Communicate with the Public*, July 25, 2017.

but their ability to obtain or use certain information may be influenced by social media companies' policies as well as law enforcement agencies' own social media policies and the rules of criminal procedure.[13]

The landscape of content available on social media platforms is broad, with users creating and sharing text, photos, and videos. Some platforms also have internal messaging services where users can communicate directly with other users of the platform.[14] Access to this social media content is influenced by factors including social media platform policies and user controls. Some content is available to a broad audience without restriction; other content contains access boundaries. Individuals generally have some control over the intended audience with whom they share content. Facebook users, for instance, can elect to share content publicly, with only Facebook contacts/friends (or some subset of friends), with Facebook friends and their friends, with a specific Facebook group, or may post information privately that no one else sees. And, depending on settings, consumers of social media content may be able to, in turn, share or re-share a friend's/contact's content, thus potentially expanding the audience of this content beyond what may have been initially intended by the individual who created or first shared it.

Accessing Public Information

When individuals post content on social media platforms without audience restrictions, anyone who visits the platforms—including law enforcement—can access this content. Law enforcement does not need to obtain court authorization to view content that has been published for any and all to see, like a sign in one's yard.[15]

---

[13] For instance, DOJ's *Justice Manual* has guidelines on personal use of social media (see Section 1-9.000, https://www.justice.gov/jm/jm-1-9000-personal-use-of-social-media) and on evidence collection, including searches and seizures (see Section 1-13.000, https://www.justice.gov/jm/jm-9-13000-obtaining-evidence). Federal law enforcement agencies are also subject to the Federal Rules of Criminal Procedure. For more information, see CRS In Focus IF11557, *Congress, the Judiciary, and Civil and Criminal Procedure*.

[14] Access to these communications may be affected by social media policies, law enforcement rules for criminal procedure, and whether or not the communications are encrypted.

[15] In 1999, DOJ convened an Online Investigations Working Group with representatives from across DOJ as well as members from the Department of the Treasury, Department of Defense, and others. A copy of the working group's November 1999 report, *Online Investigative Principles for Federal Law Enforcement Agents*, is available at https://info.publicintelligence.net/DoJ-OnlineInvestigations.pdf. It detailed a range of principles for online investigations. These principles may apply to investigations involving

In addition to content that one shares on social media, selected account-level information may also be available to a broad audience, including law enforcement, such as the information contained in a public profile. Depending on platform and user settings, this may include a host of demographic, geolocation, and other data, potentially including a list of other accounts with whom one is connected on a given social media platform. Law enforcement may use this information to learn more about an individual's social network.

Although law enforcement may be legally and technically able to access public information on social media platforms, agencies may have internal policies governing this access. These internal policies may, for instance, place restrictions on the circumstances under which law enforcement can access social media for investigations as well as the authorization needed to do so.[16]

Accessing Restricted or Private Information

Based on platform policies or user choices, some information that individuals post on social media may contain restrictions regarding the breadth of the audience that may access that information. Some of these restrictions are established by platform controls and some may be established by user preferences. In the instances when law enforcement does not have public access to information, they may rely on a number of tools and techniques to gain access to it.

For instance, law enforcement may rely on informants, or contacts of the persons about whom law enforcement is seeking information, to share social media information that they may have access to because of their status as a direct contact with the individual in question. Law enforcement may also

---

social media, though it is unclear to what extent federal law enforcement may rely on such principles today.

[16] For instance, the Honolulu Police Department requires that officers obtain approval from the Chief of Police or a designee before using social media to conduct an investigation. See Honolulu Police Department, Policy, Organization, Management, and Administration, *Policy Number 2.72: Social Media*, May 21, 2019. Studies have recommended that law enforcement develop social media policies (see, for instance, Bureau of Justice Assistance with the Global Justice Information Sharing Initiative and Criminal Intelligence Coordinating Council, *Developing a Policy on the Use of Social Media in Intelligence and Investigative Activities: Guidance and Recommendations*, February 2013). It is unclear how many agencies have these policies or whether the policies may be publicly available. The Brennan Center for Justice has collected some publicly available social media policies and collated them online at https://www.brennancenter.org/our-work/research-reports/directory-police-department-social-media-policies.

operate undercover, posing as someone who may be more likely to gain access to an individual's social media network in order to glean information.[17] Some observers have suggested that law enforcement agencies should specifically address the use of online aliases in their social media policies to draw a distinction between the information they gather that is unrestricted and publicly available and that which they gather through the use of an alias.[18]

Law enforcement may also require social media platforms to provide access to certain restricted information through a warrant, subpoena, or other court order. For instance, law enforcement may want to access private information from a particular individual's account pursuant to an investigation and may need a warrant to do so. Similarly, as some social media posts or comments on public forums are made anonymously, law enforcement would generally need a warrant to try and obtain information from the platform on the identity of the anonymous poster.

Preservation Request

In some instances, law enforcement may present social media companies with a request to preserve certain content at a particular moment in time. This may be done to prevent content from being altered during the time it takes law enforcement to obtain the proper court authorization, such as a warrant, needed to obtain access to this content. Wire and electronic service providers as well as remote computing services, including social media platforms, are required to preserve content for 90 days at the request of law enforcement. This request may be extended once for an additional 90-day period.[19] Following the January 6, 2021, attack against the U.S. Capitol, there was concern that participants in the attack and others may attempt to edit or remove content that they had posted, shared, or otherwise engaged with leading up to and following the attack. As such, reporting indicates, federal investigators requested that companies such as Facebook, Twitter, and others preserve this content that could help in their investigations.[20]

---

[17] For instance, DOJ has guidelines for FBI undercover operations. These guidelines reference undercover operations online, but they do not have specific guidance on operations involving social media. See Department of Justice, *The Attorney General's Guidelines on Federal Bureau of Investigation Undercover Operations*, May 30, 2002.

[18] U.S. Department of Justice, Community Oriented Policing Services and Police Executive Research Forum, *Social Media and Tactical Considerations for Law Enforcement*, July 2013.

[19] 18 U.S.C. §2703(f).

[20] Brooke Singman, "Big Tech 'complying' with federal requests to preserve evidence on social media amid Capitol riot probe," *Fox News*, January 28, 2021.

Platform Policies on Information Sharing with Law Enforcement

Pursuant to the Stored Communications Act (Title II of P.L. 99-508), social media platforms may disclose information about users and their communications on the platform to law enforcement under certain circumstances. For instance, platforms may disclose certain information to law enforcement with a warrant or other valid court order. Platforms may also share information with law enforcement if they, in good faith, believe that there is an emergency involving a danger of death or serious injury.[21] Social media platforms also have a lawful duty to report apparent or imminent violations of federal law pertaining to child sexual exploitation and child sexual abuse material.[22]

> Sharing Information on Child Sexual Abuse Material
>
> Violations of federal law with respect to child sexual exploitation and child sexual abuse material (CSAM) are the one area of malicious behavior on which electronic service providers—including social media platforms—must report if they have knowledge of its occurrence. The duty to report applies in instances of apparent or imminent violations of 18 U.S.C. §§2251, 2251A, 2252, 2252A, 2252B, or 2260 that involve child pornography, or what is commonly referred to as CSAM. Specifically, providers must report to the CyberTipline, which is operated by the National Center for Missing and Exploited Children (NCMEC).[23] NCMEC makes these reports available to law enforcement investigating crimes relating to child sexual exploitation.
>
> The duty to report apparent or imminent child sexual exploitation does not also place a duty on providers to actively search for this content. Rather, the duty to report only applies to content that a provider becomes aware of. Nonetheless, some social media platforms such as Facebook have started to take steps toward proactively detecting this content in their systems.[24]

---

[21] 18 U.S.C. §2702.

[22] 18 U.S.C. §2258A. This statute makes it a duty to report for all electronic service providers, which includes social media platforms.

[23] NCMEC is a resource center for law enforcement agencies working on cases of missing and exploited children. NCMEC personnel take reports of missing and exploited children through a hotline and online portal, the CyberTipline.

[24] Agnus Crawford, "Whistleblower: Facebook's response to child abuse 'inadequate'," *BBC News*, October 28, 2021. See also Facebook's policies on child safety at https://www.facebook.com/safety/onlinechildprotection.

> Policymakers have debated whether this model, of requiring electronic service providers to report apparent or imminent violations related to child sexual exploitation, can or should be replicated for other forms of malicious behavior occurring online, with a specific focus on social media platforms.

In addition to what is allowable or required by law, social media platforms establish internal policies, which may vary from platform to platform and may change over time, regarding information sharing with law enforcement.[25] They may voluntarily share information with law enforcement that is not protected by, or in violation of, the privacy agreements they have established with their users. There is also the issue of whether social media companies are disincentivized to proactively search for certain malicious content on their platforms if they are shielded from liability for content hosted on their platforms.[26]

Even if social media companies want to share certain information with law enforcement, they may not be able to do so if the information is encrypted in such a way that the company cannot access it. For instance, WhatsApp Messenger implemented default end-to-end encryption on its platform in 2016. This form of strong encryption, what some have termed *warrant proof* encryption, prevents WhatsApp from accessing the content of communications, even if presented with a warrant, because it does not hold the key to unlock the encrypted communications.[27] Meta, the parent company of WhatsApp, Facebook, and Instagram, announced that it would implement end-to-end encryption on Facebook's and Instagram's Messenger service; however, this encryption shift is reportedly delayed until at least 2023.[28]

---

[25] For instance, Facebook and Instagram policies on information sharing with law enforcement are outlined at https://www.facebook.com/safety/groups/law/guidelines/. Twitter's guidelines for law enforcement are available at https://help.twitter.com/en/rules-and-policies/twitter-law-enforcement-support.

[26] Section 230 of the Communications Decency Act of 1996 (CDA) is generally seen as protecting social media sites from liability for hosting content. A discussion of the current debate surrounding Section 230 is outside the scope of this report; however, for more information, see CRS Report R45650, *Free Speech and the Regulation of Social Media Content*.

[27] For more information on *warrant-proof* encryption and the tension between law enforcement and technology companies, see CRS In Focus IF11769, Law Enforcement and Technology: the "Lawful Access" Debate.

[28] Dan Milmo, "Meta delays encrypted messages on Facebook and Instagram to 2023," *The Guardian*, November 21, 2021.

Intelligence Gathering via Social Media

In addition to using social media to help communicate with the public and further investigations, law enforcement agencies also rely on it for intelligence gathering purposes. This is the use that arguably has generated the most questions from policymakers, analysts, and the public. There have been questions about the extent to which law enforcement is actually using social media for intelligence gathering, how they might store and use such information, whether this intelligence gathering can hinder First Amendment protected activities, whether social media monitoring may undermine privacy rights, and whether intelligence gathering disproportionally affects certain individuals or communities.[29]

Social media companies have at times weighed in on the issue of social media monitoring by law enforcement. These companies provide access to their user data to developers that build tools to improve user experiences, conduct research, and monitor social media platforms, among other things.[30] Following reports that some law enforcement agencies had been monitoring social media with developers' tools built on platforms' user data, some platforms changed their policies to expressly prohibit their user data from being used by law enforcement to monitor social media.[31]

In addition, law enforcement agencies themselves have reportedly grappled with the extent to which they should gather and rely on information and intelligence gleaned from social media. For instance, some observers have suggested that agencies such as the Federal Bureau of Investigation (FBI) may be reluctant to regularly analyze public social media posts because that could be viewed as spying on the American public and could subsequently chill free speech.[32] Others, however, have noted that the benefits to national security and public safety from analyzing social media content outweigh the risks.[33] The Attorney General's Guidelines for Domestic FBI Operations (Guidelines) specifically note that online services and resources may be used in intelligence

---

[29] See, for instance, Brennan Center for Justice et al., *Civil Rights Concerns about Social Media Monitoring by Law Enforcement*, November 6, 2019.

[30] Twitter Developer Platform, *Tap Into What's Happening to Build What's Next*, https://developer.twitter.com/en.

[31] Brennan Center for Justice, *Map: Social Media Monitoring by Police Departments, Cities, and Counties*, July 10, 2019. See also Chris Moody, Twitter Developer Platform Blog, *Developer Policies to Protect People's Voices on Twitter*, November 22, 2016.

[32] Ken Dilanian, "DHS Launches Warning System to Find Domestic Terrorism Threats on Public Social Media," *NBC News*, May 10, 2021.

[33] Ibid.

assessments that may help detect and interrupt criminal activities at their early stages. The Guidelines state that

> assessment activities may proactively involve surfing the Internet to find publicly accessible websites and services through which recruitment by terrorist organizations and promotion of terrorist crimes is openly taking place; through which child pornography is advertised and traded; through which efforts are made by sexual predators to lure children for purposes of sexual abuse; or through which fraudulent schemes are perpetrated against the public.[34]

There are numerous instances of law enforcement relying on social media in support of intelligence assessments and investigations. For instance, following the May 2020 killing of George Floyd, there were numerous protests around the country, and FBI agents "monitored social media activity for imminent acts of violence."[35] The FBI has contracted with various social media monitoring companies to "obtain early alerts on ongoing national security and public safety-related events through lawfully collected/acquired social media data."[36] In addition, DHS is reportedly considering enhancing its existing intelligence efforts to examine information from social media to better understand potential security threats and identify likely targets.[37] To do so, DHS may leverage the expertise of private companies to help analyze publicly available content posted on social media. This reevaluation of DHS's capabilities in social media analysis comes on the heels of the January 6, 2021, U.S. Capitol attack; DHS intelligence reportedly did not detect and/or report the security threats that were discussed on social media.[38]

In another example, the mayor of Chicago announced in August 2020 that the Chicago Police Department created a specialized social media task force to monitor online activity with the goal of preventing looting. The 20-person

---

[34] Department of Justice, *The Attorney General's Guidelines for Domestic FBI Operations*, September 29, 2008.

[35] Affidavit in Support of Criminal Complaint, United States v. Avery, 4:20-mj-07180, May 31, 2020.

[36] Federal Bureau of Investigation, Finance Division, Procurement Section, *Request for Proposals (RFP) No. / 15F06720R0000063*, January 28, 2020. The FBI has had agreements with companies such as DataMinr and ZeroFox; see Ken Dilanian, "Why did the FBI miss the threats about Jan. 6 on social media?," *NBC News*, March 8, 2021.

[37] Rachael Levy, "U.S. Social Media Push Would Use Outside Monitors," *Wall Street Journal*, August 16, 2021.

[38] Ibid. See also Ken Dilanian, "DHS Launches Warning System to Find Domestic Terrorism Threats on Public Social Media," *NBC News*, May 10, 2021.

unit was tasked with collecting intelligence, including through the use of data analytics and searching social media pages and accounts that had been associated with organizing looting activity. The task force was also reportedly working with other law enforcement partners, including the FBI, to investigate looting incidents that had already occurred.[39]

Going Forward

There is no specific federal legislative framework that governs law enforcement use of social media.[40] Rather, there are laws and policies governing law enforcement investigations and intelligence gathering, broadly. Some observers, however, have questioned whether the nature of social media may place it in a qualitatively different category than law enforcement's use of other investigative tools and have suggested that there should be enhanced boundaries with respect to law enforcement operations in these online spaces. For instance, some have suggested that law enforcement agencies should have written, publicly available policies on their use of social media; they should obtain local government approval before using these online spaces; they should obtain judicial approval for conducting undercover operations using social media; there should be restrictions on law enforcement contacting minors via social media; and law enforcement's use of social media should be audited.[41] Policymakers may consider these issues as they conduct oversight or debate legislation on law enforcement use of social media.

Oversight of Law Enforcement Social Media Policies

The President's Task Force on 21st Century Policing, as well as various DOJ research partnerships,[42] have recommended that law enforcement agencies

---

[39] "Chicago Authorities to Monitor Social Media Amid Looting Threats, Lightfoot Says," *NBC Chicago*, August 14, 2020.

[40] In addition, there is not yet a wide body of case law to help inform on how courts are viewing law enforcement's use of social media.

[41] See, for example, Rachel Levinson-Waldman and Angel Diaz, *How to Reform Police Monitoring of Social Media*, Brookings, July 9, 2020.

[42] Emily Tiry, Ashlin Oglesby-Neal, and KiDeuk Kim, *Social Media Guidebook for Law Enforcement*, Urban Institute, February 2019. See also Edward F. Davis III, Alejandro A. Alves, and David Alan Sklansky, "Social Media and Police Leadership: Lessons From Boston," *Harvard Kennedy School and National Institute of Justice: New Perspectives in*

develop policies governing the use of social media. For instance, the Bureau of Justice Assistance (BJA) sponsored a project in collaboration with the Global Justice Information Sharing Initiative[43] that, in 2013, recommended "all law enforcement leadership support the development of a social media-related policy and associated procedures (or enhance existing policies) to guide personnel on accessing, viewing, collecting, storing, retaining, and disseminating (or using) information from social media sites, tools, and resources as a part of their authorized investigative and criminal intelligence activities."[44] Specifically, it recommended that a social media policy should accomplish the following:

- note that use of social media will be in accordance with relevant laws, regulations, and agency policies;
- define if and when use of social media sites/tools is permitted;
- specify the authority needed to use information obtained from social media;
- note that information acquired from social media will be evaluated to assess reliability and validity;
- specify documentation, storage, and retention requirements surrounding information obtained from social media;
- define any guidelines involving off-duty personnel using social media information in connection with official duties and when/how personal equipment may be used for an authorized law enforcement purpose; and
- identify procedures for disseminating criminal intelligence and investigative products that contain information obtained from social

---

Policing, March 2014; and Bureau of Justice Assistance with the Global Justice Information Sharing Initiative and Criminal Intelligence Coordinating Council, *Developing a Policy on the Use of Social Media in Intelligence and Investigative Activities: Guidance and Recommendations*, February 2013.

43 The Global Advisory Committee (GAC) serves as a Federal Advisory Committee to the U.S. Attorney General. Through recommendations to the Bureau of Justice Assistance (BJA), the GAC supports standards-based electronic information exchanges that provide justice and public safety communities with timely, accurate, complete, and accessible information, appropriately shared in a secure and trusted environment. GAC recommendations support the mission of the U.S. Department of Justice, initiatives sponsored by BJA, and related activities sponsored by BJA's Global Justice Information Sharing Initiative (Global).

44 Bureau of Justice Assistance with the Global Justice Information Sharing Initiative and Criminal Intelligence Coordinating Council, *Developing a Policy on the Use of Social Media in Intelligence and Investigative Activities: Guidance and Recommendations*, February 2013, p. 6.

media, including any parameters for disseminating personal information.

Anecdotal reports of law enforcement officers being reprimanded for improper use of social media have highlighted the sensitive nature of law enforcement personnel using social media in their personal and professional capacities.[45] Policymakers may seek to evaluate whether federal law enforcement agencies have social media policies in place as well as how the agencies conduct oversight of officers' use of social media.

Congress can legislate directly on federal law enforcement practices, and it can also influence state, local, and tribal policies and practices through the provision or withholding of grant funding. Programs such as the Edward Byrne Memorial Justice Assistance Grant (JAG) program[46] and the Community Oriented Policing Services (COPS) program[47] have been used to incentivize activities of state and local law enforcement and may be leveraged to influence the adoption of social media policies. The federal government can also affect state, local, and tribal policies through the transfer of knowledge and expertise. For instance, BJA and its partners have provided guidance and recommendations on developing a social media policy that law enforcement agencies may reference.[48]

Data on Frequency of Social Media Use in Investigations and Intelligence Gathering

Although there have been some surveys of law enforcement on how they use social media and for which purposes, data are lacking on the extent to which law enforcement agencies leverage public information on social media platforms as well as restricted information gleaned through lawful means such

---

[45] See, for example, Donald J. Mihalek and Richard M. Frankel, "The dangers of social media for law enforcement take center stage amid series of scandals: Analysis," *NBC News*, July 11, 2019.

[46] For more information, see CRS In Focus IF10691, *The Edward Byrne Memorial Justice Assistance Grant (JAG) Program*.

[47] For more information, see CRS In Focus IF10922, *Community Oriented Policing Services (COPS) Program*.

[48] Bureau of Justice Assistance with the Global Justice Information Sharing Initiative and Criminal Intelligence Coordinating Council, *Developing a Policy on the Use of Social Media in Intelligence and Investigative Activities: Guidance and Recommendations*, February 2013.

as warrants and subpoenas. Some observers report that law enforcement has increasingly turned to social media content to assist in their investigations, while others have suggested that some law enforcement agencies are shying away from analyzing public social media posts because it may be viewed as spying on the public.[49]

Congress may consider tasking oversight entities such as the Government Accountability Office or department-level Inspectors General with reporting on issues such as whether law enforcement agencies have established clear parameters on the use of social media for investigations and intelligence gathering, whether or how agencies note the use of social media in investigative case files, and whether or how agencies tabulate metrics on their use of social media or other related tools. Congress may also request such information from law enforcement agencies directly through letters, hearings, and other oversight. A greater understanding of the purposes for and extent to which law enforcement relies on social media in its investigations and intelligence gathering may provide a stronger foundation for policy discussions going forward.

[49] Ken Dilanian, "DHS Launches Warning System to Find Domestic Terrorism Threats on Public Social Media," *NBC News*, May 10, 2021.

Chapter 4

Law Enforcement and Technology: The "Lawful Access" Debate*

Kristin Finklea

Technological advances present both opportunities and challenges for U.S. law enforcement. For example, some developments have increased the quantity and availability of digital content and information for investigators and analysts. Some observers say law enforcement's investigative capabilities may be outpaced by the speed of technological change, preventing investigators from accessing certain information they may otherwise be authorized to obtain. Specifically, law enforcement officials cite strong, end-to-end encryption, or what they have called warrant-proof encryption, as preventing lawful access to certain data. Companies employing such strong encryption have stressed they do not hold encryption keys. This means they may not be readily able to unlock, or decrypt, the devices or communications—not even for law enforcement presenting an authorized search warrant or wiretap order.

Front Door or Back Door Access

Rhetoric around the encryption debate has focused on the notion of preventing or allowing back door access to communications or data. Many view a back door as the ability for an entity, including a government agency, to access encrypted data without the user's explicit authorization. However, back door

* This is an edited, reformatted and augmented version of Congressional Research Service Publication No. IF11769, updated January 16, 2024.

In: The Future of Law Enforcement
Editor: Mohamed Swift
ISBN: 979-8-89530-863-9

access can be a security vulnerability. Despite this concern, a number of encrypted products and services have built-in back doors and thus can comply with law enforcement requests for information. For instance, many email service providers encrypt email communications and also maintain a key to those communications stored on their servers. This is also the case for cloud providers that maintain keys to the data stored on their servers. Strong, end-to-end encryption where companies do not maintain keys, however, does not contain the same opportunities for access. Also, unintended back doors, or vulnerabilities, may be discovered by technology companies, security researchers, government investigators, malicious actors, or others.

Law enforcement contends that they want front door access, where there is a clear understanding of when they are accessing a device, as the notion of a back door sounds secretive. This front door could be opened by whomever holds the key once investigators have demonstrated a lawful basis for access, such as probable cause that a crime is being committed. Whether front or back, however, building in an encrypted door that can be unlocked with a key—no matter who maintains the key—adds a potential vulnerability to exploitation by hackers, criminals, and other malicious actors. Researchers have yet to demonstrate how it would be possible to create a door that could only be accessed in lawful circumstances.

Calea

The simultaneous opportunities and challenges that evolving technology present to law enforcement have received congressional attention for several decades and have been a central point of contention between law enforcement and technology companies.

The 1990s brought concerns that digital and wireless communications made it more difficult for law enforcement agencies to execute authorized surveillance. In response, Congress passed the Communications Assistance for Law Enforcement Act (CALEA; P.L. 103-414) to help law enforcement maintain its ability to execute authorized electronic surveillance. Among other things, CALEA requires that telecommunications carriers assist law enforcement in efforts to intercept electronic communications for which it has a valid court order to carry out. There are several noteworthy exceptions to this requirement:

- Law enforcement cannot require (or prohibit) providers of wire or electronic communications services (as well as manufacturers of equipment and providers of support services) to implement "specific design of equipment, facilities, services, features, or system configurations." In other words, they cannot require providers to build in access points.
- Telecommunications carriers are not responsible for decrypting any encrypted communications (or ensuring that the government has the ability to do so), unless the company already has the ability to do so.
- CALEA applies to telecommunications carriers but specifically does not apply to "information services" such as websites and internet service providers. (Notably, the Federal Communications Commission administratively expanded CALEA's requirements to also apply to certain broadband and Voice over Internet Protocol [VoIP] providers.)

Proposed expansions of CALEA generally fall into two broad categories. Some proposed expansions may broaden the range of communications or information service providers covered by CALEA. Some have been interested in making CALEA more technology neutral, such that it could, given the rapidly changing technology landscape, apply to a wider range of communications or information service providers. Other expansions may broaden the requirements placed on telecommunication carriers—such as maintaining the ability to decrypt communications— placed on entities covered by CALEA.

Crypto Wars

Around the time that policymakers were passing CALEA, a larger discussion on encryption was taking place. The so- called crypto wars pitted the government against data privacy advocates in a debate on the use of data encryption. This tension was highlighted by law enforcement proposals to build back doors to certain encrypted communications devices as well as to block the export of strong encryption code.

Clipper Chip. During the Clinton Administration, encryption technology, known as the Clipper Chip, was introduced. This technology used a concept referred to as key escrow. The idea was that the Clipper Chip would be inserted into a communications device, and at the start of each encrypted communication session, the chip would copy the encryption key and send it to the government to be held in escrow, essentially establishing a back door for access. With authorization—such as a court authorized wiretap—government agencies would then have the ability to access the key to the encrypted communication.

Vulnerabilities in the system design were later discovered, showing that the system could be breached and the escrow capabilities disabled; as such, this system was not adopted.

Encryption Export. Pretty Good Privacy (PGP) encryption software was a widely used email encryption platform and was considered a milestone because it made military-grade cryptography available to the public. PGP proliferated when someone released a copy of it on the internet, sparking a federal investigation into whether PGP's creator was illegally exporting cryptographic software (then considered a form of "munitions" under U.S. export regulations) without a specific munitions export license. Ultimately, the case was resolved without an indictment.

Renewed Crypto Wars?

The debate over law enforcement's lawful access to encrypted information originally focused on data in motion, or real-time communications. More recent technology changes have potentially affected law enforcement capabilities to access not only real-time communications but stored content, or data at rest. A central element of the debate now involves determining what types of information law enforcement is able to access and under what circumstances.

Communications Content. Wiretap requests are submitted by law enforcement to judges, requesting permission to intercept certain wire, oral, or electronic communications in transit. According to data reported to the Administrative Office of the U.S. Courts, federal and state judges authorized 2,406 wiretaps in 2022. Over half of these (51%) were used in narcotics investigations. Of the 2,406 wiretaps, encrypted communications were encountered in 478 instances. Law enforcement could not decrypt the content in 441 (approximately 92%) of the cases where they encountered encrypted communications.

Call Detail Records. Law enforcement may request, with a subpoena or valid court order, certain call detail records from telecommunications providers. These records can include information such as the sending and receiving telephone numbers, whether or not the call was completed, call duration, and which cell towers were used to make or receive the call. These may be available retrospectively or sometimes in real time. Companies vary in the length of time they maintain call detail records and other data such as global positioning system (GPS) location information.

Notably, call detail records do not contain the content of telephone calls.

Stored Data. With a warrant or subpoena, law enforcement may attempt to obtain data stored in the cloud or on a device.

- Ease of law enforcement access to cloud-based data may depend on factors including the location of the cloud server, the service provider, and length of time information has been stored in the cloud. If the server is located overseas, for instance, law enforcement can employ the Mutual Legal Assistance process to try to obtain the data from a partner nation. Factors that may limit the scope of data stored in the cloud (and subsequently, availability to law enforcement) include whether individuals store data in or back up their devices to the cloud and whether cloud storage space and backup schedules capture the full range of data.
- With respect to devices, access to devices and the content on them may be locked and encrypted. Various factors can affect law enforcement's efforts to gain access to a device and its contents. For instance, law enforcement attempting to unlock a device with brute force would likely use software to try every possible combination of keys in an attempt to unlock the device. The success of this method may depend, among other things, on the amount of time available to try and unlock a device, device limits on passcode attempts, and the number of keys used in the passcode.

Going Forward

Policymakers may evaluate the extent to which end-to-end encryption affects law enforcement investigations and public safety. They may weigh this against privacy and data security concerns as they consider whether to expand or curtail law enforcement's lawful access to certain information. Changes could involve incentives or requirements for communications and technology companies to provide specified information to law enforcement, enhanced investigative tools, bolstered financial and manpower resources to help law enforcement better leverage existing authorities, or combinations of these and other options.

For additional resources, see CRS Report R44481, *Encryption and the "Going Dark" Debate*; CRS Report R44187, *Encryption and Evolving Technology: Implications for U.S. Law Enforcement Investigations*; and CRS Report R44827, *Law Enforcement Using and Disclosing Technology Vulnerabilities*.

Chapter 5

Law Enforcement Use of Artificial Intelligence and Directives in the 2023 Executive Order*

Kristin Finklea

The use of artificial intelligence (AI) has expanded in a variety of arenas, including by law enforcement. AI has been broadly conceptualized as computerized systems operating in ways often thought to require human intelligence. It is defined in the U.S. Code (15 U.S.C. §9401(3)) as a machine-based system that can, for a given set of human-defined objectives, make predictions, recommendations or decisions influencing real or virtual environments. Artificial intelligence systems use machine and human-based inputs to-

A. perceive real and virtual environments;
B. abstract such perceptions into models through analysis in an automated manner; and
C. use model inference to formulate options for information or action.

AI involves a host of technologies and applications. In the law enforcement realm, researchers note that while the use of AI is not yet widespread, existing tools may be enhanced with AI to expand law enforcement *capabilities* and increase their *efficiency*. Examples include the following:

---

* This is an edited, reformatted and augmented version of Congressional Research Service Publication No. IN12289, dated December 15, 2023.

In: The Future of Law Enforcement
Editor: Mohamed Swift
ISBN: 979-8-89530-863-9

- Automated license plate readers can be leveraged to employ machine, or computer, vision for capabilities such as automating the issuance of red-light violation tickets.
- Security cameras outfitted with certain AI-embedded hardware can be used for real-time facial recognition of potential suspects.
- Facial recognition technology and text analysis tools can be enhanced with AI to scan online advertisements to help identify potential crimes such as human trafficking.
- In addition to gunshot detection technology that can detect shots fired, security cameras can be outfitted with AI-enhanced software to detect weapons and alert police before shots are fired.
- AI redaction capabilities can be used to reduce possible bias in officers' narratives by removing certain identifying characteristics of suspects and victims—such as race—that could influence charges brought by prosecutors.
- Body-worn cameras can use AI software to redact or blur faces or sensitive footage before it is released to the public.
- Automated speech recognition software can use AI to help properly identify speakers' voices in audiovisual materials such as witness testimonies or interrogations.
- First responders use computer aided dispatch (CAD) systems to capture data that inform decisions on resource deployment; AI-enhanced CAD systems can improve resource allocation by using historical data, making predictions, and automating workflow.
- AI can be used along with predictive policing models to help identify individuals or places most at risk of being involved in crime.
- Law enforcement agencies can employ AI to enhance its communications with the public; they can use chatbots to respond to questions and push out emergency information.

A number of concerns have been raised about law enforcement use of AI, including whether its use perpetuates biases; one criticism is that the data on which the software are trained contain bias, thus training bias into the AI systems. Another concern is whether reliance on AI technology may lead police to ignore contradictory evidence. Policymakers may consider increased oversight over police use of AI systems to help evaluate and alleviate some of the shortcomings.

On October 30, 2023, President Biden issued Executive Order (E.O.) 14110 on the *Safe, Secure, and Trustworthy Development and Use of Artificial Intelligence*. This E.O. advances a government-wide approach to "governing the development and use of AI safely and responsibly" and directs efforts in AI policy areas involving safety and security, innovation and competition, worker support, equity and civil rights, individual protections, privacy protections, federal AI use, and international leadership.

E.O. 14110 acknowledges the risk of AI exacerbating discrimination and directs federal law enforcement in various ways. (In doing so, it references accountability focused directives for federal law enforcement previously outlined in the May 25, 2022, E.O. 14074 on *Advancing Effective, Accountable Policing and Criminal Justice Practices to Enhance Public Trust and Public Safety*.) Directives in E.O. 14110 include the following:

- The Attorney General (AG) shall coordinate and support enforcement of federal laws addressing discrimination and violations of civil rights and civil liberties related to AI. The Department of Justice's Civil Rights Division shall also coordinate with other federal civil rights offices to assess how their offices can prevent and address discrimination in automated systems—including algorithmic discrimination.
- The AG, with the Homeland Security Secretary and Office of Science and Technology Policy Director, shall submit a report to the President on the use of AI in the criminal justice system, including how AI can enhance law enforcement efficiency and accuracy, consistent with privacy, civil rights, and civil liberties protections. The report should also recommend best practices for law enforcement, including guidance on AI use, to address concerns outlined in E.O. 14074 with respect to law enforcement use of "facial recognition technology, other technologies using biometric information, and predictive algorithms, as well as data storage and access regarding such technologies."
- The interagency working group established by E.O. 14074 shall share best practices for recruiting law enforcement professionals with AI expertise and training them on responsible AI use. The AG, along with the Homeland Security Secretary, may review these and

recommend best practices for state, local, tribal, and territorial law nforcement.

- The AG shall review the Justice Department's capacity to "investigate law enforcement deprivation of rights under color of law resulting from the use of AI," including through increasing or improving training for federal law enforcement officers and prosecutors.

Policymakers conducting oversight of executive branch activities to ensure that AI is used in a fair and equitable manner may examine not only these elements of E.O. 14110 that specifically relate to federal law enforcement but also other elements—such as the development of industry standards on AI—that may in turn affect law enforcement use of AI. They may also explore whether there should be specific standards for AI use in the criminal justice sector or AI-specific requirements for criminal justice entities receiving federal grants. Additionally, policymakers may continue to debate law enforcement use of specific AI technologies in its toolbox such as facial recognition technology.

Chapter 6

Federal Support for Law Enforcement: Selected Department of Justice Programs*

Karma Ester

Summary

Congress has authorized a range of grant programs that support state, local, and tribal law enforcement. This report provides information on selected Department of Justice grants administered by the Office of Justice Programs (OJP) and the Office of Community Oriented Policing Services (COPS). Selected grant programs target police hiring, equipment procurement, officer safety and wellness, drug task forces, hate crimes prevention and investigations, community policing, school violence, and crisis intervention.

Introduction

Historically, the Department of Justice (DOJ) has provided financial assistance to state, local, and tribal law enforcement agencies to assist them with addressing crime, purchasing equipment, providing training, and supporting community policing efforts. The major offices within DOJ that administer grants are the Office of Justice Programs (OJP), the Office of Community Oriented Policing Services (COPS), and the Office of Violence

---

* This is an edited, reformatted and augmented version of Congressional Research Service Publication No. R46671, dated January 10, 2024.

In: The Future of Law Enforcement
Editor: Mohamed Swift
ISBN: 979-8-89530-863-9

Against Women (OVW).[1] This report focuses on grants administered by OJP and COPS that provide direct assistance to law enforcement agencies, but are not limited to this purpose. These include grants that support police hiring, equipment procurement, officer safety and wellness, drug task forces, community policing, hate crime prevention and investigation, school violent crime response, and crisis intervention. Law enforcement agencies must be accredited or in the process of becoming accredited to be eligible for grants.

The DOJ grant cycle is ongoing with the majority of funding solicitations being announced from March through June each year.

This report includes brief descriptions of each grant program, summary information on eligibility, purpose areas, matching requirements, links to program information, grant program solicitations, and related CRS reports.

Office of Justice Programs

The Office of Justice Programs (OJP) is a federal agency that provides grants, training, technical assistance, and other resources targeting crime reduction, victim assistance, and strengthening the juvenile and criminal justice systems.[2] Areas of focus for FY2023 funding include reentry projects; addressing contraband cellphones in correctional facilities; purchasing fentanyl and methamphetamine detection equipment; purchases of canines; virtual reality de-escalation training; gunfire detection equipment; purchasing of humane remote restraint devices; gunfire detection technology; and diversifying law enforcement personnel.

Edward Byrne Memorial Justice Assistance Grant (JAG)

JAG formula grants can be used to support a range of activities in nine program areas. These areas include the following:

---

[1] The Office of Justice Programs (OJP) includes the Bureau of Justice Assistance (BJA), Bureau of Justice Statistics (BJS), National Institute of Justice (NIJ), Office of Juvenile Justice and Delinquency Prevention (OJJDP), Office for Victims of Crime (OVC), and Office of Sex Offender Sentencing, Monitoring, Apprehending, Registering and Tracking (SMART).

[2] See Department of Justice (DOJ), OJP, "About Us," accessed April 3, 2023, at https://www.ojp.gov/about. Grants that are focused on the juvenile justice system are outside the scope of this report.

1) Law enforcement programs
2) Prosecution and court programs
3) Mental health programs
4) Crime prevention and education
5) Drug enforcement and treatment
6) Crime victim and witness programs
7) Corrections and community corrections
8) Planning, evaluation and technology improvements
9) Implementation of state crisis intervention courts and related programs or initiatives

Eligibility: States, including the District of Columbia and U.S. territories are eligible. Local units of government and federally recognized tribal governments that perform law enforcement functions may be eligible to receive an allocation based on the jurisdiction's proportion of the average number of violent crimes reported in the state for the past three years for which data are available.[3]

Match Requirement: None.

Additional Information:

- Program Overview
https://bja.ojp.gov/program/jag/overview
- FY2023 State Formula Solicitation
https://bja.ojp.gov/funding/opportunities/o-bja-2023-171793
- FY2023 Local Formula Solicitation
https://bja.ojp.gov/funding/opportunities/o-bja-2023-171790
- CRS In Focus IF10691, *The Edward Byrne Memorial Justice Assistance Grant (JAG) Program*

Project Safe Neighborhoods

This formula grant program is intended to protect communities from crime and evolving threats by identifying the most pressing violent crime problems

---

[3] Violent crimes include murder, rape, robbery, and aggravated assault. Allocations for local jurisdictions that are eligible for the Edward Byrne Memorial Justice Assistance Grant (JAG) are listed on the OJP website. See BJA, JAG Program, "FY 2023 Allocations" at https://bja.ojp.gov/program/jag/fy-2023-allocations.

in a community and developing solutions to address them. Goals include reducing violent crime, fostering community trust in law enforcement, and using data on violent crime to intervene, prevent, and improve outcomes.

Eligibility: Collaborative teams established by the U.S. Attorney's Offices (USAO) to implement strategies to address pressing violent crime problems in the USAO's district. These teams include federal, state, local, and tribal law enforcement, and community organizations and representatives.

Match Requirement: None.

Additional Information:

- Program Overview
  https://bja.ojp.gov/program/project-safe-neighborhoods-psn/overview
- FY2023 Project Safe Neighborhoods Solicitation
  https://bja.ojp.gov/funding/opportunities/o-bja-2023-171572

Matthew Shepard and James Byrd, Jr. Hate Crimes Program

This competitive grant supports state, local, and tribal law enforcement and prosecutors and their partners in investigating and prosecuting hate crimes. Funds also support outreach, education, and enhancing victim reporting tools.

Eligibility: State, territorial, local, and tribal law enforcement and prosecution agencies.

Matching Requirement: None.

Additional Information:

- Program Overview
  https://bja.ojp.gov/program/shepard-byrd-hate-crimes-program/overview
- FY2023 Solicitation
  https://bja.ojp.gov/funding/opportunities/o-bja-2023-171642

Collaborative Crisis Response and Intervention Training Program

This competitive grant seeks to implement transdisciplinary crisis response training to educate and prepare law enforcement and correctional officers to appropriately interact with people who have behavioral health conditions or disabilities. Funds may be used to plan, develop, and deploy training programs for officers in responding to crisis events in the community.

Eligibility: States, territories, cities, counties, townships, federally recognized Native American tribal governments, and campus police departments for public universities.

Matching Requirements: None.

Additional Information:

- FY2023 Solicitation https://bja.ojp.gov/funding/opportunities/o-bja-2023-171627

Comprehensive Opioid, Stimulant, and Substance Use Site-based Program Abuse Program (COSSUP)

This competitive grant program is intended to support state, local, and tribal efforts to reduce the adverse effects of opioids, stimulants, and other drugs on communities. Allowable uses have included law enforcement and first responder diversion programs, naloxone for first responders, medication-assisted treatment, and embedding social service workers with law enforcement.

Additional uses include transitional or recovery housing and support services, and embedding peers with similar experiences to assist in connecting justice involved individuals and their families with resources.

Eligibility: State, territorial, county, local governments, or federally recognized tribal governments.

Match Requirement: None.

Additional Information:

- Program Overview https://bja.ojp.gov/program/cossap/overview
- FY2023 Solicitation https://bja.ojp.gov/funding/opportunities/o-bja-2023-171527
- COSSAP Resource Center https://www.cossup.org/
- CRS Report R44987, The Opioid Epidemic and Federal Efforts to Address It: Frequently Asked Questions

Local Law Enforcement Crime Gun Intelligence Center Integration Initiative (CGIC)

This competitive grant program is administered in partnership with the Bureau of Alcohol, Tobacco, Firearms, and Explosives (ATF) and provides funding to areas experiencing precipitous increases in gun-related violent crime. Priority is given to jurisdictions with high volumes of nonfatal shootings and firearms-related homicides.

Eligibility: State, local and tribal law enforcement; other governmental agencies; governmental non-law enforcement agencies, and federally recognized Native American tribal governments

Match Requirement: None.

Additional Information:

- Program Overview https://bja.ojp.gov/program/cgic-initiative/overview
- FY2023 Solicitation https://bja.ojp.gov/funding/opportunities/o-bja-2023-171486
- ATF CGIC Fact Sheet https://www.atf.gov/resource-center/fact-sheet/fact-sheet-crime-gun-intelligence-centers-cgic
- Crime Gun Intelligence Centers https://crimegunintelcenters.org/cgic-concept/

Kevin and Avonte Program: Reducing Injury and Death of Missing Individuals with Dementia and Developmental Disabilities

This competitive grant program supports local jurisdictions' efforts to reduce the number of deaths and injuries of individuals with forms of dementia or developmental disabilities who, due to their condition, wander from safe environments.

Eligibility: Health care agencies; state, local, and tribal law enforcement; public safety agencies; and nonprofit organizations.

Match Requirement: None.

Additional Information:

- FY2023 Solicitation

https://bja.ojp.gov/funding/opportunities/o-bja-2023-171512

Preventing School Violence: BJA's STOP School Violence Program

This competitive grant program supports training for schools, students, and law enforcement to recognize, respond quickly, and help prevent acts of violence. Funds may also be used to develop anonymous reporting systems, establish intervention teams, and train school personnel to respond to mental health crises. For FY2023, some additional uses include active shooter training, trauma- informed care, bullying prevention, and diversion programs. Funds can also be used for additional specialized school personnel. No funds can be used to hire school resource officers (SROs).

Eligibility: States; units of local government; federally recognized Indian tribes; law enforcement agencies; nonprofit entities; independent school districts; and private and public institutions of higher education.

Match Requirement: None.

Additional Information:

- Program Overview
  https://bja.ojp.gov/program/stop-school-violence-program/overview
- FY2023 Solicitation
  https://bja.ojp.gov/funding/opportunities/o-bja-2023-171666
- CRS In Focus IF10836, *Department of Justice Support for School Safety Initiatives*

Body-Worn Camera Policy and Implementation Program to Support Law Enforcement Agencies

This competitive grant program funds the purchase of body-worn cameras (BWCs) and the establishing, updating, and expanding of BWC programs.

Eligibility: State, local, and tribal law enforcement agencies; correctional agencies that perform law enforcement functions (e.g., sheriff's departments);

prosecutors' offices; and state or regional consortia that support such agencies, including state administrating agencies.[4]

Match Requirement: Funds require a 50% cash or in-kind match. Funding is capped at $2,000 per BWC.

Additional Information:

- Program Overview https://bja.ojp.gov/program/body-worn-camera-policy-and-implementation-program-support-law-enforcement-agencies/overview
- FY2023 Solicitation https://bja.ojp.gov/funding/opportunities/o-bja-2023-171562

Justice and Mental Health Collaboration Program (JMHCP)

This competitive grant program supports collaboration across criminal justice and mental health systems to improve public safety responses to individuals with mental illness or co-occurring mental illness and substance abuse. Program areas have focused on embedding social workers or mental health workers with law enforcement, supporting mental health centers, and using mental health courts. BJA gives priority to rural communities and programs focusing on justice-involved females with mental health disorders, mental health courts, reentry services, and interventions to reduce recidivism.

Eligibility: States, units of local government, and federally recognized tribal governments, mental health agencies and public institutions of higher education. BJA will accept only applications that demonstrate the proposed program will be administered jointly by an agency with responsibility for criminal or juvenile justice activities and a mental health agency.

Match Requirement: Funds require a 20% match of the total cost of the project for the first two years and 40% match for the third project year. Recipients may satisfy this match requirement with either cash or in-kind services.

---

[4] State administering agencies (SSAs) are responsible for administering formula grant funds awarded directly to state governments. For a list of SSAs, see *State Administering Agencies* at https://www.ojp.gov/funding/state-administering- agencies/overview.

Additional Information:

- Program Overview
  https://bja.ojp.gov/program/justice-and-mental-health-collaboration-program-jmhcp/overview
- FY2023 Solicitation
  https://bja.ojp.gov/funding/opportunities/o-bja-2023-171522

Connect and Protect: Law Enforcement Behavioral Health Response Program

This competitive grant helps entities prepare, create or expand programs to assist collaborative law enforcement-behavioral health responses to people with mental disorders and co-occurring mental and substance use disorders who come into contact with law enforcement. Priority is given to rural areas and projects designed to promote racial equity in the justice system, reduce recidivism, and identify and treat females with either disorder that have been incarcerated.

Eligibility: State, city, township, or county governments, federally recognized tribal governments, mental health agencies, and public institutions of higher education

Match Requirement: 20% cash and/or in-kind match for the first two years and 40% match in year three.

Additional Information:

- FY2023 Solicitation
  https://bja.ojp.gov/funding/opportunities/o-bja-2023-171520

National Sexual Assault Kit Initiative (SAKI)

This competitive program is intended to help law enforcement agencies and prosecutors' offices address challenges associated with sexual assault kits that have not been submitted to a crime lab for testing.

Eligibility: State and local law enforcement agencies, federally recognized tribal governments, prosecutor's offices, units of local government, and consortia of small law enforcement agencies.[5]

Match Requirement: None.

Additional Information:

- Program Overview https://bja.ojp.gov/program/saki/overview
- FY2023 Solicitation https://bja.ojp.gov/funding/opportunities/o-bja-2023-171565

Emmett Till Cold Case Investigations and Prosecution Program

This competitive grant program provides funding to prosecutors' offices, and state, local, and tribal law enforcement to assist in the investigation and prosecution of cold case murders associated with civil rights violations and racially motivated murders committed prior to 1979.

Eligibility: State, territorial, local and federally recognized tribal law enforcement agencies and prosecutors' offices.

Match Requirement: None.

Additional Information:

- Program Overview https://bja.ojp.gov/program/emmett-till-cold-case-investigations-and- prosecution-program/overview
- FY2023 Solicitation https://bja.ojp.gov/funding/opportunities/o-bja-2023-171639

Patrick Leahy Bulletproof Vest Partnership (BVP)

The purpose of the BVP program is to reimburse law enforcement agencies for the purchase of bulletproof vests. The program reimburses departments for up to 50% of purchase costs.

---

[5] For the purposes of this solicitation, "small law enforcement agencies" are defined as agencies that have fewer than 250 sworn officers or a consortium of small agencies.

Eligibility: State, territorial, local, and federally recognized tribal law enforcement agencies.

Match Requirement: 50% match.

Additional Information:

- Program Overview https://bja.ojp.gov/program/patrick-leahy-bvp-program/overview
- Fact Sheet https://bja.ojp.gov/doc/bvp-fact-sheet.pdf

Rural Violent Crime Reduction Initiative[6]

This competitive grant program provides funding to law enforcement agencies and prosecutors' offices to implement violent crime reduction strategies, improve investigations and services to victims, and enhance collaboration between local stakeholders. Funds may also be used for salaries, overtime, and equipment.

Eligibility: State, and local law enforcement agencies serving rural communities, rural prosecutor's offices and all federally recognized tribal law enforcement agencies.

Match Requirement: None.

Additional Information:

- Program Overview https://ruralvcri.org/
- FY2023 Solicitation https://ruralvcri.org/wp-content/uploads/2023/02/RVCRI-Grant-Application- Solicitation_FINAL-3.pdf.

[6] According to the FY2023 solicitation, "To qualify as rural for this solicitation, an applicant must provide services in a rural area, but the jurisdiction's service area need not be exclusively rural. While the agency does not solely need to serve a rural area, the violent crime problem addressed must have a rural focus that allows for trackable impact. For any municipality (e.g., town, village, or borough), the area must be considered rural, and the population must not exceed 15,000. The population should be based on the latest U.S. Census enumeration."

Virtual Reality De-escalation Site-Based Initiative

This competitive program provides funding for law enforcement agencies to enhance training to respond to individuals in crisis, and improve officers' de-escalation skills using virtual reality technology.

Eligibility: State and local law enforcement agencies, federally recognized tribal governments, and state and public-controlled institutions of higher education.

Match Requirement: None.

Additional Information:

- FY2023 Solicitation
- https://bja.ojp.gov/funding/opportunities/o-bja-2023-171767

Rural and Small Department Violent Crime Reduction Program[7]

This competitive program supports small and rural agencies in combatting violent crime.

Eligibility: Small, rural, and tribal law enforcement agencies and prosecutors.

Match Requirement: None.

Additional Information:

- FY2023 Solicitation
- https://bja.ojp.gov/funding/opportunities/o-bja-2023-171729

Smart Policing Initiative Program

This competitive grant assists state, local, and tribal jurisdictions in reducing crime and improving criminal justice systems using evidence-based policing practices, information sharing, and multi-agency collaboration. Funds for

[7] According to the FY2023 solicitation, "a small agency is any law enforcement agency with 250 or fewer sworn officers…. A ural agency,' as defined under this initiative, is (a) an agency serving any area or community, no part of which is within an area designated as a standard metropolitan statistical area by the Office of Management and Budget or (b) any agency serving one or more rural census tracts."

crime reduction can be used for new personnel, overtime, technology purchases, and data analysis support.

Eligibility: State, local, and tribal law enforcement agencies; tribal governments performing law enforcement functions; and government non-law enforcement agencies acting as fiscal agents for law enforcement agencies.

Match Requirement: None.

Additional Information:

- Program Overview
https://bja.ojp.gov/program/smart-policing-initiative-spi/overview
- FY2023 Solicitation
https://bja.ojp.gov/funding/opportunities/o-bja-2023-171650

Office of Community Oriented Policing Services

The Office of Community Oriented Policing Services (COPS Office) provides information and grant resources to advance the practice of community policing by the nation's state, local, territorial and tribal law enforcement agencies.[8] Grants awarded by the COPS Office are used to hire community policing professionals, develop and test innovative policing strategies, and provide training and technical assistance to community members, local government leaders, and all levels of law enforcement.[9]

COPS Hiring Program (CHP)

This competitive grant program supports hiring new officers, rehiring officers who have been laid off, or retaining officers who are scheduled to be laid off due to budget reductions. The program covers 75% of approved salaries and benefits, not to exceed $125,000 for each awarded position during the three-year grant period. According to the COPS Office, past priority was given to applications focused on violent crime, homeland security, or school-based policing. For FY2023, the COPS Office asked grantees to focus on combating

[8] For further information on COPS, see CRS Report RL33308, Community Oriented Policing Services (COPS): In Brief and CRS In Focus IF10922, Community Oriented Policing Services (COPS) Program.

[9] See DOJ, COPS, "About the COPS Office, accessed September 20, 2023, at https://cops.usdoj.gov/aboutcops.

hate and domestic extremism, violent and gun crime, building legitimacy and trust, innovations in community policing, or police-based responses to people in crisis.

Eligibility: State, local, territorial, and federally recognized tribal law enforcement agencies.

Match Requirement: Funds require a 25% local cash match.

Additional Information:

- Program Overview
  https://cops.usdoj.gov/chp
- FY2023 Solicitation
  https://cops.usdoj.gov/pdf/2023ProgramDocs/chp/solicitation.pdf
- Fact Sheet
  https://cops.usdoj.gov/pdf/2023ProgramDocs/chp/Pre_Award_Fact_Sheet.pdf

Anti-Heroin Task Force (AHTF) Program

This competitive grant program provides funds to support investigations of illicit activities related to the distribution of heroin, fentanyl, carfentanil, the unlawful distribution of prescription opioids, and opioid trafficking. Funds may be used to pay for personnel and equipment directly related to investigations.

Eligibility: State law enforcement agencies with multijurisdictional reach and task forces with primary authority over state seizures of heroin and other opioids.[10]

Match Requirement: None.

Additional Information:

- Program Overview

---

[10] Primary law enforcement authority is defined as "the first responder to calls for service for all types of criminal incidents within its jurisdiction. Agencies are not considered to have primary law enforcement authority if they only respond to or investigate specific type(s) of crime(s); respond to or investigate crimes within a correctional institution; serve warrants; provide courthouse security; transport prisoners; and/or have cases referred to them for investigation or investigational support." See DOJ, COPS, *2020 COPS Office Anti-Heroin Task Force Program Application Guide*, March 2020, p. 88, at https://cops.usdoj.gov/pdf/2020AwardDocs/ahtf/App_Guide.pdf.

https://cops.usdoj.gov/ahtf
- FY2023 Solicitation https://cops.usdoj.gov/pdf/2023ProgramDocs/ahtf/solicitation.pdf
- Pre-Award Fact Sheet https://cops.usdoj.gov/pdf/2023ProgramDocs/ahtf/ Pre_Award_Fact_Sheet.pdf
- Pre-Award AHTF Frequently Asked Questions https://cops.usdoj.gov/pdf/2023ProgramDocs/ahtf/faq.pdf

COPS Anti-Methamphetamine Program (CAMP)

This competitive grant program provides funds to support investigations of illegal activities related to methamphetamine. Funds may be used to pay for personnel and equipment directly related to investigations.

Eligibility: State law enforcement agencies authorized to engage in or supervise anti- methamphetamine investigative activities.

Match Requirement: None.

Additional Information:

- Program Overview https://cops.usdoj.gov/camp
- FY2023 Solicitation https://cops.usdoj.gov/pdf/2023ProgramDocs/camp/solicitation.pdf
- Pre-Award Fact Sheet https://cops.usdoj.gov/pdf/2023ProgramDocs/camp/ Pre_Award_Fact_Sheet.pdf
- Pre-Award Frequently Asked Questions (FAQ) https://cops.usdoj.gov/pdf/2023ProgramDocs/camp/faq.pdf

Community Policing Development

Community Policing Development (CPD) funds are used to develop the capacity of law enforcement to implement community policing strategies. FY2023 competitive programs for law enforcement focus on crisis intervention, de-escalation training and law enforcement accreditation. Only CPD grants available to law enforcement are described in this section.[11]

Eligibility: State, local, tribal, and territorial law enforcement agencies.

Match Requirement: None.

Implementing Crisis Intervention Teams

- FY2023 Solicitation https://cops.usdoj.gov/pdf/2023ProgramDocs/cpd_cit/solicitation.pdf
- Pre-Award Fact Sheet https://cops.usdoj.gov/pdf/2023ProgramDocs/cpd_cit/Pre_Award_Fact_Sheet.pdf
- Pre-Award Frequently Asked Questions https://cops.usdoj.gov/pdf/2023ProgramDocs/cpd_cit/faq.pdf

De-Escalation Training

- FY2023 Solicitation https://cops.usdoj.gov/pdf/2023ProgramDocs/cpd_de_escalation/lea_solicitation.pdf
- Pre-Award Fact Sheet https://cops.usdoj.gov/pdf/2023ProgramDocs/cpd_de_escalation/Pre_Award_Fact_Sheet.pdf
- Pre-Award Frequently Asked Questions https://cops.usdoj.gov/pdf/2023ProgramDocs/cpd_de_escalation/faqs.pdf

Accreditation

- FY2023 Supporting Law Enforcement Agencies in Seeking Accreditation -Community Solicitation https://cops.usdoj.gov/pdf/2023ProgramDocs/cpd_accreditation/lea_solicitation.pdf
- Pre-Award Fact Sheet https://cops.usdoj.gov/pdf/2023ProgramDocs/cpd_accreditation/Pre_Award_Fact_Sheet.pdf
- Pre-Award Frequently Asked Questions https://cops.usdoj.gov/pdf/2023ProgramDocs/cpd_accreditation/faqs.pdf

---

[11] Grants open to non-law enforcement agencies include Tolerance, Diversity, and Anti-Bias Training, Emerging Issues Forums, and Innovations in Recruitment and Hiring. For further information, see https://cops.usdoj.gov/grants.

Community Policing Development Microgrants Program

This competitive grant program helps develop the capacity of law enforcement to implement community policing strategies. FY2023 funding focuses on programs targeting community-based violence intervention, officer recruitment and retention and workplace diversity, hate crimes and domestic extremism, underserved populations, and building trust and legitimacy with the community.

Eligibility: State, local, territorial, and tribal law enforcement agencies.
Match Requirement: None.
Additional Information:

- Program Overview
https://cops.usdoj.gov/cpdmicrogrants
- FY2023 Solicitation
https://cops.usdoj.gov/pdf/2023ProgramDocs/cpdmicrogrants/solicitation.pdf
- Pre-Award Fact Sheet
https://cops.usdoj.gov/pdf/2023ProgramDocs/cpdmicrogrants/Pre_Award_Fact_Sheet.pdf

Law Enforcement Mental Health and Wellness Act (LEMHWA) Implementation Projects

This competitive grant program funds efforts to improve the delivery of and access to mental health and wellness services for law enforcement. Areas of focus have included the implementation of peer support programs, access to mental health and wellness services, suicide prevention, stress reduction, and support programs for officers and their families.

Eligibility: State, local, territorial, and tribal law enforcement agencies.
Match Requirement: None.
Additional Information:

- Program Overview
https://cops.usdoj.gov/lemhwa
- FY2023 Solicitation

https://cops.usdoj.gov/pdf/2023ProgramDocs/lemhwa/Implementation_Projects_Solicitation.pdf

- Pre-Award Fact Sheet https://cops.usdoj.gov/pdf/2023ProgramDocs/lemhwa/Pre_Award_Fact_Sheet.pdf
- Frequently Asked Questions https://cops.usdoj.gov/pdf/2023ProgramDocs/lemhwa/FAQs.pdf
- CRS Report R46555, Federal Efforts to Address the Mental Health of First Responders: Resources and Issues for Congress

School Violence Prevention Program (SVPP)

This competitive grant program provides funding to improve security at schools and on school grounds. Funds may be used for security improvements, such as metal detectors, lighting, locks, and other deterrent measures; training for law enforcement officers to prevent student violence; and technology for expedited notification of law enforcement. Funds may also be used to hire civilian or non-sworn personnel. These funds may not be used to hire school resource officers.

Eligibility: Law enforcement agencies, state and local governments, and federally recognized Indian tribes, school districts, and school boards.

Match Requirement: 25% match.

Additional Information:

- Program Overview
- https://cops.usdoj.gov/svpp
- FY2023 Solicitation
- https://cops.usdoj.gov/pdf/2023ProgramDocs/svpp/solicitation.pdf
- Fact Sheet
- https://cops.usdoj.gov/pdf/2023ProgramDocs/svpp/Pre_Award_Fact_Sheet.pdf
- Frequently Asked Questions (FAQ)
- https://cops.usdoj.gov/pdf/2023ProgramDocs/svpp/faqs.pdf
- CRS Report R46872, Federal Support for School Safety and Security, Federal Support for School Safety and Security

Other Department of Justice Resources, Programs and Initiatives for Law Enforcement

In addition to providing grants to assist law enforcement, DOJ provides community resources, initiatives, and technical assistance to law enforcement agencies.[12] The following are selected programs addressing community relations, mass violence community response, and antiterrorism training for law enforcement agencies.

BJA National Training Technical Assistance (BJA NTTAC)

BJA NTTAC provides no-cost training and technical assistance to law enforcement agencies, prosecutors' offices, corrections departments, and city or county commissioners on a wide variety of criminal justice issues. Training can be provided in person or virtually.

Additional Information:

- BJA NTTAC website
  https://bjatta.bja.ojp.gov

Collaborative Reform Initiative Technical Assistance Center (CRI-TAC)

The Collaborative Reform Initiative Technical Assistance Center (CRI-TAC) program provides no cost resources and technical assistance to state, local, territorial, and tribal law enforcement agencies on a wide variety of topics (e.g., active shooter response, crisis intervention, violent crime reduction, de-escalation, and community violence prevention).

Additional Information:

- Program Overview
  https://cops.usdoj.gov/collaborativereform

[12] For a complete list of DOJ Training and Technical Assistance programs, see https://bjatta.bja.ojp.gov/.

Community Relations Service

The Community Relations Service provides training, consultation, mediation, and other support to law enforcement agencies to improve community relations, conflict resolution, and cultural awareness.

Additional Information:

- Program Overview
  https://www.justice.gov/crs/
- Programs for Law Enforcement
  https://www.justice.gov/crs/our-stakeholders/law-enforcement
- Fact Sheet
  https://www.justice.gov/file/1376521/download
- Programs and Services
  https://www.justice.gov/file/1376576/download

Mass Violence Advisory Initiative

This partnership between the Office of Justice Programs and the International Association of Chiefs of Police offers peer-to-peer counseling to law enforcement leaders whose communities have experienced a mass violence incident. This initiative, provides virtual and in-person assistance to law enforcement leaders, including incident management, public information strategies, and other support, free of charge.

Additional Information:

- Program Overview
- https://www.theiacp.org/projects/mass-violence-advisory-initiative
- Frequently Asked Questions
- https://www.theiacp.org/sites/default/files/2021-09/MVAI/MVAI%20FAQs.pdf

State and Local Anti-Terrorism Training (SLATT) Program Training and Technical Assistance (TTA)

This program offers free training addressing terrorism prevention, targeted violence, and hate crimes to state, local, and tribal law enforcement, prosecutors and others. Training is available on- site, virtually, or in an e-learning format. Access to this site is limited to registered law enforcement agencies.

Additional Information:

- Program Overview https://bja.ojp.gov/program/state-and-local-anti-terrorism-training-program/ overview

Valor Officer Safety and Wellness Initiative

This competitive program awards grants to entities that promote officer safety through specialized training and other activities, including, officer safety and wellness initiatives, crisis intervention and resolution training, active shooter training, officer suicide prevention, and researching law enforcement injuries and fatalities.

Additional Information:

- Program Overview https://bja.ojp.gov/program/valor/overview

Support for Grantees and Applicants

The Office of Justice Programs (OJP) has several resources designed to provide assistance to grant seekers. The following resources address frequently asked questions regarding grants and the application process.

- List of Programs provides a full list of OJP grant programs. https://bja.ojp.gov/program/list
- OJP Funding Resource Center provides information on funding opportunities and an overview of the OJP grant process.

https://www.ojp.gov/funding

- OJP Grant Application Resource Guide provides assistance to applicants in preparing and submitting applications. https://www.ojp.gov/funding/apply/ojp-grant-application-resource-guide
- OJP Opportunities and Awards site provides a list of currently open OJP grant opportunities, links to open solicitations and past grant solicitations. https://www.ojp.gov/funding/explore/current-funding-opportunities
- Office of Justice Programs Grants 101 provides information on grants, the grant cycle, and assistance throughout the application process. https://www.ojp.gov/funding/grants101/overview-ojp-grants-and-funding

Chapter 7

Standing Strong on the Thin Blue Line: How Congress Can Support State and Local Law Enforcement*

Committee on Homeland Security

Hearing Statement of Ranking Member Bennie G. Thompson (D-MS)

Standing Strong on the Thin Blue Line: How Congress Can Support State and Local Law Enforcement, May 15, 2024

I want to thank our panel of witnesses for being here today and for their service to our country. In honor of National Police Week, I also want to recognize the incredible contributions of law enforcement and honor those brave officers who have made the ultimate sacrifice to keep our communities safe. Our Nation is forever in their debt.

Today, the Committee is meeting to examine how Congress can support State and local law enforcement. This is an important question. National Police Week is of great importance, but congressional support for law enforcement is about more than attending a ceremony or wearing a blue ribbon on your lapel one week out of the year.

It's about supporting law enforcement not just with ceremonial words or symbolic gestures but showing up when it counts and voting for the resources our police officers need every day.

---

* This is an edited, reformatted and augmented version of Congressional Research Service Publication, dated May 15, 2024.

In: The Future of Law Enforcement
Editor: Mohamed Swift
ISBN: 979-8-89530-863-9

It's about saying no when a disgraced former President calls for defunding the FBI or certain Members threaten to cut off funding for DHS because they have political disagreements with the Biden administration.

It's about keeping dangerous weapons out of the hands of those who would seek to harm our communities, our kids, our houses of worship, our supermarkets, our gathering places, and the police sworn to protect all of us. And it's about honoring the heroic law enforcement officers — Capitol Police, Metropolitan Police, and others — who protected and defended this very Capitol and everyone in it on January 6, 2021.

While extreme MAGA Republicans try to cut funding and undermine public trust in law enforcement, Democrats are committed to providing Federal, State, local, Tribal, and territorial law enforcement with funding and support to keep our communities safe. Democrats have made historic investments in public safety, law enforcement, school security, gun violence prevention, and non-profit security for churches, synagogues, and schools. As a result, violent crime has dropped across nearly every category during the Biden administration. We are proud of doing right by law enforcement but recognize more remains to be done.

I hope to hear from our witnesses today about supporting community policing efforts across the country and how Congress can help fund those critical efforts. I also hope to hear from our witnesses about how we can encourage police forces to recruit more diverse candidates, including people of color and women, because police forces work best when they reflect the communities they serve.

Again, I thank the witnesses for joining us today and express my appreciation for all the men and women of law enforcement who serve communities across America with honor and integrity. Be assured that those words have been and will continue to be backed up by action.

Testimony
National Organization of Black Law Enforcement Executives (NOBLE) Before the U.S. House of Representatives Committee on Homeland Security
Wednesday, May 15, 2024

Chairman, Congressman Mark Green MD, Ranking Member, Congressman Bennie Thompson, and committee members, I bring you greetings on behalf of the Executive Board, members, and constituents of the National Organization of Black Law Enforcement Executives – NOBLE.

My name is Rodney Bryant, and I am the National President. NOBLE serves as the conscience of law enforcement by being committed to Justice by Action. NOBLE has 58 chapters and represents over 4,500 members worldwide that consist of chief executive officers and command-level law enforcement officials from federal, state, county, municipal law enforcement agencies, and criminal justice practitioners.

I have served more than 35 years in the law enforcement profession in various positions of increasing responsibility to include serving as patrol officer, senior police, sergeant, lieutenant, assistant commander, major, and as the 25th chief of the Atlanta Police Department. It is an honor for NOBLE to provide written testimony on the topic of "Standing Strong on the Thin Blue Line: How Congress Can Support Local Law Enforcement."

I would be remiss if I did not recognize that this week is National Police Week where we honor and remember those law enforcement officers who have made the ultimate sacrifice in the line of duty. In 2023, approximately 136 officers died in the line of duty representing a 40% reduction compared to 2022. However, one officer lost is one too many. NOBLE will continue to stand vigilant and in solidarity with law enforcement in efforts to reduce this statistic. We invite Congress to join us in this "NOBLE" pursuit.

On April 29th, our nation experienced the deadliest attack against U.S. law enforcement officers since 2016. An AR-15 semi-automatic rifle and a 40-caliber handgun were deployed in a Charlotte, NC shooting that resulted in four law enforcement officers being killed and wounding four others. I extend heartfelt prayers and condolences to the officers' families, agencies, and affected communities. NOBLE is very concerned about the level of gun violence in the United States, and specifically the correlation between violence and the proliferation of assault weapons and high-capacity ammunition magazines. It is our organization's opinion that violence—particularly gun violence is a public health issue. And, as with all public health issues, it demands a comprehensive, nonjudgmental, pragmatic, evidence-based approach to saving lives and reducing injury.

A positive step towards addressing the level of gun violence in our nation was taken with the passage of the Bipartisan Safer Communities Act. NOBLE supported this legislation. The bill combined gun safety legislation with mental health and school security resources.

Bipartisan Safer Communities Act Highlights:

- Increases funding and improves mental health, school safety, crisis intervention and anti-violence programs.
- Requires tougher background checks for younger gun buyers, those who are deemed a risk in certain cases, and closes the so- called "boyfriend loophole," barring intimate partners who have been convicted of domestic violence crimes against their significant other from having a gun even if they don't live together.
- We at NOBLE recommend that in addition to the Bipartisan Safer Communities Act, that Congress, the Law Enforcement Profession, and communities across this nation work to secure the passage of bi-partisan legislation that will at minimum address the following:
    - Mandate Universal Background Checks
    - Ban Assault Weapons
    - Ban High-Capacity Magazines
    - Mandate Safe Gun Storage
    - Relaxation of Gun
    - Laws such as Permitless Carry which exist in 29 states. It is NOBLE's belief and many in our profession that the continued relaxation of gun laws poses a real danger to law enforcement officers and the community.
    - Key Statistics
        - 2023 Mass Shootings – Approximately 656 Mass Shootings
        - Firearms Number #1 Killer of Children (ages 1-17)
        - In 2023, Firearms-related officer deaths accounted for 35% of the 136 officers killed in the line of duty.
        - Studies have shown that officers are significantly more likely to be fatally shot in states with weaker gun laws and higher levels of gun ownership.

It is my opinion that the law enforcement profession is in need of comprehensive federal legislation such as the George Floyd Justice in Policing Act. NOBLE did support the Biden Administration's Executive Order on Advancing Effective, Accountable Policing and Criminal Justice Practices to Enhance Public Trust and Public Safety. There are key elements in the order that we feel are reasonable and actionable such as accountability, workforce support, use-of-force, and resource support for mental / behavioral health services. Our organization recommends to Congress a bi-partisan effort to find common ground on a very basic constitutional right within the 14th

Amendment – Equal Protection Under The Law. For many parts of our society, citizens have not felt equally protected by a key American institution, law enforcement. In many communities of color, the first names of unarmed citizens that were killed by officers, who took an oath to protect and serve, resonate today and for generations to come. Their names are Tamir, Eric, Breonna, George, to name a few.

Lastly, I appeal to our congressional leaders of both parties to continue to support our federal law enforcement agencies in the areas of funding, public support, and policies that ensure that they maintain their readiness. It is critical that federal law enforcement resources are available to support state, county, local, and tribal law enforcement agencies. There must be a unified congressional understanding of the importance of ensuring Homeland Security for our nation which equates to strengthening all levels of public safety.

On behalf of the law enforcement leaders and constituents of NOBLE, I thank you for supporting our profession and our ability to maintain public safety. Our members stand ready to meet the needs of our communities and nation. Thank you again for this opportunity to provide testimony.

Rodney Bryant

Rodney Bryant, a more than 15-year member of the National Organization of Black Law Enforcement Executives, is the organization's 46th national president. He previously served as first vice president and second vice president, as well as sergeant-at-arms for both the national office and the Georgia Chapter. He also served as the planning committee chair for the 2017 Annual Exhibit Training and Conference in Atlanta, Georgia.

He joined the Atlanta Police Department in 1988. During his career, he climbed the ranks, serving as a patrol officer, senior police, sergeant, lieutenant, assistant commander and major. Highlights of his career include leading the command of Super Bowl LIII in 2019 and the College Football Playoff Championship in 2018. He retired in 2022 as the 25th chief of the department.

In alignment with 21st Century Policing, which asserts that law enforcement agencies must be well- trained and sensitive to the needs of the communities they serve to be effective, Bryant supports training that is tailored for each agency. He is also committed to bold leadership with respect to reducing gun violence, addressing the issue of missing and murdered women and children of color, and law enforcement recruitment with an eye toward middle management and mentoring for leadership.

Bryant earned a bachelor's degree in criminal justice from Georgia State University and a master's degree in administration at Central Michigan University.

Additionally, he is a graduate of the Federal Bureau of Investigation (FBI) National Executive Institute and is an active member of the International Association of Chiefs of Police (IACP), the Major Cities Chief Association (MCCA), the Georgia Association of Chiefs of Police (GACP), Atlanta Metropol, Inc., and the Atlanta Urban Area Security Initiative.

Police ★ Est. ★ Austin 1949 Association

Austin Police Association

"Serving Those Who Serve"

Chairman Green, members of the committee, thank you for the opportunity to testify before you today. My name is Michael Bullock and I'm the President of the Austin Police Association in Texas as well as a Senior Police Officer with the Austin Police Department.

I wish it were amidst better times that I sit here before you today, but this somber week of honoring our fellow law enforcement officers killed in the line of duty sets the tone for the tate of our profession.

In my view, the state of law enforcement is dire. We all recognize that criminal justice as a whole, is a complex policy issue for which no singular solution exists. But if we continue to do nothing – the sense of lawlessness being perpetuated in urban city centers and across the country will only get worse.

Austin is the 10th largest city in the United States with a million people living in the Capitol of Texas. Despite this, we don't even make the top 25 list when it comes to staffing. We're 700 officers short of where studies done by the city of Austin have shown we need to be. Our staffing issues can be linked to a few key events, though our struggles are shared by agencies across the country.

In 2017 the Austin City Council unanimously voted against a contract with the Austin Police Association which governs the wages, benefits, and working conditions of the men and women of the Austin Police Department. As a result, beginning in 2018 we have had more officers leave our department each year than have joined. Compounding this problem in 2020 was when our city leaders defunded our department by $150,000,000, cut 150 authorized positions, and cancelled cadet classes all for the sake of political posturing.

Our staffing has been in a freefall that's led us to a vacancy rate of over 30%. Little surprise then that after these decisions and an exodus from the department began, that a year later our number of homicides nearly doubled. The last 3 years have been the highest homicide numbers in Austin's history.

Though we are not a border city, the impact of immigration policies is felt by us as well. Our city has asked for help from the Texas State Troopers who came for a time and had a notable impact on crime. But due to the ongoing border crisis they were called away to help secure the Texas border and no longer able to help us in Austin. In May of 2023, teenagers shot and killed a man in southeast Austin when attempting to rob him. The reason they gave for this heinous crime, was they knew State Troopers had left Austin and decided to start committing crime again.

Adding additional layers of complexity to this issue is a lackadaisical attitude towards holding criminals accountable by judges and prosecutors, while at the same time seeing those same prosecutors target officers, which has in turn encouraged criminals to be increasingly violent towards law enforcement.

Over these same time periods we've seen a myriad of critical incidents take place. We have dealt with a serial bomber planting improvised explosive devices across our city killing our residents, had numerous mass shootings including one breaking out during one of our largest festivals, and most notably on our minds is an incident that took the life of one of our own.

On November 11, 2023 in the early morning hours, our APD SWAT team was called to a residence in southeast Austin where an armed subject was barricaded inside the residence, had already stabbed one his family members with two more inside, and shot at officers. Fearing for the lives of others inside the residence and knowing this vile suspect had already attempted to kill one of his own family members and willingly shot at our fellow APD officers – our SWAT team went through the door to try and save lives. After going in they were met by a hellacious barrage of gunfire from the suspect who was well armed and wearing body armor. While the suspect was ultimately taken out it came at a high price. Two of our officers were shot, one of which was Officer Jorge Pastore who paid the ultimate sacrifice.

Across this country we now see a law enforcement officer shot in the line of duty every 21 hours. This year alone we've had over 145 officers shot which has been increasing year over year.

Our job is to uphold the Constitution and enforce the laws passed by yourselves as well as your state and local counterparts. This is a charge we take seriously and one we are willing to sacrifice our lives for. I sit here before you today though pleading for your help. We need help in addressing our staffing needs, support in enforcing our laws, providing better training resources, and transcending the political rhetoric to end the war on law enforcement and restore law and order in our country. The trends we see in Austin are not isolated – and if not reversed, I fear that lawlessness is all but inevitable.

Respectfully,

Michael Bullock

Michael Bullock President
Austin Police Association

Thank you, Mr. Chairman, Ranking Member, and members of the Committee.

My name is Mike Chapman, I am the elected Sheriff of Loudoun County, Virginia. I appreciate being invited to testify at this important hearing during what is one of the most important weeks of the year for law enforcement.

Loudoun County sits about 30 miles southwest of Washington, DC, and is home to about 450,000 residents.

I am in my 46th year of law enforcement, having served as a police officer and detective in Maryland, twenty-three years with the Drug Enforcement Administration as a Special Agent from coast to coast and in three foreign assignments, and over 12 years as the elected sheriff in Virginia's largest full-service sheriff's office employing close to 900. Prior to being elected sheriff, I served three years as a law enforcement subject matter expert with Booz Allen. I bring first-hand knowledge of police work, federal experience, a private sector perspective, and the complexities associated with the elected office of sheriff.

I am here today on behalf of the National Sheriffs' Association (NSA) and serve as its Chair for Homeland Security and on its Board of Directors.

I'd like to address today's hearing "Standing Strong on the Thin Blue Line: How Congress Can Support State and local Law Enforcement." Historically and currently law enforcement collaborates well together, regardless if it is a sheriffs' office or police department. When national law enforcement organizations collectively present their concerns and positions – whether in support or opposition to legislation – Congress needs to listen. Congress' decision can significantly impede law enforcement's service, performance – i.e. investigations or even recruiting. Supplying grant money or funding is not the cure all. Backing from Congress in all aspects is essential.

This is National Police Week as America honors the day-to-day service and sacrifice of our law enforcement community. And on this day, Peace Officer Memorial Day, we honor those who have given their lives in the line of duty. This year we have already witnessed 58 line of duty deaths among law enforcement officers, with 21 of those by gunfire.

Our job is dangerous, and we need your help to serve and protect our communities - and ourselves. We ask that you recognize how law enforcement has and continues to raise the bar. The progress I have witnessed since I was hired to be a police officer in 1978 when it comes to training, professionalism, innovation, and best practices is nothing short of amazing.
It is important that you recognize this progress and publicly show your support for our profession. It is also important that you listen so that you can help us do our job better.

Let's start with intelligence gathering and police response.

Currently, there are 80 state or locally run fusion centers in 50 states and US territories. They receive grant federal grant funding which accounts for about 1/3rd the cost of operation. There is also federal, state and local coordination through six strategically placed Regional and Information Sharing Systems (RISS) centers across the U.S.

Considering that local law enforcement are the boots on the ground, it is critical that federal information flows quickly in our direction, even if the information is incomplete. The responsibility for this communication and coordination primarily falls under the Department of Homeland Security (DHS) Intelligence and Analysis (I&A). I&A is the only federal entity that is statutorily required to coordinate homeland security threat information sharing with state and local governments through fusion centers. Congress should ensure I&A is equipped and empowered to carry out that mission effectively.

In Loudoun County, I experienced a personal case study with DHS regarding poor communication, both laterally with other federal agencies, and onward to state and local agencies.

In February 2022, I was made aware that some 1,000 refugees from Afghanistan would be arriving in Loudoun County in two weeks as part of "Operation Allies Welcome" following the U.S. withdrawal from Afghanistan. This would be the first wave during a six month period – all to be located at the National Conference Center dorm-style living facility in a suburban, residential area of our county next to a middle and high school.

I immediately reached out to the DHS' Chief of Staff for additional information and to question their lack of notification earlier to local law enforcement and our public safety partners. We needed to know how well were the refugees were vetted, if the local hospital had been contacted, if school personnel and community members living within walking distance been notified, if any houses of worship had been contacted, if language capabilities services been retained, and how security would be conducted. Unfortunately, none of these concerns had been addressed. DHS subsequently postponed resettlement for 2 weeks, still not addressing these issues.

I alerted the public and organized a community stakeholders' meeting including dozens of agencies which led to specific assignments and a community forum that, for the most part, alleviated the apprehension of the community. Our local initiative made a huge difference. For the next six months potential chaos was averted, and there were no major public safety incidents. This extraordinary effort, however, would not have been necessary had DHS communicated an organized plan. We hope that this will improve in the future.

Today we face a new set of challenges on many of our college campuses and cities over matters in the Middle East. It is critical that we receive timely information from DHS to get ahead of the curve.

We need your help. We need your backing. We need improved communication from DHS to our local officers and deputies. Thank you, again, for holding this hearing, and for listening.

Loudoun County Sheriff's Office

Sheriff Michael L. Chapman

Mike Chapman was elected Sheriff, Loudoun County, VA in 2011 and took office January 2012. He was reelected to serve his fourth term in 2023. He was selected as the National Sheriffs' Association Ferris E. Lucas "Sheriff of the Year" in 2023. He was also voted "Best Public Servant" by readers of the Loudoun Times Mirror in 2022 and 2023, and Favorite Public Servant in 2021, 2022, and 2023 by readers of Loudoun Now, the two newspapers serving Loudoun County.

Sheriff Chapman directs an $133M budget and operations for the largest Sheriff's office in the Commonwealth of Virginia which handles county-wide law enforcement, the jail and the courts. The Sheriff's Office employs approximately 700 sworn deputies and 200 civilian personnel. The Loudoun County Sheriff's Office serves a population of 447,000 and an area of 519 square miles.

During his terms in office, Sheriff Chapman expanded the Drug Abuse Resistance Education (DARE) to include both Elementary and Middle Schools (named DARE Executive of the Year), established a Cold Case squad; enhanced media outreach through integrated technology and proactive social media; introduced on-line reporting; professionalized the Human Resources and hiring processes; and, through his Step Up initiative, improved service, technology, efficiency and professionalism. Sheriff Chapman initiated Crisis Intervention Team (CIT) training for deputies and dispatchers in 2012 - a program that leads the region for CIT Training. With DEA and other stakeholders, he addressed the rapidly growing national and local heroin and opioid problem and more recently has become laser-focused on fentanyl related poisonings.

Sheriff Chapman serves on the Board of Directors for the National Sheriffs' Association; the Virginia Sheriffs' Association's Board of Directors as Region VI Director, and the DARE Law Enforcement Advisory Board . He was appointed by Virginia Governor Glenn Youngkin to the Department of Criminal Justice Services Board. He served for five years as Vice President of Homeland Security for the Major County Sheriffs of America (MCSA) and was Chair of the Washington-Baltimore High Intensity Drug Trafficking Area Board. Sheriff Chapman graduated from the FBI National Executive Institute (NEI) and Law Enforcement Executive Development Association (LEEDA); the US Army War College – National Security (Certificate of Leadership Development); the National Sheriffs' Institute, the Virginia Sheriffs' Institute (VSI), Virginia Commonwealth University's Sheriffs' Institute, and earned the Virginia Department of Criminal Justice Services' Executive Certification and received the VSI Certification. He has had numerous articles published in professional periodicals to include The Hill, International Chiefs of Police The Police Chief, FBI LEEDA Insighter magazines, the Richmond Times Dispatch, and other publications.

Sheriff Chapman formerly worked for the Howard County Maryland Police Department in the Divisions of Patrol, SWAT and Criminal Investigations; and for the DEA where he directed all operations throughout the Far East, served as the Assistant Special Agent in Charge in San Francisco, CA; as DEA's Chief of Public Affairs; as the Country Attaché for Seoul, Korea; as a Supervisor in McAllen, Texas; and in field assignments in Miami, Tampa, and Pakistan. Prior to his election, Sheriff Chapman worked as a Subject Matter Expert on the Global Security/Law Enforcement team with Booz Allen and Hamilton.

Sheriff Chapman is married to the former Ann Rafferty and they have six children and ten grandchildren. He has a Bachelor of Science in Business Management, University of Maryland, and a Master's in Public Administration from Troy State University, Alabama.

Statement for the Record by Deputy Commissioner Greg Mays Tennessee Department of Safety and Homeland Security Hearing Before the Committee on Homeland Security United States House of Representatives "Standing Strong on the Thin Blue Line: How Congress Can Support Local Law Enforcement," May 15, 2024

Thank you, Chairmen Green, and Ranking Member Thompson for holding this hearing and for the invitation to testify with my fellow law enforcement leaders on some of the critical law enforcement and security issues facing the American Homeland.

The Tennessee Office of Homeland Security is a law enforcement agency with statewide jurisdiction. Our primary mission is to investigate threats to life, threats to our schools, protect our state's critical infrastructure and major events, and to work with our federal, state, and local partners to prepare for and mitigate any threats to our state. Our Department's overall mission is to serve, secure, and protect the people of Tennessee. We set about every day to accomplish our mission in several ways:

- Homeland Security employs a cadre of Homeland Security Special Agents across the State – at least one in each of our ninety-five counties. These law enforcement officers focus on threats to our schools and critical infrastructure and regularly conduct behavioral-based threat assessments. Our Homeland Security Special Agents come from varied backgrounds and bring a depth and breadth of experience to their mission to serve and protect Tennesseans.
- Homeland Security partners with the Tennessee Bureau of Investigation to co-direct the Tennessee Fusion Center – a team effort of local, state, and federal law enforcement, in cooperation with the citizens of the State of Tennessee, for the timely receipt, analysis and dissemination of terrorism information and criminal activity relating to Tennessee.
- Homeland Security helps to facilitate the distribution of federal grant funding every year from the DHS Homeland Security Grant Program. Since inception in 2003, OHS has seen over $280M come to Tennessee and go toward projects designed to make Tennesseans more secure. I'll speak more about these grants in a moment.
- Tennessee Homeland Security maintains a Cyber Security expertise focused on Homeland Security issues at the state and local level by providing training and assisting in responses to cyber-related incidents.
- Tennessee Homeland Security maintains a close watch on our state's Critical Infrastructure. DHS has designated 16 different Critical Infrastructure sectors ranging from Energy to Financial to Agriculture to Transportation. All these sectors are vital to our state. We work with law enforcement and our stakeholders to determine vulnerabilities and mitigate the threat.
- And last, but certainly not least, Tennessee Homeland Security partners with local law enforcement, the Tennessee Department of Education, local school districts, the mental health community, juvenile court systems, and communities around the state to keep our children safe by helping to develop and conduct security assessments at our state's K-12 public schools and investigate threats before they materialize on the school's doorstep.

As we gather here today during National Police Week to honor the fallen peace officers across our nation, it is also a time for us to focus on the challenges faced by law enforcement and the threats to our homeland. My testimony will focus on three areas to highlight some successes and challenges. Thank you again for the opportunity to be here.

I would like to start with security in our schools. On March 27, 2023, Nashville was rocked by a shooting at the Covenant School. Three children and three adults lost their lives in addition to the shooter who was killed by police while she was still shooting at arriving officers from a second story window of the school. This shooting so close to home further steeled our resolve to do everything we can to prevent something similar from happening again.

We approach school security in Tennessee by focusing on three main areas of concern:

- First, physical security such as door locks, cameras, barriers, access control procedures – sometimes a simple solution works best.
- Secondly, proper response protocols must be in place and exercised. If a tragic event does happen, law enforcement must be trained to respond appropriately and stop the killing. School students and administrators must be trained and have a plan to shelter in place or evacuate as appropriate. All these plans must be exercised regularly – a new state law in Tennessee requires it. We saw in the Covenant shooting the rapid and professional response of officers from the Metro Nashville Police Department. There is no doubt the bravery and rapid response of the officers saved lives that horrible day.
- The third focus of concern is perhaps the most complex. We must investigate every credible threat and evaluate the subject's capability and intent to act violently. Research such as the U.S. Secret Service's National Threat Assessment Center study published in 2021, titled "Averting Targeted School Violence" looked at sixty-seven averted school attacks. The study found 94% of school shooters told someone they were going to do it. The other 6% in the study were behaving so oddly that bystanders reported them. So, in all these cases, we see that law enforcement officers, educators, mental health counselors, and concerned community members must be listening and ready to report and act on any threatening behavior or statements.

The Office of Homeland Security partners with schools to encourage this type of reporting. Of course, some kids feel more comfortable communicating electronically. So, In Tennessee, we instituted the SafeTN App to allow students (or members of the community) to anonymously report threatening behavior. The app also provides resources for anyone contemplating suicide or self-harm. The Tennessee Office of Homeland Security operates a 24/7 threat desk where these incoming calls for help or action are acted upon immediately.

As I mentioned earlier, the Governor of Tennessee proposed, and the TN General Assembly funded, a Homeland Security Special Agent in each of Tennessee's ninety-five counties to help coordinate the multi-agency approach to school security and to conduct these behavioral-based threat investigations.

Tennessee's local law enforcement officers play a critical role in school safety by acting as School Resource Officers (SROs). Last year, the Governor proposed, and General Assembly provided, funding to place one SRO in each of Tennessee's K-12 public and charter schools. This grant funding is managed by the Office of Homeland Security and is available directly to law enforcement agencies to hire, train, and equip law enforcement officers to serve in the important SRO role. Of the $140M allocated on July 1, 2023:

- Over $101M has been awarded upfront for salary, benefits, training, and equipment.
- 154 law enforcement agencies applied and were funded.
- 1356 schools are covered by this state grant.
- As of 3/31/24, 1309 of 1356 schools were staffed with an SRO (97%)

Is this approach to school security working? Although we don't claim to have solved the issue of school security, we are seeing positive results. For example, in the fall of 2023, Homeland Security agents, working with local Sheriff's Deputies, began an investigation of a student who had come to school in full tactical gear and made a bomb threat.

The investigation indicated that subject had a fascination with the military, weapons, and explosives and that he also fantasized about killing people. Further investigation revealed the subject owned several knives and smoke grenades. Information was discovered that revealed the subject was frequently a victim of bullying by other students. A search warrant of the subject's cell phone showed evidence of making threats of being a terrorist, a member of the Taliban, conducting a school shooting, and shooting police. The subject underwent a court ordered mental evaluation where he was determined to have homicidal tendencies. The subject was admitted to a mental health facility for further evaluation and care.

We work a significant number of cases just like this one. Since the beginning of this academic year - approximately August 1, 2023 - the Office of Homeland Security has logged over 322 threats to schools in Tennessee – or more than one threat to a school every day. And this number reflects only those threats which are known to us – either reported through our reporting mechanisms or reported by schools directly to us, or reported by local, state, or federal agencies to us. We do not know the actual total number of school threats in the state because the local schools and law enforcement agencies are not required to report them to us. The problem is big.

Nothing is more important than the safety and security of our children. Law enforcement will continue to prioritize the security of our schools.

I would now like to pivot to the subject of grants. Tennessee has benefitted greatly from the Federal Homeland Security Grant Program since its inception in 2003. As you know, three individual grant programs make up the federal Homeland Security Grant Program:

- State Homeland Security Program (SHSP)
- Urban Area Security Initiative (UASI) – Nashville area only
- Operation Stone Garden (for border states)

Federal funding for these state and territorial preparedness grant programs (SHSP, UASI, and Operation Stone Garden) has dropped 44% since FY2010—including a 10% cut alone for FY2024.

These programs that states and territories rely on for homeland security funding have all seen declines. On top of the decline in aggregate dollar amounts, given inflation, the purchasing power of each dollar provided has dropped more than 20% since 2014.

These grant programs are a very worthwhile endeavor and we have had much success responding to manmade and natural disasters because of them. For example, in the immediate aftermath of the Nashville Christmas Day bombing in 2020, which damaged a piece of critical infrastructure and shut down 911 communications centers in the region, equipment acquired through the HSGP such as command posts, alternate communications equipment, rescue equipment, and training for responders was deployed and aided in the Response and Recovery efforts. With much of the equipment acquired through this program at the local level, it has served multiple functions for manmade and natural disasters and has created enduring capabilities in all of Tennessee's ninety-five counties.

Another very important federal grant program is the Nonprofit Security Grant Program (NSGP). This program provides support for target hardening and other physical security enhancements for nonprofit organizations that are at high risk of a terrorist attack. In Tennessee, requests for funding under this program have skyrocketed from 10 applicants in 2019 to 103 applicants last year – a tenfold increase. This year's application process is currently open and expected to see increases in applicants from last year.

These grant funds have saved lives.

On July 31, 2023, a suspect attempted to gain entry into the Margolin Hebrew Academy in Memphis with the apparent intent to kill those inside this Jewish school. After unsuccessful attempts to gain entry through locked doors, the subject fired shots outside the school and fled.

He was encountered by police a short distance away and was shot and taken into custody by police after brandishing a weapon. The school credited recent security upgrades with avoiding tragedy. Specially, the school wrote a letter to my office crediting the Nonprofit Security Grant Program (NSGP). The letter read in part,

> "I want to take this opportunity to express my deepest gratitude to both of you for your invaluable support in securing and administering the NSGP for enhancing our security measures. The implementation of the latest security grant allowed us to reinforce our entrances with new doors and access control, ultimately preventing the shooter from gaining entry. Additionally, the cameras installed from a previous grant played a pivotal role in assisting law enforcement in locating and neutralizing the shooter swiftly."

Again, these grant funds save lives. And as federal funding of these programs declines, the needs are increasing.

In Tennessee, the need to help protect our non-profits and houses of worship does not rely on federal funding alone. The Tennessee General Assembly recently allocated money for a new state grant program for nonprofits and houses of worship. Like the federal nonprofit grant, we have seen a sharp increase in requests for these limited funds. In the FY23 state program, we received over $2.2M in requests, far outstripping the $750,000 of state funds we had available to award.

Finally, I'd like to speak briefly about an emerging threat to Tennessee and our nation where we need help from the federal government. Part of my role as Deputy Commissioner for Homeland Security is to evaluate the potential for future threats and take mitigation measures now to protect Tennessee.

When I peek over the horizon to anticipate what may be coming, one challenge I see is weaponized Unmanned Aerial Systems, or drones. The proliferation of drones has become a problem from a security and law enforcement perspective. While the federal government has taken steps to regulate use of drones and to some degree license users, little is available for state and local law enforcement in the way of countering drones that may be used as a method of attack.

It's no secret this drone threat is real. Drones can be used to smuggle payloads, transport contraband, and carry lethal payloads or other weaponized materials. We've seen weaponized drones recently in the war in Ukraine, and in attacks on Israel.

In the United States, we've seen an increasing number of drones in sensitive locations. For example, last fall, in two higher profile instances, a drone flew over an Ohio State football game, as well as a Baltimore Ravens playoff game. In Tennessee, we saw drones flying over public gatherings and causing safety concerns for law enforcement aircraft in the area.

Since drones are classified as aircraft by the FAA, only certain federal agencies, including DHS and DOJ, currently have the legal authorization to mitigate threats from UAS. While many states have taken steps to regulate where drones can be flown, states do not have the authorization to mitigate a drone in-flight—they can only monitor its flight path and penalize those who fly in prohibited areas.

I believe the probability of a weaponized drone attack in the United States should be a top priority for all of us who hold positions of responsibility for the security of our nation's homeland. I ask this Committee to prioritize Counter-UAS (C-UAS) for funding and expanded cooperation with states in this area.

I have mentioned several times today the importance of partnerships. Law Enforcement in Tennessee and around the country take pride in working together to support each other under very difficult conditions. These partnerships – which are crucial to success – were never more evident to me than on Christmas Day 2020 when a vehicle borne explosive device was detonated in downtown Nashville, all but destroying a city street. Only a few hours after the explosion, I found myself standing in the rubble on 2nd Ave and observing federal, state, and local law enforcement all working together to determine what happened and why. The partnerships, information sharing, and preparedness funding contributed to quickly identifying the perpetrator, confirming he was deceased, and later confirming that he acted alone.

As the Deputy Commissioner of Tennessee's Office of Homeland Security, keeping the people and places in Tennessee safe and secure is on my mind every day. Our dedicated group of highly experienced law enforcement and public safety personnel always stand ready to serve, secure, and protect the people of Tennessee. But a single law enforcement or public safety agency cannot do it alone. We need each other. We need the support of the United States Congress and the support of the American people.

I thank you once again for the opportunity to be here today.

Chapter 8

The Community Oriented Policing Services (COPS) Program: Potential Issues for Reauthorization*

Nathan James

Summary

The Community Oriented Policing Services (COPS) program is one of the primary sources of federal support for state and local law enforcement in the United States. The program is administered by the COPS Office in the Department of Justice (DOJ).

The COPS program was established by the Violent Crime Control and Law Enforcement Act of 1994 (P.L. 103-322). While the initial authorization created multiple grant programs under COPS, the program that provided grants to hire law enforcement officers to engage in community policing activities was the one that received the greatest attention. P.L. 103-322 authorized appropriations for the COPS program from FY1995 to FY2000. The COPS program was last reauthorized by the Violence Against Women and Department of Justice Reauthorization Act of 2005 (P.L. 109-162). This act changed the structure of the COPS program and authorized appropriations from FY2006 to FY2009. The COPS program has not been reauthorized since, though legislation to do so has been introduced in nearly every Congress since authorized appropriations for the program expired at the end of FY2009. Even absent reauthorization, several laws have been enacted since P.L. 109-162 that have expanded the scope of the COPS program, including, most recently, by the Recruit and Retain Act (P.L. 118- 64), which allowed

* This is an edited, reformatted and augmented version of Congressional Research Service Publication No. R48151, updated October 1, 2024.

In: The Future of Law Enforcement
Editor: Mohamed Swift
ISBN: 979-8-89530-863-9

COPS grants to be used for programs to make it easier to hire new officers and to promote careers in law enforcement.

Annual appropriations for the COPS program averaged nearly $1.5 billion from FY1995 to FY1999. Annual COPS funding largely decreased from FY2000 to FY2014, with a few exceptions. The decrease in funding during these years was partially a result of moving funding away from hiring programs, a change in the account structure for the COPS program (funding that was previously provided under the COPS account, but which was eventually transferred to other grant making organizations at DOJ, was moved to other grant-related accounts), and likely related to a ban on congressionally directed funding that started in FY2011. COPS funding has increased since FY2015, which is the result of increasing funding for hiring programs and for existing and new nonhiring initiatives such as anti-heroin task forces, active shooter training, and grants under the Matching Grant Program for School Security. Also, since FY2022, appropriations for the COPS account have included funding for community funding projects.

This report discusses issues policymakers might consider, if they take up legislation to reauthorize the COPS program. It starts by providing legislative and funding histories for the COPS program. It then discusses select issues for Congress related to potential reauthorization legislation. This includes issues that are specific to the structure of the COPS program, such as the limit on the total amount a law enforcement agency can receive to hire an officer, how funding is allocated among large and small jurisdictions, and how appropriations for COPS compare to the authorization for the program. It also includes discussion of the role of the COPS program in addressing two larger issues facing law enforcement: decreases in law enforcement staffing and their potential effect on crime, and the use of force by officers and law enforcement's relationship with communities of color.

The mission of the Community Oriented Policing Services (COPS) program is to advance community policing in jurisdictions across the United States.[1] The COPS program awards grants to state, local, and tribal law enforcement agencies, so they can hire and train law enforcement officers in community policing, purchase and deploy new crime-fighting technologies, and develop and test new and innovative policing strategies.

The COPS program was originally authorized by the Violent Crime Control and Law Enforcement Act of 1994 (P.L. 103-322; 1994 Crime Act). Though the 1994 Crime Act established multiple programs under COPS, the

---

[1] U.S. Department of Justice, Community Oriented Policing Services Office, *About the COPS Office*, https://cops.usdoj.gov/aboutcops.

program that provided grants to hire law enforcement officers to engage in community policing activities was the one that received the greatest attention. The program supported the Clinton Administration's goal to fund 100,000 new law enforcement officer positions.[2] Initial authorization of appropriations for the COPS program expired at the end of FY2000. The COPS program was last reauthorized from FY2006 to FY2009 through the Violence Against Women and Department of Justice Reauthorization Act of 2005 (P.L. 109-162; 2005 DOJ reauthorization).

Legislation to reauthorize the COPS program has been introduced in nearly every Congress since authorized appropriations expired at the end of FY2009.[3] Legislation was also introduced in the 117th and 118th Congresses that would have expanded the allowable uses of COPS grants to address staffing shortages by allowing the grants to be used for, among other things, paying hiring and retention bonuses and funding recruiting activities. During an April 2024 Senate Judiciary Committee hearing on the COPS program, several members of the committee noted the need to reauthorize the program.[4]

This report discusses issues policymakers might consider if they take up legislation to reauthorize the COPS program. It starts by providing legislative and funding histories for the COPS program. It then discusses select issues for Congress related to potential reauthorization legislation. This includes issues that are specific to the structure of the COPS program, such as the limit on the total amount a law enforcement agency can receive to hire an officer, how funding is allocated among large and small jurisdictions, and how appropriations for COPS compare to the authorization for the program. It also includes discussion of the role of the COPS program in addressing two larger issues facing law enforcement: decreases in law enforcement staffing and their potential effect on crime, and the use of force by officers and law enforcement's relationship with communities of color.

---

[2] U.S. Department of Justice, *The Clinton Administration's Law Enforcement Strategy: Combatting Crime with Community Policing and Community Prosecution*, March 1999, p. 1.

[3] See, for example, the COPS Improvements Act of 2009 (H.R. 1139, 111th Cong.), COPS Improvements Act of 2011 (H.R. 1896, 112th Cong.), COPS Improvements Act of 2014 (S. 2254, 113th Cong.), COPS Improvements Act of 2015 (S. 2401, 114th Cong.), COPS Reauthorization Act of 2018 (S. 2774, 115th Cong.), COPS Reauthorization Act of 2021 (S. 3374, 117th Cong.), and COPS Reauthorization Act of 2023 (S. 1306, 118th Cong.).

[4] U.S. Congress, Senate Committee on the Judiciary, *Oversight of the Community Oriented Policing Services (COPS) Grant Program*, 118th Cong., 2nd sess., April 10, 2024.

Legislative History

The COPS program was first authorized by Title I of the 1994 Crime Act. The program was subsequently reauthorized by the 2005 DOJ reauthorization. Though appropriations for the COPS program have not been reauthorized since the 2005 DOJ reauthorization, laws have been enacted that have modified the scope of the COPS program. This section of the report provides an overview of legislation related to the COPS program. It does not provide a comprehensive account of every change made to the program's authorization; rather, it highlights significant changes to the authorization that have shaped the current structure of the program.

Violent Crime Control and Law Enforcement Act of 1994

The 1994 Crime Act authorized the Department of Justice (DOJ) to award COPS grants to state, local, and tribal governments, other public and private entities, and multijurisdictional or regional consortia to "increase police presence, to expand and improve cooperative efforts between law enforcement agencies and members of the community to address crime and disorder problems, and otherwise to enhance public safety." To further this stated purpose of the COPS program, the act authorized DOJ to make grants to (1) hire law enforcement officers and train them in community policing; (2) rehire law enforcement officers who were laid off due to budget cuts to serve in community policing; and (3) procure equipment, technology, or support systems, or pay overtime, if it would increase the number of officers serving in community policing equal to or greater than the increase in the number of officers that would result from a grant for a similar amount to hire or rehire law enforcement officers to serve in community policing. The act also authorized DOJ to award grants for a Troops-to-Cops program, which could be used to hire former members of the armed services to work as community policing officers. Under the act, authority to award hiring grants expired on September 13, 2000.

In addition, the act authorized DOJ to award COPS grants for other programs, projects, and activities (nonhiring programs) that would

- increase the number of law enforcement officers engaging members of the community on proactive crime prevention and control strategies;
- provide specialized training to law enforcement officers to enhance their conflict resolution, mediation, problem solving, service, and other skills needed to partner with members of the community;
- increase police participation in multidisciplinary early intervention teams;
- develop new technologies to help law enforcement agencies reorient their focus from reacting to crimes to preventing crimes;
- develop and implement programs to help citizens engage in efforts with law enforcement agencies to prevent crime and to increase their access to the criminal justice system;
- establish programs to decrease the amount of time law enforcement officers must spend attending court hearings;
- establish and implement programs that partner law enforcement officers and young persons in proactive efforts to control and prevent crime in the community;
- establish management and administrative systems to facilitate adoption of community-oriented policing as an organizational philosophy;
- establish, implement, and coordinate crime prevention and control programs with other federal programs to better address the comprehensive needs of the community; and
- help purchase service weapons for law enforcement officers.

The act established a 25% match requirement for COPS grants. Further, the act required that for any grant for hiring or rehiring a law enforcement officer that is longer than one year, the match provided by the grant recipient is required to increase each year.[5] The act also established a $75,000 per officer maximum amount for grants for hiring or rehiring a law enforcement officer.

The act required DOJ to award not less than 0.5% of the total amount of grant funding available each fiscal year to each qualifying state, unless all applications from the state have been funded. It also provided that half of the annual funding for the COPS program must be awarded to jurisdictions of

---

[5] For example, over the course of a three-year hiring grant, a grantee could provide a 15% match the first year, a 25% match the second year, and a 40% match the third year.

150,000 or fewer people and the other half must be awarded to jurisdictions of more than 150,000 people.

The act required that those applying for a COPS grant submit an application for funding that

- includes a long-term strategy and an implementation plan that reflects consultation with community groups and appropriate private and public agencies;
- demonstrates a specific public safety need;
- explains the applicant's inability to address public safety needs without grant funding;
- identifies related governmental and community initiatives that complement or will be coordinated with the proposal;
- certifies there has been appropriate coordination with all affected agencies;
- outlines the initial and ongoing level of community support for implementing the proposal, including financial and in-kind contributions;
- specifies plans for obtaining necessary support and continuing the proposed program, project, or activity following the conclusion of the grant;
- specifies plans for how the applicant will pay an increasingly higher share of the officer's salary and benefits, if the application is for a grant for hiring or rehiring additional career law enforcement officers;
- assesses the effect, if any, of the increase in police resources on other components of the criminal justice system;
- explains how the grant will be utilized to reorient the law enforcement agency's mission toward community-oriented policing or enhance its involvement in or commitment to community-oriented policing; and
- provides assurances that the applicant will, to the extent practicable, seek, recruit, and hire members of racial and ethnic minority groups and women in order to increase their ranks within the agency.

The act authorized DOJ to waive one or more of the application requirements for jurisdictions of fewer than 50,000 people and for any applications for grants for nonhiring programs under $1 million, and to "otherwise make special provisions to facilitate the expedited submission, processing, and approval of such applications."

The act also required DOJ to include a monitoring component for any COPS grant. Monitoring must include systematic identification and collection of data about activities, accomplishments, and programs throughout the life of the program, project, or activity and presentation of such data in a usable form.[6] Further, it required selected grant recipient programs to be evaluated by a local evaluator or as part of a national evaluation, pursuant to guidelines established by DOJ.

The act authorized DOJ to use any component of the department to administer the COPS program. It authorized appropriations for the program at $1.332 billion for FY1995, $1.850 billion for FY1996, $1.950 billion for FY1997, $1.700 billion annually for both FY1998 and FY1999, and $268.0 million for FY2000.

P.L. 105-302

P.L. 105-302 amended the COPS authorization to allow DOJ to award grants to "establish school- based partnerships between local law enforcement agencies and local school systems by using school resource officers who operate in and around elementary and secondary schools to combat school-related crime and disorder problems, gangs, and drug activities."

---

[6] The COPS Office notes in the FY2024 COPS Hiring Program grant solicitation that "awarded organizations will be responsible for submitting Programmatic Performance Reports on a semiannual basis and SF-425—Federal Financial Reports on a quarterly basis. In addition, awarded organizations will be responsible for the timely submission of a final Closeout Report and any other required final reports" and that "the COPS Office may take a number of monitoring approaches, such as site visits, enhanced office-based award reviews, alleged noncompliance reviews, and periodic surveys to gather information and to ensure compliance"; U.S. Department of Justice, Community Oriented Policing Services Office, *FY204 COPS Hiring Program*, p. 34, https://cops.usdoj.gov/pdf/2024ProgramDocs/chp/solicitation.pdf.

The Prosecutorial Remedies and Other Tools to End the Exploitation of Children Today (PROTECT) Act of 2003

The PROTECT Act of 2003 (P.L. 108-21) amended the COPS authorization to allow DOJ to award grants to assist state and tribal governments with enforcing sex offender registry laws.[7]

Violence Against Women and Department of Justice Reauthorization Act of 2005

The 2005 DOJ reauthorization changed the structure of and reauthorized appropriations for the COPS program.

The act amended the COPS authorization to make the COPS program a "single grant program under which the Attorney General makes grants to States, units of local government, Indian tribal governments, other public and private entities, and multi-jurisdictional or regional consortia" for a variety of purposes. These purposes were the nonhiring programs enumerated in the initial COPS authorization along with those added by P.L. 105-302 and the PROTECT Act. The 2005 DOJ reauthorization removed the authorization for the separate hiring and Troops-to-Cops programs. Under the new grant program DOJ was authorized to make grants to hire new law enforcement officers and rehire laid-off officers for community policing activities. Despite making this an allowable purpose under the new grant program, the act did not extend the date on which DOJ's authority to make hiring grants expired (September 13, 2000). The act also authorized DOJ to award COPS grants to "procure equipment, technology, or support systems, or pay overtime, to increase the number of officers deployed in community-oriented policing" and to "pay for offices hired to perform intelligence, anti-terror, or homeland security duties." In addition, the act modified the technologies for which the grants could be used to help law enforcement agencies reorient their focus from reacting to crimes to preventing crimes to include "interoperable communications technologies, modernized criminal record technology, and forensic technology." The act reauthorized COPS appropriations at $1.047 billion each year from FY2006 to FY2009.

---

[7] For more information on sex offender registry laws, see CRS Report R46863, Federal Requirements for State and Military Registered Sex Offender Management.

Tribal Law and Order Act of 2010

The Tribal Law and Order Act of 2010 (P.L. 111-211) authorized DOJ to award grants to tribal governments receiving direct law enforcement services from the Bureau of Indian Affairs (BIA) for many of the purposes for which COPS grants can be awarded.[8] The act also required DOJ to award grants to tribal governments to assist them in carrying out any of the purposes for which COPS grants can be used. Per the act, tribal governments are not required to provide matching funds for the cost of the program and grant funds can be used to cover indirect costs.[9] The act authorized $40 million per fiscal year from FY2011 to FY2015 for grants to tribal governments.

The Protecting Our Lives by Initiating COPS Expansion (POLICE) Act of 2016

The POLICE Act of 2016 (P.L. 114-199) authorized DOJ to award COPS grants to allow law enforcement officers to participate in nationally recognized, scenario-based active shooter training.

21st Century Cures Act

The 21st Century Cures Act (P.L. 114-255) authorized DOJ to awards COPS grants to

- provide specialized training to law enforcement officers in recognizing individuals who have a mental illness, and in how to properly interact with such individuals;
- establish programs that enhance the ability of law enforcement agencies to address the mental health, behavioral, and substance abuse problems of individuals encountered by law enforcement officers in the line of duty;

---

[8] For more information on how BIA provides law enforcement services on tribal lands, see CRS In Focus IF12569, *Law Enforcement on Tribal Lands*.

[9] For more information on indirect costs, see U.S. Department of Justice, *DOJ Grants Financial Guide*, January 2024, Section 3.11, pp. 87-90.

- provide specialized training to correctional officers to recognize individuals who have a mental illness; and
- enhance the ability of correctional officers to address the mental health of individuals under their supervision.

Law Enforcement Mental Health and Wellness Act of 2017

The Law Enforcement Mental Health and Wellness Act of 2017 (P.L. 115-113) authorized DOJ to award COPS grants to establish peer mentoring mental health and wellness pilot programs in state, local, and tribal law enforcement agencies.

Substance Use-Disorder Prevention that Promotes Opioid Recovery and Treatment (SUPPORT) for Patients and Communities Act

The SUPPORT for Patients and Communities Act (P.L. 115-271) authorized DOJ to use funding appropriated for the COPS program to make grants to state law enforcement agencies with "high seizures of precursor chemicals, finished methamphetamine, laboratories, and laboratory dump seizures for the purpose of locating or investigating illicit activities, such as precursor diversion, laboratories, or methamphetamine traffickers."

The act also authorized DOJ to use funding appropriated for the COPS program to make grants to state law enforcement agencies with "high per capita rates of primary treatment admissions, for the purpose of locating or investigating illicit activities, through Statewide collaboration, relating to the distribution of heroin, fentanyl, or carfentanil or relating to the unlawful distribution of prescription opioids."

Recruit and Retain Act

The Recruit and Retain Act (P.L. 118-64) authorized DOJ to award COPS grants to support hiring efforts for law enforcement agencies that have experienced declines in recruits by reducing application-related fees, such as fees for background checks, psychological evaluations, and testing.

The act required the COPS Office to award grants to law enforcement agencies that have partnered with an elementary or secondary school or college for recruiting activities, which can include the following:

- helping students explore potential future career opportunities in law enforcement;
- strengthening recruitment by law enforcement agencies that have had a decline in recruits or high rates of resignations or retirements;
- enhancing community interactions between youth and law enforcement agencies that are designed to increase recruiting; and
- supporting other recruitment activities such as dedicated programming for students, work-based learning opportunities, project-based learning, mentoring, community liaisons, career or job fairs, worksite visits, job shadowing, apprenticeships, or skills-based internships.

The act limited spending for these purposes to not more than $3 million of the amount of funding made available for the COPS program for these purposes. The act also required that grantees not spend more than 2% of funding they receive for hiring or rehiring officers on administrative costs.[10]

Appropriations for the COPS Program

Table 1 provides appropriations data for the COPS program since its inception. From FY1995 to FY1999, the annual appropriation for the program averaged nearly $1.5 billion and most of the annual funding was for hiring programs. The relatively high levels of funding during this period, compared to post-FY2000 appropriations, were largely the result of the effort to fund 100,000 new law enforcement officer positions.

[10] Documents from the COPS Office indicate that COPS hiring grants cannot be used for administrative costs. Frequently asked questions published by the COPS Office regarding the FY2024 solicitation for the COPS hiring program state, "CHP [COPS hiring program] funding may not be used for indirect costs. CHP only pays for approved entry-level salaries and fringe benefits of full-time sworn officers over three years." U.S. Department of Justice, Community Oriented Policing Services Office, *FY24 COPS Hiring Program (CHP) Pre-Award Frequently Asked Questions (FAQ)*, p. 9, https://cops.usdoj.gov/pdf/2024ProgramDocs/chp/faqs.pdf.

After the initial push to fund the 100,000 new officers, the COPS program changed into a conduit for supporting a wider range of local law enforcement needs. Starting in FY1998, an increasing portion of the annual appropriation for COPS was dedicated to programs that helped law enforcement agencies purchase new equipment, combat methamphetamine production, upgrade criminal history record systems, and improve their forensic science capabilities. Increased funding for nonhiring initiatives under the COPS account coincided with decreased funding for hiring programs. By FY2005, appropriations for hiring programs were nearly nonexistent, and funding for them was eliminated for FY2006 and FY2007. Funding for hiring programs was revived when the American Recovery and Reinvestment Act of 2009 (P.L. 111-5) provided $1 billion for the COPS hiring program. Appropriations for hiring programs from FY2009 to FY2012 were the result of efforts to help local law enforcement agencies facing budget cuts (as a result of the recession) either hire new law enforcement officers or retain officers they would have otherwise had to lay off. Appropriations continued to be provided for hiring programs even as the effects of that recession waned.

There was a notable reduction in the total amount of funding provided for the COPS program after FY2012 relative to previous fiscal years. Prior to FY2012, the least amount of annual funding (in nominal dollars) provided for the program was $472 million for FY2006. Although COPS funding has increased over the past several fiscal years, annual funding from FY2012 to FY2021 remained significantly lower than it was before FY2012. Lower annual appropriations for the COPS program during these fiscal years can likely be generally attributed to (1) a decrease in the amount of funding provided for hiring programs, (2) a ban on congressionally directed spending, and (3) restructuring of the COPS account. Increases in annual COPS funding starting in FY2022 are attributable to a partial reversal of some of these trends.

Congress prohibited congressionally directed spending—so-called earmarks—from FY2011 to FY2021. This ban substantially decreased funding for the Law Enforcement Technology and the Methamphetamine Clean-up programs, which were being administered by the COPS Office. By FY2012, there was no funding for the Law Enforcement Technology program and the only funding remaining for the Methamphetamine Clean-up program was transferred to the Drug Enforcement Administration to assist with the clean-up of clandestine methamphetamine laboratories. Funding for the Methamphetamine Clean-up program ceased in FY2018.

From FY2010 to FY2012, appropriations for several programs that were funded under the COPS account—such as Project Safe Neighborhoods, DNA backlog reduction initiatives, Paul Coverdell grants, offender reentry programs, the National Criminal History Improvement program, and the Bulletproof Vest Grant program—were moved to the State and Local Law Enforcement Assistance (S&LLEA) account in the annual Commerce, Justice, Science, and Related Agencies (CJS) appropriations legislation. Programs funded under this account are administered by the Office of Justice Programs (OJP). Prior to the programs being moved to the S&LLEA, appropriations for them were transferred from the COPS Office to OJP for administration. In general, from FY2001 to FY2011 appropriations for programs that were transferred to OJP accounted for one-third to one-half of the annual funding for the COPS account. In recent fiscal years, differing proportions of the COPS account have again been transferred to OJP. Since FY2017, Congress has also provided funding for the Regional Information Sharing System (RISS) program under the COPS account, which is transferred to OJP.

Funding for the COPS program has increased over the last 10 fiscal years, from $208 million for FY2015 to $685 million for FY2024. Increased funding for the COPS account during this time is the result of increasing funding for hiring programs and for nonhiring initiatives such as anti- heroin task forces, active shooter training, and grants under the Matching Grant Program for School Security. Also, for FY2024 funding was provided for the COPS Law Enforcement Technology program for the third straight fiscal year, which had been eliminated when Congress implemented its ban on congressionally directed spending.

Table 1. Appropriations for the COPS Program, FY1995-FY2024

(in millions of dollars)

Fiscal Year	*Total Appropriation*	*Hiring Programs Appropriation*	*Percentage Transferred to OJP*
1995	$1,300	$1,057	0%
1996	1,400	1,128	0%
1997	1,420	1,339	0%
1998	1,633	1,338	0%
1999	1,520	1,201	4%
2000	913	481	21%
2001	1,042	408	30%
2002	1,105	385	33%
2003	978	199	35%
2004	748	114	36%
2005	598	10	38%

Table 1. (Continued)

Fiscal Year	*Total Appropriation*	*Hiring Programs Appropriation*	*Percentage Transferred to OJP*
2006	472	—	53%
2007	542	—	51%
2008	587	20	41%
2009	1,551	1,000	18%
2010	792	298	26%
2011	495	247	34%
2012	199	141	0%
2013	209	155	0%
2014	214	151	0%
2015	208	135	0%
2016	212	137	0%
2017	222	137	16%
2018	276	150	13%
2019	304	153	12%
2020	343	156	11%
2021	386	157	10%
2022	532	157	8%
2023	683	225	6%
2024	685	157	6%

Source: FY1995-FY2017 appropriations were provided by the U.S. Department of Justice, Office of Community Oriented Policing Services; FY2018-FY2024 appropriations were taken from the explanatory statement to accompany the annual Commerce, Justice, Science, and Related Agencies Appropriations Act and from the text of the Bipartisan Safer Communities Act (P.L. 117-159).

Notes: Amounts include all supplemental funding, and are in nominal dollars. Amounts for hiring programs reflect all set-asides (see Table A-1 for more information).

Select Issues for Reauthorization

There are several issues that policymakers might consider, if Congress takes up legislation to reauthorize the COPS program; this section discusses some of these.

Cap on Hiring Grants

The authorization for the COPS program sets a cap of $75,000 per officer for hiring grants. A provision in the annual CJS appropriations act since FY2012 has increased this cap to $125,000.[11] Because hiring grants are three years in duration, a grant would cover $41,667 of a new or rehired officer's salary and benefits each year.

Table 2. Percentile annual salaries for police and sheriff patrol officers

May 2023

Percentile	Annual Salary
10%	$45,200
25%	$54,770
50%	$72,280
75%	$92,410
90%	$111,700

Source: Bureau of Labor Statistics, Occupational Employment and Wages, May 2023, 33-3051, Police and Sheriff Patrol Officers.

According to the Bureau of Labor Statistics (*Table 2*), the total salary for a law enforcement officer making the median salary over a three-year period is $216,840, meaning that a grant recipient would be required to pay the remaining $91,840, which is equivalent to a 42% match. Law enforcement agencies employing officers making a salary in the 25th percentile would be able to cover a majority of the officer's three-year salary costs with grant funds and come close to the statutory 25% match requirement (a $125,000 grant would cover 76% of the officer's salary over the three-year grant period).

Policymakers might consider whether to increase the $75,000 per officer cap on hiring grants in the COPS authorization (which has effectively been $125,000 since FY2012 because of a provision in the CJS appropriations act) to reflect the higher salaries for law enforcement officers since the COPS program was created in 1994. If policymakers chose to increase the cap on hiring grants, they might also consider whether to establish a mechanism so

[11] For example, the language in the FY2024 CJS appropriations act (P.L. 118-42) states that "$256,168,839 is for grants under section 1701 of title I of the 1968 Act (34 U.S.C. 10381) for the hiring and rehiring of additional career law enforcement officers ... *Provided*, That, notwithstanding section 1704(c) of such title (34 U.S.C. 10384(c)), funding for hiring or rehiring a career law enforcement officer may not exceed $125,000 unless the Director of the Office of Community Oriented Policing Services grants a waiver from this limitation."

that the cap increases in subsequent years, such as indexing the cap to inflation. While a higher cap might make it easier for grant recipients to cover the cost of hiring new officers, it might also mean that the COPS Office would make fewer awards, assuming that appropriations for the hiring program do not increase at a rate commensurate with the increasing cap.

Changing Allocation Among Jurisdictions

The current authorization for the COPS program requires the COPS Office to award half of annual funding for the program to jurisdictions of 150,000 or fewer people (*small jurisdictions*) and the other half to jurisdictions of more than 150,000 people (*large jurisdictions*).

Data from the Bureau of Justice Statistics (BJS) 2020 Law Enforcement Management and Administrative Statistics (LEMAS) survey indicate that there are 175 local police departments serving large jurisdictions and 11,538 serving small jurisdictions.[12] The police departments serving large jurisdiction employ the equivalent of 202,430 full-time officers and the departments serving small jurisdictions employ the equivalent of 263,006 full-time officers.[13] The data show that large police departments make up a small percentage of all police departments and these departments employ a disproportionately large number of officers. The police departments serving large jurisdictions account for 1.5% of all police departments, but they employ 43.5% of all officers in local police departments.

Congress might consider whether to change the way that COPS grants are allocated between small and large jurisdictions. The current requirement to split funding between small and large jurisdictions provides small jurisdictions, which tend to have fewer resources, with access to COPS funding. Requiring half of the annual funding to be awarded to these jurisdictions ensures that they will be able to receive COPS grant funds and they will not get out-competed for grants by larger jurisdictions that might be able to employ personnel who have expertise in applying for grants. However, there are many more small jurisdictions competing against each other for grants than there are large jurisdictions. Policymakers could consider a more

---

[12] CRS analysis of data from the 2020 LEMAS survey.

[13] Law enforcement agencies that responded to the survey indicated the number of full-time and part-time officers they employed. The number of part-time officers was divided in half and added to the number of full-time officers to calculate the number of full-time equivalent officers. This assumes that two part-time officers are equal to one full-time officer.

gradated division of annual COPS funding.[14] Should Congress seek to alter the distribution of grant funding, it could consider a number of adjustments. For instance, removing the current requirement to allocate half of funds to small jurisdiction and the other half to large jurisdictions and placing a limit on the number of officers a law enforcement agency can apply for, could leave more funding available for smaller agencies.[15] Other adjustments could be made to facilitate different targeting priorities.

Altering the Structure of the COPS Authorization

Congress changed the structure of the COPS program in the 2005 DOJ reauthorization. When the COPS program was initially authorized, there were distinct programs with specific purposes under COPS. The reauthorization changed the COPS program into a single grant program under which DOJ could award grants for a variety of enumerated purposes. However, appropriations under the COPS account do not reflect the structure of the COPS authorization. Congress continues to appropriate funding for specific purposes under the COPS account (e.g., hiring programs, active shooter training, anti-methamphetamine and anti-heroin task forces, school security programs) rather than providing funding for the general COPS program that would give DOJ some discretion regarding which purposes would be funded each fiscal year.

If policymakers decide to take up legislation to reauthorize the COPS program, they might consider whether to amend the COPS authorization to reflect what has been emphasized in the COPS account (i.e., distinct programs with specific purposes). Policymakers could also evaluate the list of authorized purposes for which COPS grants can be awarded, which is now up to 23, to determine if any should be repealed given that some have never received funding or have not been funded in more than a decade (see Table A-1 for a detailed breakdown of COPS funding, by program, for the past 10 fiscal years).

---

[14] For example, Congress could require the COPS Office to award 25% of annual funding to each quartile of agencies based on the size of jurisdiction they serve.

[15] Currently, requests for officer positions through the COPS hiring program are capped at 20% of the number of sworn officers employed by the requesting agency, with a maximum of 50 officers for any agency. The COPS Office imposed this restriction administratively; it is not statutory. U.S. Department of Justice, Community Oriented Policing Services Office, *FY24 COPS Hiring Program (CHP) Pre-Award Frequently Asked Questions (FAQ)*, p. 7.

Authorizing the COPS Office

The law that first authorized the COPS program did not authorize an office to administer the program. Rather, DOJ created the COPS Office administratively.[16] The COPS Office is the only grant-making agency in DOJ that does not have an authorization. Both OJP (34 U.S.C. §10101) and the Office of Violence Against Women (34 U.S.C. §10442) are authorized in statute. In addition, the grant making bureaus and offices in OJP have their own statutory authorization:

- Bureau of Justice Assistance (34 U.S.C. §10141)
- Bureau of Justice Statistics (34 U.S.C. §10132)
- National Institute of Justice (34 U.S.C. §10122)
- Office of Juvenile Justice and Delinquency Prevention (34 U.S.C. §11111)
- Office of Sex Offender Sentencing, Monitoring, Apprehending, Registering, and Tracking (34 U.S.C. §20945)
- Office for Victims of Crime (34 U.S.C. §20111)

The authorizations for these agencies provide for considerations such as who will head the agency, how that official will be appointed, who the official reports to, the agency's responsibilities and jurisdiction, and where the agency resides in DOJ's organizational structure.

If Congress takes up legislation to reauthorize the COPS program, policymakers might consider whether to authorize the COPS Office in statute. While the COPS Office has existed uninterrupted since the program's inception, its structure is established through rulemaking, which means that its functions could be changed without congressional consent. For example, the Trump Administration in FY2019 and FY2020 proposed merging the COPS Office with OJP to "streamline services, save taxpayer dollars, and eliminate duplication among DOJ's grant components."[17] If Congress chooses to pursue this, authorizing the COPS Office would allow Congress to establish the

---

16 U.S. Department of Justice, "Establishment of the Office of Community Oriented Policing Services," 60 *Federal Register* 8932, February 16, 1995. For more information on executive branch authority to shape the federal bureaucracy, see CRS Report R44909, *Executive Branch Reorganization*, and CRS Legal Sidebar LSB10158, *Organizing Executive Branch Agencies: Who Makes the Call?*

17 U.S. Department of Justice, FY2019 Performance Budget, Community Oriented Policing Services, February 12, 2018, p. 3.

office's role in DOJ, its responsibilities, and its organizational structure (such as whether the director should be Senate-confirmed).

Law Enforcement Staffing

Recent reports of law enforcement agencies losing officers because of retirement, leaving the profession, or moving to another (usually larger and better paying) agency has raised concerns among some policymakers about law enforcement staffing levels and their effects on public safety. Legislation has been introduced in 118th Congress that would allow COPS funding to be used to pay hiring and retention bonuses, support recruitment efforts, and supplement current officers' salaries.[18]

The most recent data from the Census Department's Annual Survey of Public Employment and Payroll show that the number of law enforcement officers decreased from 2019 to 2022 (Table 3). The decrease in law enforcement officers from 2019 to 2022 did not greatly change the number of officers per 1,000 people. There were 2.2 law enforcement officers per 1,000 people in the United States in 2019, and 2.1 law enforcement officers per 1,000 people each year from 2020 to 2022.

Table 3. Law enforcement officers in the United States, 2013-2022

Year	Number of Law Enforcement Officers	Rate per 1,000 People
2013	672,060	2.1
2014	678,896	2.1
2015	683,850	2.1
2016	687,643	2.1
2017	698,277	2.1
2018	710,428	2.2
2019	711,387	2.2
2020	702,508	2.1
2021	695,380	2.1
2022	692,917	2.1

Source: Census Bureau's Annual Survey of Public Employment and Payroll. Rate calculated by the Congressional Research Service using U.S. population estimates from the Census Bureau.

---

[18] See, for example, the Enhancing COPS Hiring Program Grants for Local Law Enforcement Act (H.R. 3376); the Recruit and Retain Act of 2024 (H.R. 3325 and S. 546); the Invest to Protect Act of 2023 (H.R. 3184 and S. 1144); the COPS on the Beat Grant Program Parity Act of 2023 (S. 1530); and the Filling Public Safety Vacancies Act (S. 972).

A survey conducted by the Police Executive Research Forum (PERF) suggests that the number of law enforcement officers increased in 2023.[19] The PERF survey is not representative of all law enforcement agencies in the United States. PERF reported that 214 agencies responded to their 2024 survey and that large agencies (those with 250 or more officers) were overrepresented in the results. That being said, in aggregate, the responding agencies reported that they employed more sworn officers in January 2024 (151,335) than they did in January 2023 (150,714). However, the survey also found that the number of officers employed by these agencies was 4.9% less than the number they employed in January 2020 (159,199). PERF found variation across agencies, noting that small (1-49 officers) and medium (50-249 officers) agencies reported having more officers in January 2024 than they did in January 2020, while large agencies had fewer officers in January 2024 compared to January 2020.

Data from the PERF survey provide some insight into the decrease in the number of law enforcement officers in the United States from 2019 to 2022. Respondents to the survey indicated that there was a decrease in the total number of sworn officers hired in 2020 compared to 2019.

However, the number of officers hired increased in each of the three following years. Even though law enforcement agencies were hiring more officers, there was an increase in the number of resignations and retirements in 2020, 2021, and 2022.[20] The number of resignations and retirements decreased in 2023.

Interest in law enforcement staffing levels stems from concerns among some policymakers about what effect it might have on public safety. The assumption that more law enforcement officers will result in lower levels of crime is based in economic theory. In theory, criminals act in rational ways, meaning that they balance the costs and benefits of different courses of action. As such, criminals will engage in criminal activity if they believe that the potential benefits outweigh the potential costs. Having more law enforcement

---

[19] Police Executive Research Forum, "New PERF Survey Shows Police Agencies Have Turned a Corner with Staffing Challenges," April 27, 2024.

[20] Law enforcement agencies were not alone in losing personnel due to resignations during this period, which coincided with the COVID-19 pandemic, and is sometimes referred to as the Great Resignation. It has been reported that state and local governments lost 1.5 million jobs at the onset of the pandemic, and while employment rebounded somewhat by the end of 2021, state and local governments employed about 928,000 fewer people than they did before the pandemic. Liz Farmer, "The Great Resignation's Impact on Local Government," Rockefeller Institute of Government blog, January 20, 2022, https://rockinst.org/blog/the-great-resignations-impact-on-local-government/.

officers theoretically increases the probability that criminals will be caught and punished, thereby increasing the costs associated with criminal activity and deterring criminal behavior. More arrests can also result in more criminals being incarcerated, which could have an incapacitation effect; in other words, criminals will not be able to commit more crimes because they are imprisoned. More law enforcement officers could also potentially decrease crime though specific deterrence (i.e., tracking specific offenders, who in turn reduce their criminal activity).

Those concerned about the effect of fewer law enforcement officers on public safety point to studies showing that having more police officers contributes to decreases in crime. They argue these studies suggest a decrease in police force size will result in more crime. The research on the relationship between the size of police forces and crime is mixed (see the text box below).

Research suggests that the complete absence of law enforcement—during a police strike, for example—can result in an increase in crime,[21] but there is little research on the effects of a marginal decrease in the number of law enforcement officers. An exception is a 2021 study of two neighboring jurisdictions that revealed increases in violent and property crimes after Newark, NJ, laid off 13% of its police officers in 2010, while the adjacent Jersey City, NJ, was able to forgo layoffs, and experienced decreases in violent and property crimes during the same period.[22]

Effects of the Number of Law Enforcement Officers on Crime

There is a robust body of research on the effects of increases in the number of law enforcement officers on crime levels. Researchers at various points in time have conducted studies to summarize the body of research on this topic. Generally, research on the effects of more law enforcement officers on crime levels has produced mixed results, and when research finds a positive effect, the size of the effect tends to be small. Methodological

[21] YongJei Lee, John E. Eck, and Nicholas Corsaro, "Conclusions from the History of Research into the Effects of Police Force Size on Crime—1968 Through 2013: A Historical Systematic Review," *Journal of Experimental Criminology*, vol. 12 (2016), pp. 433-434 (hereinafter, "Lee et al., "Effects of Police Force Size on Crime").

[22] Eric L. Piza and Vijay F. Chillar, "The Effect of Police Layoffs on Crime: A Natural Experiment Involving New Jersey's Two Largest Cities," *Justice Evaluation Journal*, vol. 4, no. 2 (2021), pp. 163-183.

issues with these studies might make it difficult to measure how much of an effect more law enforcement officers have on crime.[23]

- One meta-analysis conducted in 2004 found that increasing the number of law enforcement officers is associated with a decrease in the amount of both violent and property crime. The researcher estimated that the increase in the number of law enforcement officers between 1991 and 2001 accounted for a 5% to 6% reduction in crime.[24]
- A 2006 review of studies on the effects of law enforcement on violent crime found mixed results. The studies in the review confirmed all possible results—law enforcement led to increases in violent crime, led to decreases in violent crime, and had no effect on violent crime.[25] The researchers concluded that there is not a consistent body of evidence to support the assertion that hiring more law enforcement officers can decrease violent crime.
- A 2015 meta-analysis found evidence that the number of law enforcement officers had an effect on crime rates, though the effect was small.[26] The authors concluded that the number of law enforcement

---

[23] One of the challenges in studying the relationship between the number of law enforcement officers and crime is unraveling the simultaneity problem (i.e., when the value of one variable is determined by the value of a second variable, but at the same time the value of the second variable is determined by the value of the first variable). In the context of the relationship between the number of law enforcement officers and the amount of crime, the number of law enforcement officers is contingent upon the amount of crime (cities might hire additional officers in response to rising crime rates), but the amount of crime is determined by the number of officers (crime might decrease if more officers are hired or crime could appear to increase because more crimes are reported). If statistical models do not control for this problem, it could appear that having more officers leads to more crime. Researchers have noted that the statistical methods utilized to test the relationship between the number of law enforcement officers and crime might not be sensitive enough to detect a link between the two variables. They note, "in contrast to the quasi- and randomized controlled experimental literature, nonexperimental studies are easy to implement, but their collective findings may be too weak and unreliable to inform policy." There has been little change in the overall number of law enforcement officers in the United States since the early 1990s, which could make it hard to detect the effect of marginal increases in law enforcement officers on crime. Lee et al., "Effects of Police Force Size on Crime," pp. 446-447.

[24] Steven D. Levitt, "Understanding Why Crime Fell in the 1990s: Four Factors That Explain the Decline and Six That Do Not," *Journal of Economic Perspectives*, vol. 18, no. 1 (Winter 2004), p. 176.

[25] John E. Eck and Edward R. Maguire, "Have Changes in Policing Reduced Violent Crime? An Assessment of the Evidence," in *The Crime Drop in America, Revised Edition*, eds. Alfred Blumstein and Joel Wallman (New York, NY: Cambridge University Press, 2006), pp. 210-214.

[26] Michael L. Carriaga and John L. Worrall, "Police Levels and Crime: A Systematic Review and Meta-Analysis," *The Police Journal*, vol. 88 (December 2015), pp. 265-346.

officers have a small, negative effect on overall crime rates. But they also note that "when this relationship is examined across individual crime types, the effect decreases in magnitude, loses statistical significance and, in some cases, changes direction."[27]

- A 2016 meta-analysis concluded that the relationship between the size of a police force and crime is "negative, small, and not statistically significant."[28] The authors concluded that "merely increasing police force size does nothing to reduce crime."[29] The authors also found that more recent studies did not support a link between increased numbers of law enforcement officers and lower crime. The same was true for studies utilizing more rigorous research designs or statistical techniques.
- More recent research has found that an increase in the number of law enforcement officers can decrease crime. A 2019 study used a natural experiment created by cities that received COPS hiring grants in 2009 under the American Recovery and Reinvestment Act of 2009 (P.L. 111-5); it estimated hiring grants increased police forces by 3.2% and crime rates in cities that received grants were 3.5% lower relative to cities that did not receive a grant.[30] A 2022 study found that additional police had an effect on homicide, but consistent with some past research, the effect was small. The study found that one additional law enforcement officer is associated with 0.1 fewer homicides, meaning it would require hiring 10 new officers to prevent 1 homicide.[31]

Concerns about law enforcement staffing levels and their effects on crime might raise questions for policymakers about the scope of the COPS program. If Congress wants to fund the COPS program as a means of supporting public safety, the research on the effects of increasing the number of law enforcement officers on crime might raise questions about whether this is an effective way of accomplishing that goal. It has been argued that having the police engage in evidence-based practices such as hot-spots policing, problem-oriented policing, and focused deterrence is more effective at reducing crime than just increasing the number of law enforcement officers.[32] If Congress takes up

[27] Ibid., p. 328.
[28] Lee et al., "Effects of Police Force Size on Crime," p. 445.
[29] Ibid., p. 446.
[30] Steven Mello, "More COPS, Less Crime," *Journal of Public Economics*, vol. 172 (April 2019), pp. 147-200.
[31] Aaron Chalfin et al., "Police Force Size and Civilian Race," *American Economics Review: Insights*, vol. 4, no. 2 (June 2022), pp. 139-158.
[32] Lee et al., "Effects of Police Force Size on Crime," pp. 440-441.

legislation to reauthorize the COPS program, policymakers might consider whether to allow COPS grants to be used to aid law enforcement agencies in adopting evidence-based policing practices instead of or in addition to hiring additional law enforcement officers. On the other hand, law enforcement agencies might need a minimum level of staffing in order to engage in proactive, evidence-based policing activities while still being able to provide other policing services, such as responding to calls for service.[33]

In light of recent reports about law enforcement agencies losing officers due to resignations, transfers, or retirements, policymakers might consider whether to allow COPS funds to be used for purposes other than law enforcement officers' salaries that could help agencies hire and retain officers. Congress took a step in this direction through amendments made by the Recruit and Retain Act (see above). Policymakers might consider whether to make further changes to the COPS program regarding recruiting and retaining law enforcement officers by allowing grant recipients to use COPS grants for hiring or retention bonuses, to provide housing stipends for officers who live in the jurisdiction, to help officers repay student loans or take college courses that could help them advance in the department, or to fund studies of ways to streamline the hiring process or reshape the curriculum at training academies. Congress might also consider whether to allow COPS grants to be used for programs to promote law enforcement careers in high schools and colleges or to create internship or apprenticeship programs; or whether to allow the grants to be used to hire non-sworn personnel to handle administrative tasks, which could allow officers to spend more time on patrol and responding to calls for service.

Law Enforcement Reform

Several high-profile deaths of people at the hands of law enforcement officers, particularly young Black men, over the past decade have contributed to ongoing demands for law enforcement reforms. Congressional efforts on this front culminated with the House's consideration and passage of the George Floyd Justice in Policing Act of 2020 (H.R. 7120, 116th Congress) in June 2020 and the George Floyd Justice in Policing Act of 2021 (H.R. 1280, 117th

---

[33] Jeremy M. Wilson and Alexander Weiss, *A Performance-Based Approach to Police Staffing and Allocation*, U.S. Department of Justice, Community Oriented Policing Services Office, Washington, DC, 2014, pp. 15-16.

Congress) in March 2021. Both pieces of legislation would have placed conditions on COPS grants as a means of promoting law enforcement reforms. Both bills would have

- prohibited COPS grant recipients from entering into a contract, such as a collective bargaining agreement, that would prevent DOJ from seeking or enforcing equitable or declaratory relief against a law enforcement agency engaging in a pattern or practice of unconstitutional misconduct, or that conflicts with any terms or conditions contained in a consent decree;
- required COPS grant recipients to have policies and procedures designed to eliminate racial profiling and show that they have eliminated any existing practices that permit or encourage racial profiling;
- made state and local governments ineligible for COPS funding unless they have a law that prohibits the use of no-knock warrants in drug cases;
- made state and local governments ineligible for COPS funding unless they have a law that prohibits the use of chokeholds or carotid holds by state and local law enforcement officers; and
- made state and local governments ineligible for COPS funding unless they have a law that makes it a criminal act for a law enforcement officer to engage in a sexual act with an individual in their custody.

Both bills would have also authorized COPS grants to be used to

- create civilian review boards;
- recruit, hire, incentivize, retain, develop, and train new career law enforcement officers or current law enforcement officers who move to communities where there are poor relationships between community members and the police or
- where there are high crime rates and officers will reside in or close to these communities;
- collect data on the number of law enforcement officers who move to the communities in which they work and its effect on crime; and
- develop strategies to recruit, hire, promote, retain, develop, and train a diverse and inclusive law enforcement workforce.

Some advocates and policymakers have argued that more resources should be invested in more general programs that could help reduce criminal behavior, such as antipoverty programs and mental health services, rather than investing additional resources in hiring more police officers.

Others have argued that non-law enforcement personnel should respond to situations that do not involve threats of violence and where the presence of an armed officer could potentially escalate a situation. There have also been arguments for alternative responses to violence, such as interventions by community violence interruption organizations that try to break the cycle of violence and save lives without the involvement of law enforcement.

Even though the research is mixed on the effect of increasing the number of law enforcement officers in a jurisdiction, experts in the field note that having an adequate number of law enforcement officers is important to providing effective policing. Research suggests that attrition in law enforcement agencies can contribute to a greater workload for remaining officers; reduced morale, effectiveness, operational capacity, and service delivery; and accelerated loss of the highest-performing officers.[34] The Council on Criminal Justice also asserts that by diversifying recruitment efforts, law enforcement agencies can improve their relationship with the community.

Recruiting more female officers could decrease the use of force because they are more likely to use communication skills instead of resorting to physical force, as a de-escalation strategy.[35]

Recruiting and retaining more officers who are well suited to engage the public and hiring officers that reflect the demographics of the communities in which they work could increase community trust, if these officers are trained, supervised, and held accountable in ways that engender trust.[36] In addition, increasing the quality and diversity of police recruits may help lessen the likelihood of discriminatory policing.[37]

If Congress takes up legislation to reauthorize the COPS program, policymakers might consider whether to allow COPS grants to be used to support reforms at law enforcement agencies, such as those proposed in the George Floyd Justice in Policing acts. From FY2021 to FY2023, the

---

[34] Jeremy M. Wilson et al., "Police Retention: A Systematic Review of the Research," *Policing: A Journal of Policy and Practice*, vol. 17 (2023), p. 10.

[35] Council on Criminal Justice, Task Force on Policing, *Recruitment, Diversity, and Retention*, May 2021, p. 7.

[36] Ibid.

[37] Ibid.

explanatory statement to accompany the CJS appropriations act directed the COPS Office to use funding for community-policing development for specific purposes, such as crisis intervention and de-escalation training, supporting law enforcement agency accreditation, and diversity and antibias training. Congress could consider codifying these or other specifications in the authorization for the COPS program. Congress might also consider whether to allow law enforcement agencies to apply for COPS grants to support programs that provide alternative responses in certain situations, such as mental health professionals either responding with or in lieu of a law enforcement officer during calls for service involving individuals suffering from a mental health crisis or nonsworn personnel handling most traffic enforcement.

The George Floyd Justice in Policing reform legislation would have incentivized law enforcement reforms by placing conditions on COPS funding. Congress could consider providing similar or new reform incentives in a reauthorization bill. One question policymaker might face is how the incentive would be structured. The reform legislation would have made state and local governments ineligible to apply for funding if they did not have certain measures in place. Congress could promote reforms through a similar requirement, or policymakers could consider providing preferential consideration for grant applicants who meet particular requirements. Some provisions of the reform legislation would have required grant recipients to do something as a condition of receiving funding. One issue with that is that COPS grants have a limited implementation period and reform efforts can take time to implement. Also, unlike a formula grant program such as the Edward Byrne Memorial Justice Assistance Grant (JAG) program,[38] state and local governments are much less likely to receive a portion of COPS funding each year as long as the program is funded. The lack of regular, annual funding might raise questions about how effective it would be to place reform-related requirements on COPS grants. In addition, if Congress did pass such requirements, recipients would not have to adhere to them after grant funding ends.

[38] For more information on the JAG program, see CRS In Focus IF10691, *The Edward Byrne Memorial Justice Assistance Grant (JAG) Program*.

Defining Community Policing

Under the authorization for the COPS program, grants can be awarded for hiring or rehiring law enforcement officers "for deployment in community-oriented policing," to procure technology to "to increase the number of officers deployed in community-oriented policing," or to facilitate the adoption of "community-oriented policing as an organization-wide philosophy." However, the authorization for the program does not contain a definition of community-oriented policing.[39]

It is not always clear what actually constitutes community-oriented policing. The COPS Office states community policing is a "philosophy that promotes organizational strategies that support the systematic use of partnerships and problem-solving techniques to proactively address the immediate conditions that give rise to public safety issues such as crime, social disorder, and fear of crime."[40] Two scholars, in their review of trends in policing, describe community policing as "a catchphrase that has been used to describe a potpourri of different strategies" and that "one complication in determining the extent to which [community policing] has transformed policing is determining exactly what it is."[41] A 2018 review of proactive policing strategies conducted by the National Academies of Sciences, Engineering, and Medicine stated that "despite [community policing's] longevity as a reform—it dates back more than three decades—there is still considerable variation in how community-oriented policing is defined."[42] The academy noted that community policing started with an emphasis on community-focused tactics, such as foot patrol, neighborhood watch, and community meetings or newsletters.[43] However, community policing practices evolved to include collective efficacy and empowerment; procedural justice and legitimacy; and efforts to increase police accountability through citizen review boards, body-worn cameras, and improved complaint processes.[44] In a literature review of community oriented policing and problem oriented policing, community oriented policing is described as "a broad

---

[39] See 34 U.S.C. §10389 (definitions).

[40] U.S. Department of Justice, Office of Community Oriented Policing Services, *Community Policing Defined*, 2014, https://cops.usdoj.gov/RIC/Publications/cops-p157-pub.pdf.

[41] Edward R. Maguire and William R. King, "Trends in the Policing Industry," *Annals of the American Academy of Political and Social Science*, vol. 593 (May 2004), p. 23.

[42] National Academies of Sciences, Engineering, and Medicine, *Proactive Policing: Effects on Crime and Communities* (Washington, DC: National Academies Press, 2018), p. 64.

[43] Ibid., pp. 64-65.

[44] Ibid., p. 65.

policing strategy that relies heavily on community involvement and partnerships, and on police presence in the community, to address local crime and disorder."[45]

While there are different conceptualizations of community policing, some common elements emerge from the literature:[46]

- *An emphasis on partnerships:* Community policing posits that the police can rarely solve public safety problems alone; therefore, law enforcement should develop partnerships with community stakeholders (e.g., other government agencies, community members, nonprofit organizations/service providers, businesses, and the media) to develop solutions to problems and promote trust in police.
- *Citizen input:* Under community policing, law enforcement should engage the public in making decisions about public safety priorities, addressing identified problems, and making decisions about how their communities should be policed. In addition, the police should carefully consider citizen input when making policy decisions that affect the community.
- *A focus on prevention and problem solving:* Community policing promotes proactive efforts to address conditions that are contributing to public safety problems rather than responding to crime after it occurs. One of the more
- commonly cited problem-solving models in the community policing literature is SARA (scanning, analysis, response, and assessment). *Scanning* involves identifying and prioritizing problems. *Analysis*

---

[45] U.S. Department of Justice, Office of Justice Programs, Office of Juvenile Justice and Delinquency Prevention, *Community-Oriented Policing and Problem-Oriented Policing, Literature Review: A Product of the Model Program Guide,* https://ojjdp.ojp.gov/model-programs-guide/literature-reviews/community-oriented-problem-oriented- policing#2-0, last updated January 2023.

[46] See, for example, U.S. Department of Justice, Community Oriented Policing Services Office, *Community Policing Defined*, 2014, https://cops.usdoj.gov/RIC/Publications/cops-p157-pub.pdf; Gary W. Cordner, "Community Policing: Elements and Effects," in *Critical Issues in Policing*, 6th ed., eds. Roger G. Dunham and Geoffrey P. Alpert (Long Grove, IL: Waveland Press, 2010), pp. 432-449; U.S. Department of Justice, Office of Justice Programs, Bureau of Justice Assistance, *Understanding Community Policing: A Framework for Action*, NCJ 148457, August 1994, https://www.ncjrs.gov/pdffiles/commp.pdf; and Sarah Lawrence and Bobby McCarthy, *What Works in Community Policing? A Best Practices Context for Measure Y Efforts*, University of California Berkeley School of Law, The Chief Justice Earl Warren Institute on Law and Social Policy, November 2013, https://www.law.berkeley.edu/files/What_Works_in_Community_Policing.pdf.

involves researching what is known about the problems. *Response* includes developing solutions to permanently reduce the number and extent of the problems. *Assessment* involves evaluating the success of the response to the identified problems.

- *Changing officer assignments:* One of the key tenets of community policing is a focus on long-term geographic assignments. This means assigning officers to a place (i.e., a specific beat) for an extended period of time to facilitate interactions between the officers and residents and foster a sense of mutual accountability for what happens in the neighborhood.
- *Fostering positive interactions:* Policing involves some negative or coercive interactions with members of the public, such as making arrests, issuing tickets, stopping people based on reasonable suspicion, or ordering people to desist disruptive behavior. As such, under community policing law enforcement also works to develop ways to have positive interactions with the public. The theory is that positive interactions can help offset the negative interactions, foster a sense of familiarity and trust, and allow police officers to become more knowledgeable about people and conditions on their beat.
- *Organizational change:* Community policing emphasizes the need for flatter organizations (i.e., reduced layers of hierarchy) and decentralized authority. These changes are necessary so that officers can act more independently, be more responsive to their communities, and take responsibility for their roles in community policing. In addition, management should empower officers to be proactive and creative in solving public safety problems and developing relationships with the community. Community policing also places an emphasis on organizational culture, mission, and values, and less emphasis on rules and policies, with the idea that if officers are instilled with certain values they will generally make good decisions. Evaluations of officers' performance should be based on the quality of their community policing and problem-solving activities instead of traditional performance indicators (e.g., tickets issued, arrests made, calls handled).
- *Access to information:* Community policing relies on collecting and producing data on a range of police functions—not just enforcement and call-handling activities—as a means to developing solutions to community problems and providing citizen-focused services.

> Community policing also emphasizes the need for police to conduct crime analysis at a more localized level (e.g., a neighborhood) so that officers can identify and respond to problem hotspots.

There may be some questions about whether COPS grants move law enforcement agencies to embrace community policing agency-wide rather than just at the officer level. According to the COPS Office, the agency has received more than $20 billion in funding and it has awarded grants to over 13,000 of the 18,000 law enforcement agencies in the United States.[47] However, data from BJS indicate that as of 2020, 32% of police departments have a written community policing plan, though a majority of police departments serving jurisdictions of 50,000 or more people have such a plan.[48] BJS's data indicate that nearly 40% of police officers work in agencies that do not have a community policing plan.[49] A 2014 study concluded that COPS grants awarded to law enforcement agencies serving 50,000 or fewer people in the mid-1990s did not promote widespread adoption of community policing principles among these agencies.[50]

During the mid- to late 1990s, the COPS Office awarded billions of dollars in grants for law enforcement agencies to hire officers to engage in community policing. However, some scholars argue that there is not great consistency in what constitutes community policing, and the concept of community policing can just be a way for law enforcement agencies to present their old ways in a new package. For instance, two scholars have previously noted, "[law

---

[47] U.S. Department of Justice, Community Oriented Policing Services Office, *About COPS*, https://cops.usdoj.gov/ aboutcops; and U.S. Department of Justice, Community Oriented Policing Services Office, *U.S. Department of Justice FY2025 President's Budget, Office of Community Oriented Policing Services*, March 2024, p. 4.

[48] BJS reported that 92% of police departments serving jurisdictions of 1 million or more residents have a written community policing plan; 74% of departments serving jurisdictions of 500,000-999,999 residents have a plan; 62% of departments serving 250,000-499,999 residents and 100,000-249,999 residents have plan; 58% of departments serving jurisdictions of 50,000-99,999 residents have a plan; 48% of departments serving jurisdictions of 25,000-49,999 residents have a plan; 38% of departments serving jurisdictions of 10,000-24,999 residents have a plan; 28% of departments serving jurisdictions of 2,500-9,999 residents have a plan; and 24% of departments serving jurisdictions of 2,499 residents or fewer have a plan. Sean E. Goodison and Conor Brooks, *Local Police Departments, Procedures, Policies, and Technology, 2020—Statistical Tables*, U.S. Department of Justice, Office of Justice Programs, Bureau of Justice Statistics, NCJ 307405, Washington, DC, November 2023, p. 17.

[49] Ibid.

[50] Scott W. Phillips and S. Marlon Gayadeen, "The Coercive Impact of Federal Grants: COPS Grants and the Diffusion of the Community Policing Philosophy," *Police Journal: Theory, Practice and Principles*, vol. 87 (2014), pp. 49-60.

enforcement agencies] are managing to reconstitute their image away from the citizen-controller paradigm based in the autonomous legal order and towards a more comforting Normal Rockwell image—police as kind, community care-takers."[51] They contend that community policing is more about police transforming their image rather than the substance of their work.

Some research suggests that community policing might help improve the perception of the legitimacy of the police, but it has a limited effect on reducing crime and citizens' fear of crime. Policing scholars at George Mason's Center for Evidence-Based Crime Policy note

> Evidence for the effectiveness of community policing is mixed. Several systematic and narrative reviews find that its impact on crime prevention is limited and that it has little impact on reducing citizens' fear of crime However, community policing was originally intended to emphasize the non-crime-fighting roles of the police, such as building community trust, and to increase citizen satisfaction with and confidence in the police.... [A 2014 study found] that community policing is associated with significant increases in citizen ratings of satisfaction with the police and also has positive benefits for police legitimacy and citizen perceptions of disorder.[52]

At the same time, and consistent with the debate over what community policing is, these experts also note

> As with many areas of policing, research guidance on implementing community-oriented policing is limited. A key challenge is the diversity of strategies that have been deployed under the umbrella of community policing over time and across different agencies. The extent to which departments who claim to be doing community policing engage in community partnerships, systematic problem-solving, and organizational transformation varies substantially, and there is not always a formal process for citizen engagement in identifying and responding to problems.[53]

---

[51] Victor E. Kappeler and Peter B. Kraska, "A Textual Critique of Community Policing: Police Adaption to High Modernity," *Policing: An International Journal of Policing Strategies & Management*, vol. 21, no. 2 (1998), p. 306.

[52] Cynthia Lum et al., An Evidence Assessment of the Recommendations of the President's Task Force on 21st Century Policing—Implementation and Research Priorities, Center for Evidence-Based Crime Policy, George Mason University, Fairfax, VA, 2016, p. 28.

[53] Ibid., p. 29.

Before allocating more funding for COPS hiring grants, policymakers might consider whether there need to be clearer expectations for how law enforcement agencies use the officers hired with the grants, or at least whether there should be some limitations on COPS-funded officers' activities. For example, policymakers could consider legislation that would prevent law enforcement agencies from placing COPS-funded officers on SWAT teams or specialized units that engage in aggressive enforcement of specific offenses.

Clarifying the Purpose of the COPS Program

The COPS program has had multiple goals since its inception, some of which arguably may not have fully aligned at times. This may be a good time to assess program goals.

On one hand, the COPS program was created as a means of adding 100,000 new law enforcement officers to police forces across the country. As discussed above, more recent legislation introduced in Congress has viewed the COPS program as a way to help law enforcement agencies boost their ranks. In this sense, the COPS program is a means of aiding law enforcement hiring. On another hand, one of the stated purposes of the COPS program was to promote the adoption of community policing by helping law enforcement agencies hire officers to engage in community policing activities. The COPS program has also been viewed as a way to address violent crime in the United States by placing more officers on the streets.

If policymakers take up legislation to reauthorize the COPS program, they might consider which goals to prioritize and whether any goals conflict. For example, there are questions about how much of an effect the COPS program had on agencies adopting community policing practices, as discussed previously. A law enforcement agency hiring a few officers to engage in community policing might not reorient the entire agency toward this practice. Past literature on the issue of community policing suggests that in order for community policing to be effective it requires organizational change rather than having a small number of officers conducting community policing activities.[54] Plus, if a law enforcement agency retains officers whose salaries

[54] See, for example, U.S. Department of Justice, Community Oriented Policing Services Office, Community Policing Defined, 2014, https://cops.usdoj.gov/RIC/Publications/cops-p157-pub.pdf; Gary W. Cordner, "Community Policing: Elements and Effects," in Critical Issues in Policing, 6th ed., eds. Roger G. Dunham and Geoffrey P. Alpert (Long Grove, IL: Waveland Press, 2010), pp. 432-449; U.S. Department of Justice, Office of Justice

were initially funded with COPS grants, they are not required to continue using those officers for community policing after the grant period expires and they assume responsibility for funding the positions. If policymakers want to promote the adoption of community policing in more agencies across the country, they might consider whether focusing on helping law enforcement agencies hire new officers is the best way to accomplish this goal.

If policymakers want the COPS program to be a source of support for law enforcement, this might raise a question about if it is necessary to require law enforcement agencies to hire officers for community policing. As discussed above, several amendments to the COPS program since it was created by the 1994 Crime Act have added purposes that focus more on supporting law enforcement operations or programs rather than advancing community policing. If Congress views the COPS program as a way to help state and local governments address violent crime, for instance, policymakers might consider whether the COPS program should retain as heavy a focus on helping law enforcement agencies hire new officers or whether greater emphasis should be placed on providing funding to help law enforcement agencies in other ways (e.g., to encourage adoption of evidence-based crime prevention programs and practices).

Continuing the COPS Program

Policymakers might also consider whether to continue supporting the COPS program. While many cities saw an increase in violent crime in 2020 and 2021, which coincided with the COVID- 19 pandemic and protests related to George Floyd's death in Minneapolis, MN, violent crime decreased in 2022 and 2023.[55] While violent crime in some cities is still above the level it was before 2020, it is generally at historically low levels. This, combined with concerns about what effects more police have on communities of color and the mixed

---

Programs, Bureau of Justice Assistance, Understanding Community Policing: A Framework for Action, NCJ 148457, August 1994, https://www.ncjrs.gov/pdffiles/commp.pdf; and Sarah Lawrence and Bobby McCarthy, What Works in Community Policing? A Best Practices Context for Measure Y Efforts, University of California Berkeley School of Law, The Chief Justice Earl Warren Institute on Law and Social Policy, November 2013, https://www.law.berkeley.edu/files/What_Works_in_Community_Policing.pdf.

[55] Ernesto Lopez and Bobby Boxerman, Crime Trends in U.S. Cities: Year-End 2023 Update, Council on Criminal Justice, January 2024, https://counciloncj.org/crime-trends-in-u-s-cities-year-end-2023-update/.

research on the effect of more police on crime rates, might raise questions about whether there should be continued funding for the COPS program and whether those funds could be allocated to other programs to address violence.

Some questions have been raised about whether the COPS program addresses issues that should be the focus of federal policy. For instance, a Heritage Foundation report published several years ago asserts that crime is not a national issue—rather, it is an issue that all states share in common—and it would be most appropriate for Congress's role in addressing crime to focus on criminal matters that are squarely within the purview of federal law enforcement.[56] It suggests that local governments are better positioned to fund law enforcement agencies because there is more direct oversight of how those agencies use those funds.[57] More direct oversight means that law enforcement agencies have an incentive to spend funds provided by state and local governments in a manner consistent with legislative and constituent goals.[58] Also, if law enforcement agencies do not spend their funding properly, it is easier for local governments to reallocate those funds for other uses.[59] While the COPS Office has the responsibility of monitoring how grant funds are spent, there might be a question about if the office can effectively monitor its grant load given its level of resources and with grant recipients being spread across the country.[60] Past audits of COPS grants conducted by DOJ's Office of the Inspector General (OIG) have found that some grantees have misused COPS funding, including improperly charging salaries and fringe benefits to

[56] Brian Walsh and David Muhlhausen, COPS Reform: Why Congress Can't Make the COPS Program Work, Heritage Foundation, September 26, 2008, https://www.heritage.org/crime-and-justice/report/cops-reform-why-congress-cant- make-the-cops-program-work.

[57] Ibid.

[58] Ibid.

[59] Ibid.

[60] The COPS Office's FY2025 congressional budget submission indicates that the COPS Office has 100 authorized FTEs. The COPS Office did not provide a break out of how many of these positions are grant managers.

COPS grants and supplanting local funds.[61] It is possible that these audit findings do not apply to COPS grants in general.[62]

There are also questions about whether the COPS program met its original goals of funding 100,000 new law enforcement officers. A 2005 study conducted by the Government Accountability Office found that COPS funding paid for a total of about 88,000 additional officer- years from 1994 to 2001.[63] An evaluation of the COPS program sponsored by the National Institute of Justice found that under the best-case scenario, of the 105,000 officer and officer equivalents funded by the COPS program by May 1999, an estimated 84,600 officers would have been hired by 2001 before declining to 83,900 officers by 2003.[64] Under the worst-case scenario, an estimated 69,000 officers would have been hired by 2001 before declining to 62,700 officers by 2003. A more recent study that examined the effects of COPS hiring grants awarded from 2009 to 2016 found that for each officer position funded through a hiring grant, the sworn police force size increased between 0.3 and 0.5

---

[61] See, for example, U.S. Department of Justice, Office of the Inspector General, *Audit of the Office of Community Oriented Policing Services Hiring Program Grant Awarded to the Camden County Police Department, Camden, New Jersey*, Audit Report 22-009, Washington, DC, November 2021; U.S. Department of Justice, Office of the Inspector General, *Audit of the Office of Community Oriented Policing Services Hiring Program Grant Awarded to the Essex County Sheriff's Office, Newark, New Jersey*, Audit Report 20-095, Washington, DC, August 2020; U.S. Department of Justice, Office of the Inspector General, *Audit of the Office of Community Oriented Policing Services Hiring Program Grant Awarded to the Arlington Police Department, Arlington, Texas*, Audit Report 20-070, Washington, DC, June 2020; U.S. Department of Justice, Office of the Inspector General, *Audit of the Office of Community Oriented Policing Services Tribal Resources Grant Program Awards to the Choctaw Nation of Oklahoma, Durant, Oklahoma*, Audit Report GR-60-19-013, Washington, DC, September 2019; U.S. Department of Justice, Office of the Inspector General, *Audit of the Office of Community Oriented Policing Services Grants Awarded to DeKalb County, Georgia*, Audit Report GR-40-15-002, Washington, DC, October 2014; U.S. Department of Justice, Office of the Inspector General, *Audit of the Office of Community Oriented Policing Services 2009 COPS Hiring Recovery Program Grant Awarded to the Toledo Police Department, Toledo, Ohio*, Audit Report GR-50-14-007, Washington, DC, July 2014; and U.S. Department of Justice, Office of the Inspector General, *Audit of the Office of Community Oriented Policing Services Hiring Recovery Program Grant Administered by the City of Tulsa, Oklahoma*, Audit Report GR-60-14-005, Washington, DC, March 2014.

[62] U.S. Department of Justice, Office of the Inspector General, review of grants made to the Honolulu Police Department and Polk County, FL, found no issues with how those grants were managed.

[63] U.S. Government Accountability Office, *Community Policing Grants: COPS Grants Were a Modest Contributor to Declines in Crime in the 1990s*, GAO-06-104, October 2005, p. 57.

[64] Jeffery A. Roth et al., *National Evaluation of the COPS Program*, U.S. Department of Justice, Office of Justice Programs, National Institute of Justice, NCJ183643, August 2000, http://www.ncjrs.gov/pdffiles1/nij/183643.pdf.

officers.[65] The study indicates that while COPS hiring grants did increase the number of law enforcement officers, one funded position did not result in one additional officer on the force.[66]

There may be some questions as well about whether COPS grants move law enforcement agencies to embrace community policing agency-wide rather than just at the officer level, as discussed previously.

---

[65] Steven Mello, *Empirical Analysis of COPS Hiring Program Grants, 2009-2016*, U.S. Department of Justice, Community Oriented Policing Services Office, 2024, p. 9.

[66] There are several reasons why a law enforcement agency might not be able to turn a funded position into a new officer on the force: the agency might not be able to find enough qualified candidates, a candidate might not pass a background check, candidates might not complete academy training, or an officer might be let go or resign during his or her probationary period.

Appendix. Funding for Programs Under the COPS Account

Table A-1. Appropriations for the COPS Account, by Program: FY2015-FY2024

(in millions of dollars)

FY2015		FY2016	FY2017	FY2018	FY2019	FY2020	FY2021	FY2022	FY2023	FY2024
COPS Hiring Program	180	187	195	223	229	235	237	246	324	256
Transfer to Tribal Resources Grant Program	33	30	—	30	27	27	30	32	34	34
Community Policing Development	8	10	5	10	7	7	—	—	—	—
Regional Information Sharing Program	—	—	35	36	37	38	40	42	44	44
POLICE Act	—	—	8	—	—	—	—	—	—	—
Tribal Access Program	—	—	—	—	3	3	3	3	4	4
Law Enforcement Mental Health and Wellness	—	—	—	—	2	5	8	8	10	10
Collaborative Reform Model	5	10	10	—	—	—	—	5	8	8
Community Policing Development	—	—	—	—	—	—	35	40	45	25
Crisis Intervention Teams	—	—	—	—	—	—	10	10	11	—
De-escalation Training	—	—	—	—	—	—	15	15	16	—
Accreditation Support	—	—	—	—	—	—	5	8	9	—
Community Policing Development Micrograms	—	—	—	—	—	—	3	5	6	—
Diversity and Anti-bias Training	—	—	—	—	—	—	2	2	3	—
Methamphetamine Enforcement and Clean-up	7	11	10	—	—	—	—	—	—	—
Transfer to the Drug Enforcement Administration	7	11	10	—	—	—	—	—	—	—
Law Enforcement Equipment and Technology Program	—	—	—	—	—	—	—	112	178	247
Anti-methamphetamine Task Forces	7	7	7	8	8	13	15	15	16	16
Anti-heroin Task Forces	7	7	10	32	32	35	35	35	35	35
Regional Gang Task Forces	7	—	—	—	—	—	—	—	—	—
POLICE Act	—	—	—	10	10	10	11	11	12	12

FY2015		FY2016	FY2017	FY2018	FY2019	FY2020	FY2021	FY2022	FY2023	FY2024
STOP School Violence Act	—	—	—	—	25	50	53	73	73	73
Law Enforcement Officer De-escalation Training	—	—	—	—	—	—	—	—	—	20

Source: Appropriations were taken from the explanatory statement to accompany the annual Commerce, Justice, Science, and Related Agencies appropriations acts and the text of the Bipartisan Safer Communities Act (P.L. 117-159).

Notes: Amounts in italics are set-asides.

Chapter 9

Community Oriented Policing Services (COPS) Program*

Nathan James

Background

Under the initial authorization for the Community Oriented Policing Services (COPS) program (Title I of the Violent Crime Control and Law Enforcement Act of 1994, P.L. 103-322, "the 1994 Crime Act"), grants could be awarded for (1) hiring new police officers or rehiring police officers who have been laid off to engage in community policing, (2) hiring former members of the armed services to serve as law enforcement officers engaged in community policing, and (3) supporting community policing nonhiring initiatives, such as training law enforcement officers in crime prevention and community policing techniques or developing technologies that support crime prevention strategies.

The COPS program was reauthorized by the Violence Against Women and Department of Justice Reauthorization Act of 2005 (P.L. 109-162). The act changed the COPS program from a multi-grant program to a single-grant program under which DOJ can make grants to state, local, and tribal governments, and other public and private entities for a variety of enumerated purposes (see 34 U.S.C.§10381(b)).

Congress has continued to appropriate funding for the COPS program even though authorized appropriations for the program expired in FY2009.

---

* This is an edited, reformatted and augmented version of Congressional Research Service Publication No. IF10922, updated May 9, 2024.

In: The Future of Law Enforcement
Editor: Mohamed Swift
ISBN: 979-8-89530-863-9

COPS Funding

From FY1995 to FY1999, the annual appropriation for the COPS program averaged nearly $1.4 billion. The relatively high levels of funding during this time period, compared to post-FY2000 appropriations, were largely the result of efforts to place 100,000 new law enforcement officers on the streets.

After the initial push to hire and fund 100,000 new law enforcement officers, Congress started to change the COPS program into a conduit for supporting a wider range of local law enforcement needs. Starting in FY1998, an increasing portion of the annual appropriation for COPS was dedicated to programs that helped law enforcement agencies purchase new equipment, combat methamphetamine production, upgrade criminal history record systems, and improve their forensic science capabilities. Increasing funding for nonhiring initiatives under the COPS account coincided with decreasing funding for hiring programs. By FY2005, appropriations for hiring programs were nearly nonexistent, and Congress eliminated funding for them for FY2006 and FY2007. Funding for hiring programs was revived when the American Recovery and Reinvestment Act of 2009 (P.L. 111-5) provided $1 billion for the COPS program.

Appropriations for hiring programs from FY2009 to FY2012 were the result of Congress's efforts to help local law enforcement agencies facing budget cuts as a result of the recession either hire new law enforcement officers or retain officers they would otherwise have to lay off. Appropriations continued to be provided for hiring programs even as the effects of that recession waned.

There was a notable reduction in the total amount of funding provided for the COPS program after FY2012 relative to previous fiscal years. Prior to FY2012, the least amount of annual funding (in nominal dollars) provided for the COPS program was $472 million for FY2006. Although COPS program funding has increased over the past several fiscal years (Table 1), annual funding from FY2012 to FY2021 remained significantly lower than it was before FY2012. Lower annual appropriations for the COPS program during these fiscal years can be attributed to three trends: (1) a decrease in the amount of funding provided for hiring programs, (2) a ban on congressionally directed spending, and (3) Congress's restructuring of the COPS account. However, increases in annual COPS funding starting in FY2022 are attributable to a partial reversal of some of these trends.

Congress had a ban on congressionally directed spending from FY2011 to FY2021. This ban substantially decreased funding for the Law Enforcement

Technology and the Methamphetamine Clean-up programs, which were being administered by the COPS Office. By FY2012, Congress did not appropriate any funding for the Law Enforcement Technology program and the only funding remaining for the Methamphetamine Clean-up program was transferred to the Drug Enforcement Administration to assist with the cleanup of clandestine methamphetamine laboratories.

Congress ceased providing funding for the Methamphetamine Clean-up program in FY2018.

From FY2010 to FY2012, Congress moved appropriations for several programs that were funded under the COPS account—such as Project Safe Neighborhoods, DNA backlog reduction initiatives, Paul Coverdell grants, offender reentry programs, the National Criminal History Improvement program, and the Bulletproof Vest Grant program—to the State and Local Law Enforcement Assistance (S&LLEA) account. Programs funded under this account are administered by the Office of Justice Programs (OJP). Prior to the programs being moved to the S&LLEA, appropriations for them were transferred from the COPS Office to OJP for administration. In general, from FY2001 to FY2011, appropriations for programs that were transferred to OJP accounted for one-third to one-half of the annual funding for the COPS account. In recent fiscal years, differing proportions of the COPS account has again been transferred to OJP. Since FY2017, Congress has provided funding for the Regional Information Sharing System (RISS) program under the COPS account, which is transferred to OJP.

Funding for the COPS program has increased in the last seven fiscal years, from $208 million for FY2015 to $685 million for FY2024. Increased funding for the COPS account is the result of Congress increasing funding for hiring programs, and for nonhiring initiatives such as anti- heroin task forces, active shooter training, and grants under the Matching Grant Program for School Security. Also, for FY2024 Congress provided funding for the COPS Law Enforcement Technology program for the third straight fiscal year, after eliminating the program in FY2010.

Debate over the COPS Program, Law Enforcement Reform, and Violent Crime

Recently, funding for the COPS program, especially the hiring program, has become a flashpoint in the debate over policing reform. Some proponents of law enforcement reform argue that law enforcement agencies police communities of color in a biased way, and absent efforts to address underlying social factors, more police officers means that more people of color, especially Black men, will be subject to biased policing. Proponents of reform argue that funding should be used for programs that address social problems (e.g., poverty, homelessness, lack of access to mental health care) in order to reduce involvement with the criminal justice system rather than increasing the number of police officers.

Table 1. COPS's total budget authority, funding for hiring programs, and transfers to OJP, FY2015-FY2024

Amounts in millions of nominal dollars

Fiscal Year	Total Budget Authority	Funding for Hiring Programs	Proportion Transferred to OJP
2015	208	135	0%
2016	212	137	0%
2017	222	137	16%
2018	276	150	13%
2019	304	153	12%
2020	343	156	11%
2021	386	157	10%
2022	532	157	8%
2023	683	225	6%
2024	685	157	6%

Sources: FY2015-FY2017 appropriations were provided by the U.S. Department of Justice, Office of Community Oriented Policing Services; FY2018-FY2024 appropriations were taken from the explanatory statement to accompany the annual Commerce, Justice, Science, and Related Agencies Appropriations Act.

Note: Total budget authority includes carryover from previous fiscal years.

President Biden has indicated his support for the COPS program as a way to promote law enforcement reform through community policing efforts. In his plan for criminal justice reform, President Biden stated

> policing works best when officers are out of their cruisers and walking the streets, engaging with and getting to know members of their communities. But in order to do that, police departments need resources to hire a sufficient number of officers.... However, the [COPS] program

has never been funded to fulfill the original vision for community policing.... As a condition of the grant, hiring of police officers must mirror the racial diversity of the community they serve.

Since FY2021, funding has been provided under the COPS account for programs to promote policing reform efforts, such as funding for de-escalation training, improving law enforcement's response to people with mental health problems, helping law enforcement agencies gain accreditation, and anti-bias and diversity training. While there was also continued funding for the COPS hiring program, for FY2024 the COPS Office gave additional consideration to applicants that indicated they would use funding to (1) recruit officers from the communities in which they would serve, (2) recruit officers who are willing to relocate to areas characterized by fragmented relations between police and community residents or to areas of high crime, and (3) require officers to complete evidence-based cultural sensitivity training.

The COPS program has also been integral to the debate over what steps Congress can take to aid state and local governments in their efforts to address violent crime. While there is debate over whether additional police officers alone can help reduce violent crime (see CRS In Focus IF12022, State and Local Law Enforcement Officer Staffing for a brief discussion), some policymakers have argued for additional funds for the COPS hiring program as one avenue to help cities address increases in violent crime. In its FY2025 congressional budget submission for the COPS program, the Biden Administration requested increased funding for the COPS hiring program to support the hiring of 2,000 additional officers and to "increase the capacity of law enforcement agencies to implement community policing strategies that strengthen partnerships for safer communities and enhance law enforcement's capacity to prevent, solve, and control crime – especially violent crime – through funding for additional officer and deputy positions." Some proponents of policing reform efforts argue that (1) policymakers have emphasized the need to increase the number of law enforcement officers as a means of tackling violent crime when they have not taken sufficient steps to address how the police treat people of color and (2) the focus on recent increases in violent crime in certain U.S. cities is detracting from efforts to follow through on law enforcement reform proposals.

Chapter 10

Issues in Law Enforcement Reform: Responding to Mental Health Crises*

Nathan James
Johnathan H. Duff
Jill C. Gallagher
and Isobel Sorenson

Summary

The manner in which police have handled mental health-related encounters has come under increased scrutiny during the last few decades, especially regarding the use of force. Through hearings and legislation, policymakers have demonstrated an interest in improving the police's response to individuals who are experiencing a mental health crisis.

When considering options for improving law enforcement's response to people experiencing a mental health crisis, policymakers have looked to specialized responses employed by local governments across the country. These responses include the following:

- Crisis Intervention Teams (CITs), in which specially trained law enforcement officers respond to calls for service involving people having a mental health crisis and liaise with mental health providers.
- Co-Responder Teams (CRTs), which pair law enforcement officers with trained clinicians who together respond to

* This is an edited, reformatted and augmented version of Congressional Research Service Publication No. R47285, dated October 17, 2022.

In: The Future of Law Enforcement
Editor: Mohamed Swift
ISBN: 979-8-89530-863-9

emergency calls involving individuals experiencing a mental health crisis.

- Mobile Crisis Teams (MCTs), which utilize community-based mental health professionals to respond to individuals experiencing mental health crises. These teams typically do not involve the police initially, though police can be called upon when appropriate.

Research on specialized responses to people experiencing a mental health crisis suggests that CITs, CRTs, and MCTs may improve some outcomes, such as improving police officers' perceptions of and response to people with mental illness and connecting people to mental health services. However, it remains less clear whether these changes translate into actual improved outcomes for people with mental health needs, such as fewer arrests and reduced use of force against them.

The Department of Justice (DOJ) and the Substance Abuse and Mental Health Services Administration (SAMHSA) provide funding that is intended to help improve law enforcement's response to people experiencing a mental health crisis. For example, DOJ's Justice and Mental Health Collaboration programs provide grants to help state, local, and tribal governments increase access to mental health care and other treatment services for people in need. SAMHSA's Mental Health Awareness Training grant program provides law enforcement and other first responders with training on how to recognize mental health conditions, provide initial help to those experiencing a mental health crisis, and connect individuals to appropriate care.

There are several issues policymakers might consider if Congress were to take up legislation to improve law enforcement's response to people experiencing a mental health crisis, including the following:

- aiding state and local governments with expanding their capacity to provide a continuum of mental health services, such as psychiatric emergency receiving units and inpatient mental health services;
- providing funding for preventative interventions to aid people before the onset of mental health conditions;
- providing funding for law enforcement agencies that want to provide CIT training to their officers and those that want to start CRT or MCT programs;
- collecting data on law enforcement officers' interactions with people experiencing a mental health crisis by expanding current DOJ efforts to collect data on law enforcement activities;

- providing additional funding for more staff and equipment to aid 911 call centers with handling calls for service involving people experiencing a mental health crisis;
- promoting more uniform laws and policies regarding training that law enforcement officers receive on how to respond to individuals experiencing a mental health crisis and actions officers can take to divert them from the criminal justice system; and
- supporting research on CRTs and MCTs.

Law enforcement officers[1] are frequently the first responders to individuals experiencing a mental health crisis.[2] The manner in which police have handled mental health-related encounters has come under increased scrutiny during the last few decades.[3] For example, people with mental illness and mental health advocacy groups have raised concerns about interactions between individuals with mental health disorders and police officers, especially those that involved the use of force.[4] One study estimated that one in four people with a mental health condition has been arrested at some point in their lifetime and 1% of calls for service for the police involve people with a mental disorder.[5]

Law enforcement officers often have little training in mental health crisis management and response.[6] In general, police are not formally trained to recognize, assess, and treat mental health conditions, relying instead on

---

[1] Throughout this report, the terms *law enforcement officer* and *police officer* or *police* will be used interchangeably.

[2] For the purposes of this report, a *mental health crisis* is defined as "any situation in which a person's behavior puts them at risk of hurting themselves or others and/or prevents them from being able to care for themselves or function effectively in the community." Teri Brister, *Navigating a Mental Health Crisis: A NAMI Resource Guide for Those Experiencing a Mental Health Emergency*, National Alliance on Mental Illness, Arlington, VA, 2018, p. 5.

[3] Jennifer D. Wood and Amy C. Watson, "Improving Police Interventions During Mental Health-Related Encounters: Past, Present, and Future," *Policing and Society*, vol. 27, no. 3 (2017), pp. 289-299 (hereinafter, "Wood and Watson, 'Improving Police Interventions During Mental Health-Related Encounters'").

[4] James D. Livingston, "Contact Between the Police and People with Mental Disorders: A Review of Rates," *Psychiatric Services*, vol. 67, no. 8 (August 2016), p. 850 (hereinafter, "Livingston, 'Contact Between the Police and People with Mental Disorders'").

[5] Livingston, "Contact Between the Police and People with Mental Disorders."

[6] H. Richard Lamb, Linda E. Weinberger, and Walter J. DeCuir, Jr., "The Police and Mental Health," *Psychiatric Services*, vol. 53, no. 10 (2002), pp. 1266-1271 (hereinafter, "Lamb et al., 'The Police and Mental Health'").

experiences learned on-the-job.[7] This has led some to characterize law enforcement officers as the so-called secret social service for their largely unrecognized role in triaging individuals with mental health needs.[8]

Some research suggests that people with mental health conditions are more likely to be subjected to violence by the police. For example, one study of police-public encounters in New York City and Baltimore found that people with serious mental illness were more likely than the general population to be involved in violent incidents with the police, even after controlling for criminal behavior.[9] Research also suggests that people with complex mental health needs are disproportionately killed during interactions with law enforcement.[10] One study found that the death rate for people who had signs of a mental illness during police interactions (20 deaths per million) is nearly seven times higher than it is for people without signs of a mental illness (3 deaths per million).[11]

This body of research, along with recent high-profile incidents in which police responses to individuals with mental health needs have had fatal outcomes, have led to a renewed interest in improving police response to mental health crises.[12] Congress has taken an interest in addressing the role of law enforcement in the mental health crisis response system.[13] For example, Congress has supported grant programs that encourage police training or

---

[7] Eddie Kane, Emily Evans, and Farhad Shokraneh, "Effectiveness of Current Policing-Related Mental health Interventions: A Systematic Review," *Criminal Behavior and Mental Health*, vol. 28 (2018), pp. 108-119; and Thomas M. Green, "Police As Frontline Mental Health Workers: The Decision to Arrest or Refer to Mental Health Agencies," *International Journal of Law and Psychiatry* (1997).

[8] Maurice Punch, "The Secret Social Service," The British Police 102 (1979): 17.

[9] Hyun-Jin Jun, Jordan E. DeVylder, and Lisa Fedina, "Police Violence Among Adults Diagnosed with Mental Disorders," *Health and Social Work*, vol. 45, no. 2 (May 2020), pp. 81-89.

[10] Amam Z. Saleh, Paul S. Appelbaum, and Xiaoyu Liu et al., "Deaths of People with Mental Illness During Interactions with Law Enforcement," *International Journal of Law and Psychiatry*, vol. 58 (2018), pp. 110-116 (hereinafter, "Saleh et al., 'Deaths of People with Mental Illness During Interactions with Law Enforcement'").

[11] Saleh et al., "Deaths of People with Mental Illness During Interactions with Law Enforcement," p. 114.

[12] Minyvonne Burke, "Policing Mental Health: Recent Deaths Highlight Concerns Over Officer Response," *NBC News*, May 16, 2021, https://www.nbcnews.com/news/us-news/policing-mental-health-recent-deaths-highlight-concerns-over- officer-response-n1266935; and Lamb et al., "The Police and Mental Health," pp. 1266-1271.

[13] See, for example, U.S. Congress, Senate Committee on the Judiciary, Subcommittee on Criminal Justice and Counterterrorism, *Behavioral Health and Policing: Interactions and Solutions*, subcommittee hearing, 117th Cong., 1st sess., April 22, 2021.

partnerships with behavioral health professionals to improve the response to persons experiencing a mental health crisis.[14]

Mental Health and Violence

Law enforcement officers may respond to mental health-related emergencies because of the threat of harm or violence (to the individual experiencing the crisis or to others). Most mental health crises do not involve the threat of violence and most people with mental health conditions do not pose a significant threat of violence.[15] Some research suggests that a small segment of individuals with serious mental illness may be slightly more prone to violence than those without a mental health condition, though acts of violence in this population are not common.[16] Data suggest that people with serious mental illness are more likely to be victims of violent crime rather than perpetrators.[17] Still, some mental health-related emergencies can be volatile, and in some situations it may be most appropriate for a law enforcement officer to be present. Studies have found that law enforcement officers believe that people with mental illness are significantly more prone to violence than people without mental illness, which may result in higher levels of force being used during mental health emergencies. This suggests the importance of appropriate training for responses to these situations.[18]

This report discusses specialized law enforcement programs for responding to individuals experiencing mental health crises. Mental health crises can include various emergencies such as suicidal ideation, symptoms of psychosis (e.g., hallucinations, delusions), threats of harm to others, or other significant acute psychological or emotional distress. These situations can involve individuals with serious mental illness, other diagnosed mental health

---

[14] See, for example, the Bipartisan Safer Communities Act (P.L. 117-159).

[15] Tori DeAngelis, "Mental Illness and Violence: Debunking Myths, Addressing Realities," *Monitor on Psychology*, vol. 52, no. 3, (April/May 2021), p. 31 (hereinafter "DeAngelis, 'Mental Illness and Violence'").

[16] See, for example, Richard Van Dorn, Jan Volavka, and Norman Johnson, "Mental Disorder and Violence: Is There a Relationship Beyond Substance Use?" *Social Psychiatry and Psychiatric Epidemiology*, vol. 47, no. 3 (2012), pp. 487- 503.

[17] H. Khalifeh, S. Johnson, and L. M. Howard et al., "Violent and Non-Violent Crime Against Adults with Severe Mental Illness," *The British Journal of Psychiatry*, vol. 206 (2015), pp. 275-282.

[18] Michael T. Rossler and William Terrill, "Mental Illness, Police Use of Force, and Citizen Injury," *Police Quarterly*, vol. 20, no. 2 (June 2017), p. 191.

conditions, or no psychological disorders at all.[19] The report begins by describing specialized responses that local governments have employed to improve their responses to individuals experiencing mental health crises. It briefly discusses the research on the effectiveness of these alternative responses and then turns to a review of federal programs that could provide support for these programs. Lastly, the report discusses some considerations for policymakers should Congress take up further legislation to address this issue.

Specialized Responses to Mental Health Crises

Over the past several decades, local governments have adopted specialized approaches to respond to calls involving individuals experiencing a mental health-related emergency. A survey of police agencies found that these models tend to fall into one of three categories (see Figure 1):

- Crisis Intervention Teams (CITs), in which specially trained police officers provide initial crisis response in the field and liaise with mental health providers;
- Co-Responder Teams (CRTs), in which mental health clinicians embedded in police agencies respond alongside law enforcement officers in the field; and
- Mobile Crisis Teams (MCTs), in which mental health clinicians responding with or without law enforcement assistance or triage.[20]

Each of these models provides a type of street triage, aiming to incorporate mental health expertise into crisis response.[21] A primary goal of these

---

[19] See, for example, Deborah M. Stone, Thomas R. Simon, and Katherine A. Fowler et al., Vital Signs: Trends in State Suicide Rates - United States, 1999-2016 and Circumstances Contributing to Suicide - 27 States, 2015, Centers for Disease Control and Prevention, Morbidity and Mortality Weekly Report, vol. 67, no. 22, June 8, 2018.

[20] Randy Borum, Martha Williams Deane, and Henry Steadman et al., "Police Perspectives on Responding to Mentally Ill People in Crisis: Perceptions of Program Effectiveness," *Behavioral Sciences and the Law*, vol. 16 (1998), pp. 393- 405; and Martha Williams Deane, Henry Steadman, Randy Borum et al., "Emergency Partnerships Between Mental Health and Law Enforcement," *Psychiatric Services*, vol. 50, no. 1 (1999), pp. 99-101, as cited in Wood and Watson, "Improving Police Interventions During Mental Health-Related Encounters."

[21] Stephen Putnis, Devon Perfect, and Abirami Kirumbarajan et al., "A Systematic Review of Co-Responder Models of Police Mental Health 'Street' Triage," *BMC Psychiatry*, vol. 18

programs is to connect individuals in crisis with community mental health services and divert them from the justice system or acute care health services (such as hospital emergency departments).[22] Many observers believe that decreasing the likelihood that an individual in crisis will end up in police custody is the most appropriate way to support people with acute or chronic mental health needs and prevent reoccurrence of a crisis and repeated contact with the criminal justice system.[23]

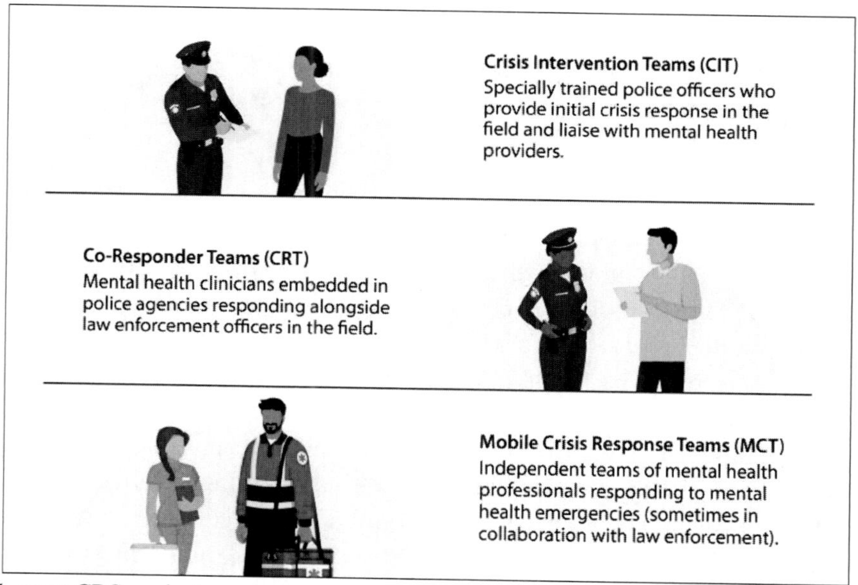

Source: CRS analysis.
Notes: Some areas may employ more than one model at a time.

Figure 1. Common Models of Mental Health Crisis Response.

There is considerable variation in program design and heterogeneity in application of these programs—even across communities employing the same model. One review identified 19 different approaches to street triage across these three models.[24] For example, co-responder teams might adopt a first

(2018), p. 256 (hereinafter, "Putnis et al., 'A Systematic Review of Co-Responder Models'").
[22] G.K. Shapiro, A. Cusi, and M. Kirst et al., "Co-Responding Police-Mental Health Programs: A Review," *Administration and Policy in Mental Health and Mental Health Services Research*, vol. 42, no. 5 (2015), pp. 606-620 (hereinafter, "Shapiro et al., 'Co-Responding Police-Mental Health Programs'").
[23] Shapiro et al., "Co-Responding Police-Mental Health Programs."
[24] Puntis et al., "A Systematic Review of Co-Responder Models."

response approach in which the CRT responds initially to a perceived mental health crisis. They could also employ a second response (or post-response) approach in which other emergency personnel (e.g., traditionally trained law enforcement officers or emergency medical technicians) arrive to the scene first and call for the CRT if a mental health crisis is identified.[25] Some CRTs are only dispatched after a call is placed to an emergency control room (e.g., 911), some take calls directly from police officers in the field, some are dispatched in response to a call from either source, and some have their own independent line for receiving calls.[26]

Crisis Intervention Teams

CITs are a first responder model in which specially trained law enforcement officers respond to calls for service involving people experiencing a mental health crisis. The CIT model is the most widely used of the three most common mental health crisis response approaches. CITs originated in Memphis, TN, in 1988 when the Memphis Police Department (MPD) partnered with the Memphis chapter of the National Alliance on Mental Illness, the University of Memphis, and the University of Tennessee to develop a specialized unit in response to public outcry over the death of a man with schizophrenia during an encounter with MPD (hence, the CIT model is sometimes referred to as the Memphis model).[27] The stated goal of the program is to reduce deaths that can occur during interactions between the police and people experiencing a mental health crisis and to divert these individuals, when appropriate, away from the criminal justice system and into treatment.[28]

Police officers who serve on CITs typically undergo 40 hours of training, during which they learn how to recognize symptoms of major mental health conditions, interact with and gain perspective from people who have suffered mental health crises and their families, engage in role playing exercises to help

---

[25] Katie Bailey, Staci Rising Paquet, and Bradley R. Ray et al., "Barriers and Facilitators to Implementing an Urban Co-Responding Police-Mental Health Team," *Health and Justice*, vol. 6, no. 21 (2018).

[26] Puntis et al., "A Systematic Review of Co-Responder Models," p. 261.

[27] Wood and Watson, "Improving Police Interventions During Mental Health-Related Encounters," p. 292.

[28] Michael S. Rogers, Dale E. McNeil, and Renee L. Bender, "Effectiveness of Police Crisis Intervention Training Programs," *Journal of the American Academy of Psychiatry and the Law*, vol. 47, no. 4 (2019), p. 415 (hereinafter, "Rogers et al., 'Effectiveness of CIT Programs'").

them develop de-escalation skills, and conduct site visits of community facilities that provide follow-up services to people with mental health needs after a treatment referral is made by law enforcement.[29] Police officers who serve on CITs traditionally volunteer for the team.[30]

The Memphis model includes changes that go beyond training a portion of the agency's officers on proper responses to people experiencing a mental health crisis. The model also involves

- training dispatchers to recognize calls for service that have a high probability of being mental health-related and dispatching CITs;
- developing partnerships between law enforcement agencies, mental health services, mental health advocates, and other stakeholders; and
- establishing a centralized drop-off emergency mental health care facility that will accept all patients.[31]

According to the CIT Center at the University of Memphis, there are approximately 3,000 CIT programs in the United States.[32] However, it is not clear how many of these agencies are implementing the full Memphis model (as opposed to just providing some of their officers with the 40 hours of CIT training).[33] It has been noted that the Memphis model was designed to be flexible enough to "allow communities to tailor their efforts to local needs, resources, and limitations,"[34] though some fidelity to the model is required for effectiveness.

---

[29] Charles Dempsey, Cameron Quanbeck, and Clarissa Bush et al., "Decriminalizing Mental Illness: Specialized Policing Responses," *CNS Spectrums*, vol. 25, no. 2 (2020), p. 182, hereinafter "Dempsey et al., 'Decriminalizing Mental Illness.'"

[30] Wood and Watson, "Improving Police Interventions During Mental Health-Related Encounters," p. 292.

[31] Amy C. Watson and Michael T. Compton, "What Research on Crisis Intervention Teams Tells Us and What We Need to Ask," *Journal of the American Academy of Psychiatry and the Law*, vol. 47, no. 4 (2019), p. 423 (hereinafter, "Watson and Compton, 'What Research on CITs Tells Us and What We Need to Ask'"). These drop-off emergency mental health care facilities are sometimes referred to as *psychiatric receiving units* or *crisis stabilization centers*. See "Access to Mental Health Services" later in this report.

[32] University of Memphis, CIT Center, http://www.cit.memphis.edu/.

[33] Wood and Watson, "Improving Police Interventions During Mental Health-Related Encounters," p. 292.

[34] Amy C. Watson, Michael T. Compton, and Leah G. Pope, Crisis Response Services for People with Mental Illness or Intellectual or Developmental Disabilities: A Review of the Literature on Police-Based and Other First Response Models, Vera Institute of Justice, New York, NY, 2019, p. 27 (hereinafter, "Watson et al., Crisis Response Services for People with Mental Illness").

Co-Responder Teams

CRTs pair law enforcement officers with clinicians who respond to emergency calls involving individuals experiencing a mental health crisis. CRTs are being implemented as a part of a larger CIT effort, part of other police-mental health collaboration programs, or on their own.[35] The goals of CRTs are to (1) reduce unnecessary emergency department visits, psychiatric hospitalizations, and arrests; (2) increase safety for officers and subjects; and (3) provide connections to community-based mental health treatment.[36] CRTs accomplish these outcomes by deescalating crises, preventing injuries to individuals in crisis and the response team, linking individuals experiencing psychiatric emergencies to appropriate care in the community, and reducing pressure on both the local justice and health care systems.[37] The theory underlying CRT programs is that a joint response is preferable as police are specialists in handling situations involving illegal activity while mental health professionals are specialists in providing clinical care to individuals in crisis.[38]

As mentioned previously, there are variations in how CRTs operate and how they are deployed. Co-responding programs can differ greatly in the populations they serve, including regarding funding levels, program guidelines, hours of operation, procedures, staff expertise, equipment, and training.[39] In some cases, CRTs include police officers and clinicians who ride together in the same vehicle—either a squad car, unmarked police car, or ambulance.[40] In other cases, the clinician provides support to the police officer remotely, either via phone or police radio. With the exception of models that utilize remote consultation, CRTs are not available to respond 24 hours a day in most jurisdictions that have implemented them.[41]

Mobile Crisis Teams

MCTs utilize community-based mental health professionals to respond to mental health crises, with law enforcement deployed as needed. Unlike CITs

---

[35] Watson et al., Crisis Response Services for People with Mental Illness, p. 14.
[36] Watson et al., Crisis Response Services for People with Mental Illness, p. 15.
[37] Shapiro et al., "Co-Responding Police-Mental Health Programs."
[38] Shapiro et al., "Co-Responding Police-Mental Health Programs."
[39] Shapiro et al., "Co-Responding Police-Mental Health Programs."
[40] Puntis et al., "A Systematic Review of Co-Responder Models," p. 258.
[41] Puntis et al., "A Systematic Review of Co-Responder Models," p. 261.

and CRTs, MCTs typically do not involve the police initially, though police can be called upon when appropriate.[42] Conversely, police can request that an MCT respond if the circumstances are deemed appropriate. Calls for service can be screened through a dedicated helpline or through a 911 call center.[43] In either case, an MCT is dispatched to respond to the call if it meets defined criteria (e.g., the subject of the call appears to be experiencing a mental health crisis and there is no evidence he or she is engaged in violent activity), as specified by the jurisdiction.[44] MCTs are usually operated by a mental health agency instead of a police department, and provide onsite crisis management through assessment, intervention, consultation, referral to services, and follow-up to help ensure that the individual connects with the recommended services.[45]

Several cities have implemented MCT programs, mostly on a pilot basis (see the *Appendix* for examples). There are no comprehensive data on which cities use MCTs or the characteristics of these teams. Most available accounts indicate that pilot programs offer teams in a specific portion of the city during certain hours. Many cities take a layered approach to mental health calls by utilizing an MCT for some calls but also maintaining a CIT and/or a CRT.

The CAHOOTS Program (Eugene, OR)

The oldest and most established MCT is the Crisis Assistance Helping Out on the Streets (CAHOOTS) in Eugene, OR. The CAHOOTS program has been operating since 1989. CAHOOTS is not a part of the Eugene Police Department (EPD), but it does use City of Eugene-marked vehicles and receives funding from the city through a contract with EPD.[46] CAHOOTS teams are staffed by personnel from the White Bird Clinic, a mental health services provider in the city. CAHOOTS is the primary responder in many cases involving people who are intoxicated, mentally ill, or disoriented, and they transport people for necessary nonemergency medical care. People can

[42] Watson et al., Crisis Response Services for People with Mental Illness, p. 39.
[43] Ashley Abramson, "Building mental Health into Emergency Responses," Monitor on Psychology, vol. 52, no. 5, July 1, 2021, pp. 30-31 (discussing a model used in Long Island, NY, where 911 call takers can dispatch a team of clinical professionals; and a model used in Austin, TX, where callers can opt for mental health services).
[44] Watson et al., Crisis Response Services for People with Mental Illness, p. 39.
[45] Watson et al., Crisis Response Services for People with Mental Illness, p. 39.
[46] Eugene Police Department, "CAHOOTS," https://www.eugene-or.gov/4508/CAHOOTS.

call the nonemergency police line or 911 and request CAHOOTS.[47] EPD triages calls for service through their call center and dispatches a CAHOOTS van (which has a paramedic and an experienced crisis worker) to the scene when it is determined that a non-law enforcement response is warranted.[48] Sometimes, CAHOOTS will be called to a scene by a police officer who initially responded to a call when that officer determines the situation would be better handled by mental health professionals.

The CAHOOTS program has served as a model for other cities exploring options for redirecting mental health calls away from the police and to mental health professionals. It was reported that since the summer of 2020, over 400 municipalities contacted CAHOOTS organizers asking for advice on how establish their own programs.[49]

Other Models

In addition to the three most common mental health and law enforcement crisis response programs discussed above, other strategies have also emerged. For example, one model used in the United Kingdom embeds mental health specialists in contact control rooms (which are akin to 911 call centers in the United States) along with emergency dispatchers.[50] These mental health professionals advise call handlers and sometimes deal directly with individual callers. Other models use street triage teams that conduct outreach with people with mental illness in the community to connect them to services in hopes of preventing a mental health crisis.[51]

---

[47] Ben Adam Climer and Brenton Gicker, "CAHOOTS: A Model for Prehospital Mental Health Crisis Intervention," *Psychiatric Times*, January 29, 2021, https://www.psychiatrictimes.com/view/cahoots-model-prehospital-mental- health-crisis-intervention.

[48] In Eugene, 911 call takers can dispatch Eugene Police, CAHOOTS, and local fire and emergency medical services (EMS) response agencies. The decision on resources to send that a 911 call taker makes is "outlined by department policy but is informed by the knowledge, training and experience of our dispatchers. Dispatchers must consider public and responder safety, the presence of weapons, elements of criminal activity, and the needs of the citizens for every emergency." See https://www.eugene-or.gov/Document Center/View/56581/911-Process-Infographic.

[49] Julianne Hill, "Police Are Often the First Responders to Mental Health Crises, but Tragedies Are Prompting Change," *ABA Journal*, April 1, 2021.

[50] Eddie Kane, Emily Evans, and Farhad Shokraneh, "Effectiveness of Current Policing-Related Mental Health Interventions: A Systematic Review," *Criminal Behavior and Mental Health*, vol. 108 (2018).

[51] Several communities have explored various approaches to responding to mental health calls before deciding on a single model. The City of Minneapolis, for example, developed and

Some communities rely on emergency medical technicians (EMTs) or paramedics to provide services to individuals with mental health needs. Some public safety agencies are embracing and encouraging training for EMTs and leveraging outside resources to train EMTs to lead or support a CRT or CIT. The National Association of Emergency Medical Technicians (NAEMT) serves as a clearinghouse for training and education and provides information for first responders so they can assist in a mental health crisis.[52] NAEMT provides links to training offered by the International Critical Incident Stress Foundation, Inc., (CISF), which trains individuals interested in becoming a part of a crisis management team. The National Council for Mental Well Being offers a course in Mental Health First Aid, a skills-based training course that teaches participants about mental health and substance-use issues.

The International Association of Chiefs of Police (IACP) created the One Mind Campaign, which encourages training and coordination across local mental health agencies, public safety agencies, and community organizations to improve interactions between law enforcement officers and individuals with mental health conditions. The goal of the initiative is for these agencies and organizations to become "of one mind."[53] To join the campaign, law enforcement agencies must pledge to implement four strategies over a 12-36 month timeframe, including (1) establishing a partnership with one or more community health organizations, (2) developing and implementing a model policy addressing law enforcement response to individuals with mental health conditions, (3) training and certifying 100% of sworn officers (and selected non-sworn staff, such as dispatchers) in mental health awareness courses by providing Mental Health First Aid training, and (4) providing CIT training to a minimum of 20% of sworn officers (and selected non-sworn staff).

---

funded approaches such as sending non-police response teams, including mental health workers and emergency medical technicians (EMTs) to mental health crisis calls; training 911 dispatchers to assess mental health calls and dispatch the best response team; and embedding mental health professionals in 911 call centers to triage mental health calls and identify the best response. See League of Women Voters, "Reimagining Public Safety: Efforts to Reimagine Public Safety," https://lwvmpls.org/2-04-reforming- 911-calls/.

[52] National Association of Emergency Medical Technicians (NAEMT), "Awareness, Education, and Training," https://www.naemt.org/initiatives/wellness/ems-mental-health/awareness-education-and-training.

[53] International Association of Chiefs of Police (IACP), "One Mind Campaign," https://www.theiacp.org/projects/one- mind-campaign.

988: Suicide Hotline or 911 for Mental Health?

On July 16, 2022, the 988 Suicide & Crisis Lifeline (988 Lifeline; formerly the National Suicide Prevention Lifeline) transitioned from a 10-digit number (1-800-273-8255) to the 3-digit hotline number (988). The 988 Lifeline is a national hotline that provides immediate crisis counseling and referral services for individuals experiencing suicidal thoughts or other mental distress. Currently, the 988 Lifeline routes calls by area code to the crisis center nearest that area code. The crisis center is staffed by trained crisis workers. Call center staff are equipped to counsel callers, provide local referrals for follow-up treatment, or (in some cases) transfer callers to 911 to dispatch local emergency personnel. There is an interest in some jurisdictions for potentially expanding the 988 Lifeline from a counseling and referral hotline to a dispatching service able to deploy local crisis responders to mental health emergencies, similar to 911.[54] In 2020, the Substance Abuse and Mental Health Services Administration (SAMHSA) issued national guidelines for behavioral health crisis care, identifying the 988 Lifeline as a potential hub for community crisis response.[55] In this format, the 988 Lifeline would not only serve as a suicide counseling hotline— as it does currently—but as a centralized call center able to dispatch mobile crisis response and link individuals with community services. While some localities may begin piloting more comprehensive systems soon (such as coordinated 911-988 programs),[56] most communities would require significant efforts and additional resources to achieve this goal.

Research on the Mental Health Crisis Responses Models

Research suggests that CRTs and MCTs may improve some outcomes related to law enforcement interactions with people experiencing a mental health

---

[54] See, for example, Bipartisan Policy Center, *Answering the Call 988: A New Vision for Crisis Response*, Washington, DC, June 2022.

[55] Substance Abuse and Mental Health Services Administration (SAMHSA), *National Guidelines for Behavioral Health Crisis Care*, Best Practices Toolkit, Rockville, MD, 2020.

[56] In November 2021, a consortium of mental health providers produced a report, *Consensus Approach and Recommendations for the Creation of a Comprehensive Crisis Response System*. The report made several recommendations related to 911 and 988, including the need for planning "to ensure the two systems operate in a complementary fashion, not as parallel or exclusive systems," [and] "clarity on roles and protocols for cross-system referrals."

crisis.[57] For instance, CRTs and MCTs both appear particularly effective at connecting people to mental health services.[58] CRTs also appear to improve outcomes for individuals experiencing a mental health crisis.[59] Research suggests that CRTs reduced the number of people being taken into police custody and unnecessary emergency department visits.[60] An evaluation of a MCT pilot program in Denver, CO, suggests that the program not only diverted people with mental health problems from the criminal justice system by providing care to these individuals but it also decreased crime in the areas served by MCTs.[61]

CIT programs appear to be particularly effective at changing police officers' perceptions of and response to people with mental illness.[62] Several studies found that CIT training has positive effects on law enforcement participants. For example, CIT training appears to improve police officers' attitudes and behaviors toward people with mental health conditions. One study found that CIT-trained officers

- demonstrate improvements in knowledge, attitudes, and self-efficacy toward interacting with people with mental illness;
- have a greater understanding of stigmas associated with mental illness;
- have beliefs about mental illness that are shaped by medical knowledge;
- demonstrate a reduced preference for using force against people with mental illness; and
- show a preference for de-escalating situations and linking people with mental illness to treatment.[63]

---

57 CITs are the most widely evaluated of the three models of specialized responses to people with mental illness. There is less research on the effectiveness of and outcomes related to CRTs and MCTs. In addition, a significant proportion of the CRT research comes from Canada, the United Kingdom, and Australia, where CRTs are more common and have been in existence longer.

58 Watson et al., *Crisis Response Services for People with Mental Illness*.

59 Puntis et al., "A Systematic Review of Co-Responder Models," pp. 256-266; and Watson et al., *Crisis Response Services for People with Mental Illness*.

60 Puntis et al., "A Systematic Review of Co-Responder Models," pp. 256-266; and Watson et al., *Crisis Response Services for People with Mental Illness*.

61 Thomas S. Dee and Jaymes Pyne, "A Community Response Approach to Mental Health and Substance Abuse Crises Reduces Crime," *Science Advances*, vol. 8, no. 23 (2022).

62 Rogers et al., "Effectiveness of CIT Programs."

63 Amy C. Watson, Michael T. Compton, and Jeffrey N. Draine, "The Crisis Intervention Team (CIT) Model: An Evidence-Based Policing Practice," *Behavioral Sciences and the Law*,

While research suggests that CIT programs might be effective at changing police officers' attitudes and approaches to interacting with people experiencing a mental health crisis, it is less clear whether these changes translate into improved outcomes for people with mental health needs who have contact with the police. One study found that arrests after CIT implementation declined over time,[64] while a 2016 meta-analysis found that CITs do not reduce the arrest of or use of force against people with mental illness.[65]

Despite the meta-analysis on CITs effects on the results of interactions between the police and people in a mental health crisis, for most of these crisis response models, research remains limited and evaluations looking at multiple outcomes of the models sometimes yield mixed results. For example, in their review of research on crisis response services, several experts concluded that overall, the literature demonstrates that MCT services have high rates of consumer and provider satisfaction and can effectively increase community-based service use, reduce reliance on psychiatric ED [emergency departments], and link people to community-based care once discharged from an ED.[66]

The authors noted that most existing studies on crisis response models have methodological limitations, hindering the ability to draw definitive conclusions for all outcomes related to these programs. Many of the studies evaluate just one program in a single city, for example, limiting the ability to generalize the results to other jurisdictions. Thus, more conclusive determinations on the effectiveness of mental health crisis response programs await a more robust body of research.

---

vol. 35, no. 5-6 (September-December 2017), pp. 431-441 (hereinafter, "Watson et al., 'The Crisis Intervention Team (CIT) Model: An Evidence-Based Policing Practice'").

64 Stephanie Franz and Randy Borum, "Crisis Intervention Teams May Prevent Arrests of People with Mental Illnesses," *Police Practice and Research*, vol. 12, no. 3 (June), p. 2011.

65 The meta-analysis found that CIT-trained officers were less likely than non-CIT-trained officers to arrest people with mental illness, but the result was not statistically significant. See Sema A. Taheri, "Do Crisis Intervention Teams Reduce Arrests and Improve Officer Safety? A Systematic Review and Meta-Analysis," *Criminal Justice Policy Review*, vol. 27, no. 1 (2016), pp. 76-96. The conclusions of Taheri's meta-analysis resulted in the National Institute of Justice (NIJ) rating CITs as having "No Effects" on reducing arrests of or use of force against people with mental illness. See https://crimesolutions.ojp.gov/ratedpractices/81#mao. Other experts assert that due to the limitations of the research on CITs, it is too early to draw conclusions about their effectiveness in reducing arrests and use of force against people with mental illness. See, for example, Watson and Compton, "What Research on CITs Tells Us and What We Need to Ask," pp. 422-426.

66 Watson et al., Crisis Response Services for People with Mental Illness, p. 44.

Federal Programs Related to Law Enforcement and Mental Health Crisis Response

Both the U.S. Department of Justice (DOJ) and SAMHSA[67] within the U.S. Department of Health and Human Services (HHS) provide funding to state and local governments to help improve their response to individuals experiencing a mental health crisis and those with mental health disorders.

Department of Justice Grant Programs

Justice and Mental Health Collaboration Program

Congress has appropriated funding for the Adult and Juvenile Collaboration program (34 U.S.C. §10651) since FY2006 and DOJ awards these funds through its Justice and Mental Health Collaboration program. Under the authorization for the program, grants can be awarded to state, local, and tribal governments for a variety of purposes related to improving the criminal justice system's response to people with mental health disorders.

Under the program, grants can be awarded to plan and implement programs to promote public safety by ensuring access to adequate mental health and other treatment services for adults or juveniles with mental health disorders that are overseen cooperatively by (1) a criminal or juvenile justice agency or a mental health court and (2) a mental health agency. Specifically, planning and implementation grants can be used to

- create or expand mental health courts or other court-based programs for preliminarily qualified offenders;
- offer specialized training to criminal and juvenile justice and mental health professionals on identifying the symptoms of people with mental health disorders in order to respond more effectively to these individuals;

[67] In addition to the two SAMHSA programs mentioned, there are a number of SAMHSA grants, such as the Community Mental Health Service Block Grants (MHBG), that offer significant flexibilities when it comes to allowable activities. Grants like the MHBG could be used to support activities such as response to mental health crises, but they are not specifically dedicated to that purpose. Of note, Congress included a set-aside for "evidence-based crisis systems" in the FY2021 and FY2022 annual appropriations for the MHBG.

- support programs operated cooperatively by criminal and juvenile justice and mental health agencies that provide mental health treatment, and where appropriate, substance abuse treatment; and
- support collaboration between state and local governments with respect to people with mental health disorders in the justice system.

Grants under this program can also be awarded to improve law enforcement's response to people with mental health disorders. Grants can be used to

- offer law enforcement and campus security personnel training in procedures to identify and respond to incidents involving individuals experiencing a mental health crisis;
- implement receiving centers that assess people in law enforcement custody for suicide risk and mental health and substance abuse treatment needs;
- establish new or improve existing computerized information systems to provide timely information to criminal justice system personnel so they can improve their response to individuals with mental health disorders;
- provide support for law enforcement academy, in-service, and continuing education training and other programs that instruct law enforcement personnel on how to identify and respond to people with mental health disorders or co- occurring mental health and substance use disorders; and
- establish and expand cooperative efforts to promote public safety through the use of effective intervention with individuals with mental health disorders.

Further, grants can be awarded for activities such as sequential intercept mapping, which is a process for studying how people with mental health conditions work their way through the criminal justice system. It also involves developing opportunities for the criminal justice and mental health systems to collaborate on ways to address the risks and needs of these individuals. The process includes identifying gaps in service for people with mental health conditions in the criminal justice system and developing programs to address these gaps. These programs can include emergency and crisis services; specialized police-based responses; court hearings and disposition alternatives; reentry from jails and prisons; and community supervision, treatment, and support services. Grants can also be used to implement intervention programs, which can include hiring personnel and providing support services to prevent involvement in the criminal justice system.

Community Oriented Policing Services (COPS) Office CIT Program

For FY2021 and FY2022, the COPS Office has awarded grants for CIT under its Community Policing Development program. Grants are awarded to law enforcement agencies to help them implement CITs, which can include "embedding behavioral or mental health professionals with law enforcement agencies, training for law enforcement officers and embedded behavioral or mental health professionals in crisis intervention response, or a combination of these."[68] Grants can be used to pay law enforcement officer overtime, mental health professionals' salaries or contracts, and personnel training costs.

Edward Byrne Memorial Justice Assistance Grant (JAG) Program

JAG is a formula grant program that provides funds to states, the District of Columbia, each territory, and local and tribal governments for a variety of criminal justice initiatives.[69] Grant recipients can use their JAG funds for state and local initiatives, technical assistance, training, personnel, equipment, supplies, contractual support, and criminal justice information systems for, among other things, mental health and related law enforcement and corrections programs, including behavioral programs and crisis intervention teams. The JAG program gives grant recipients flexibility in deciding how to spend their funds, so while state, local, and tribal governments could use JAG funding for programs to improve the criminal justice system's response to people with mental health needs, they are not required to do so.

---

[68] U.S. Department of Justice (DOJ), Community Oriented Policing Services Office (COPS), *FY2022 Crisis Intervention Teams Program, Community Policing Development*, fact sheet, May 2022, p. 1.

[69] For more information on the JAG program, see CRS In Focus IF10691, *The Edward Byrne Memorial Justice Assistance Grant (JAG) Program*.

Substance Abuse and Mental Health Services Administration Grant Programs

Law Enforcement and Behavioral Health Partnerships for Early Diversion Grants

SAMHSA administers the Law Enforcement and Behavioral Health Partnerships for Early Diversion (or Early Diversion) grant program as part of its criminal and juvenile justice programming. The purpose of this program is to establish or expand programs that divert adults with a serious mental illness from the criminal justice system to community-based services prior to arrest and booking.[70] SAMHSA's Early Diversion grant program supports three programs in Colorado, Connecticut, and Tennessee.[71]

Mental Health Awareness Training

SAMHSA'S Mental Health Awareness Training (MHAT) grant program provides resources for training law enforcement and other first responders on how to recognize a mental health condition, provide initial help in a mental health crisis, and connect individuals to appropriate care. The MHAT program—also known as Mental Health First Aid—is structured similarly to standard first aid training: an eight-hour course that instructs participants in how to identify, understand, and respond to the signs of a mental health crisis. SAMHSA partners with the National Council for Mental Wellbeing to administer MHAT grants. Originally part of Project AWARE, the MHAT program received its own authorization in Section 9010 of the 21st Century Cures Act (P.L. 114-255).

Considerations for Congress

If policymakers choose to take steps related to supporting specialized law enforcement responses to mental health crises, there are several issues Congress could consider, including the following:

---

70 U.S. Department of Health and Human Services (HHS), SAMHSA, *Fiscal Year 2023 Justification of Estimates for Appropriations Committees*, https://www.samhsa.gov/sites/default/files/samhsa-fy-2023-cj.pdf.

71 SAMHSA, *Law Enforcement and Behavioral Health Partnerships for Early Diversion*, https://www.samhsa.gov/ criminal-juvenile-justice/grants-grantees/early-diversion.

- further aiding state and local governments with expanding their capacity to provide mental health services,
- providing funding for preventative interventions to aid people before the onset of mental health conditions,
- promoting more training for law enforcement officers on how to respond to people experiencing a mental health crisis,
- promoting responses that utilize mental health professionals,
- collecting data on law enforcement officers' interactions with people experiencing a mental health crisis,
- providing additional funding to aid 911 call centers with handling calls for service involving people experiencing a mental health crisis,
- promoting more uniform laws and policies regarding how law enforcement agencies respond to mental health crises, and
- supporting research on alternative law enforcement responses.

Access to Mental Health Services

There is a growing sentiment that diverting individuals to mental health services during a crisis would reduce burdens on both the criminal justice and local health care systems.[72] Cities that have implemented specialized law enforcement mental health crisis response programs have found the availability of adequate community mental health resources to be essential to program effectiveness.[73] However, research suggests that police officers have perceived the mental health resources in their area as "inadequate, cumbersome, or absent altogether."[74] Improving law enforcement's response to individuals experiencing a mental health crisis depends on the availability of appropriate mental health services. As one study noted, even if appropriate police intervention occurs, without adequate supportive housing programs, short and long-term mental health bed availability, and sufficient mental

---

[72] See, for example, Katie Bailey, Staci Rising Paquet, and Bradley R. Ray et al., "Barriers and Facilitators to Implementing an Urban Co-Responding Police-Mental Health Team," *Health and Justice*, vol. 6, no. 21 (2018).

[73] See, for example, William Wells and Joseph A. Schafer, "Officer Perceptions of Police Responses to Persons with a Mental Illness," *Policing: An International Journal of Police Strategies & Management*, vol. 29, no. 4 (2006), pp. 578- 601 (hereinafter, "Wells and Schafer, 'Officer Perceptions of Police Responses to Persons with a Mental Illness'").

[74] Wells and Schafer, "Officer Perceptions of Police Responses to Persons with a Mental Illness," p. 581.

health and substance use disorder treatment programs, many individuals will likely continue to experience crises that require police response.[75]

For individuals needing mental health services, acute care medical facilities such as hospital emergency departments or incarceration in jails are often the only options in many communities.[76] In areas with few psychiatric inpatient beds or limited mental health services, treatment may actually be more accessible in jail than in the community.[77] With limited options for custodial care of individuals with mental health needs, law enforcement and other first responders are often left with few resources when encountering people experiencing a mental health crisis.[78]

Inpatient Bed Availability

Effective treatment for individuals experiencing a mental health crisis typically involves a spectrum of services provided at continuum of care facilities. For many individuals, mental health needs can be met through community-based outpatient services. For those with complex mental health conditions or a serious mental illness, or those in an acute crisis, inpatient care may be the most effective care.[79] Most estimates suggest that the supply of psychiatric inpatient beds in hospitals in the United States is not adequate to meet the demand for institutional care. While there is no agreed-upon number for system adequacy, experts have recommended 40-60 psychiatric inpatients

---

[75] Jacqueline B. Helfgott, Matthew J. Hickman, and Andre P. Labossiere, "A Descriptive Evaluation of the Seattle Police Department's Crisis Response Team Officer/Mental Health Professional Partnership Pilot Program," *International Journal of Law and Psychiatry*, vol. 44 (2016), pp. 109-122.

[76] Emergency department (ED) care must be provided regardless of a patient's ability to pay under the Emergency Medical Treatment and Labor Act (EMTALA) requirements. Thus, local EDs often become a safety net when other alternatives are unavailable. See David Bender, Nalini Pande, and Michael Ludwig, *A Literature Review: Psychiatric Boarding*, HHS, Assistant Secretary for Planning and Evaluation (ASPE), Office of Disability, Aging and Long-Term Care Policy, October 29, 2008, https://aspe.hhs.gov/sites/default/files/migrated_legacy_files//43101/PsyBdLR.pdf; and Wood and Watson, "Improving Police Interventions During Mental Health-Related Encounters."

[77] One report described a practice referred to as *mercy booking*, in which law enforcement officers perceived detention in jail as the only available access point to psychiatric treatment, even when officers recognize that it would likely not serve the person in need as well as other services. See Lamb et al., "The Police and Mental Health," pp. 1266-1271.

[78] Walid Fakhoury and Stefan Priebe, "Deinstitutionalization and Reinstutionalization: Major Changes in the Provision of Mental Healthcare," *Psychiatry*, vol. 6, no. 8 (August 2007), pp. 313-316.

[79] See, for example, National Association of State Mental Health Program Directors, *Beyond Beds: A Series of Working Papers*, 2017-2021, https://nasmhpd.org/content/tac-assessment-papers.

beds per 100,000 people.[80] According to a Pew Charitable Trust national average for states is 11.7 beds per 100,000.[81] A 2015 study conducted by the National Association of State Mental Health Program Directors found that most states (35 of the 46 with available data) were experiencing shortages of psychiatric hospital beds.[82] The psychiatric bed shortage is due, in part, to a lack of mental health treatment facilities offering inpatient care. According to SAMHSA's National Mental Health Services Survey (N-MHSS), approximately 15% of mental health treatment facilities offered inpatient care in 2018 (Figure 2).

---

[80] California Hospital Association, *California's Acute Psychiatric Bed Loss*, Sacramento, CA, February 2019, https://calhospital.org/wp-content/uploads/2021/04/psychbeddata2017.pdf; and The Pew Charitable Trusts, *Amid Shortage of Psychiatric Beds, Mentally Ill Face Long Waits for Treatment*, Stateline Article, August, 2, 2019, https://www.pewtrusts.org/en/research-and-analysis/blogs/stateline/2016/08/02/amid-shortage-of-psychiatric-beds-mentally-ill-face-long-waits-for-treatment (hereinafter, "Pew, *Amid Shortage of Psychiatric Beds, Mentally Ill Face Long Waits for Treatment*").

[81] Pew, *Amid Shortage of Psychiatric Beds, Mentally Ill Face Long Waits for Treatment*. The Treatment Advocacy Center—a nonprofit advocacy organization—has estimated that the country needs an additional 123,300 state psychiatric beds to meet current demand. See Doris A. Fuller and Elizabeth Sinclair, Treatment Advocacy Center, *Going, Going, Gone: Trends and Consequences of Eliminating State Psychiatric Beds, 2016*.

[82] Ted Lutterman, Robert Shaw, and William Fisher et al., *Trends in Psychiatric Inpatient Capacity, United States and Each State, 1970 to 2014*, National Association of State Mental Health Program Directors, Beyond Beds Assessment #2, Alexandria, VA, August 2017, https://nasmhpd.org/sites/default/files/TACPaper.2.Psychiatric-Inpatient-Capacity_508C.pdf.

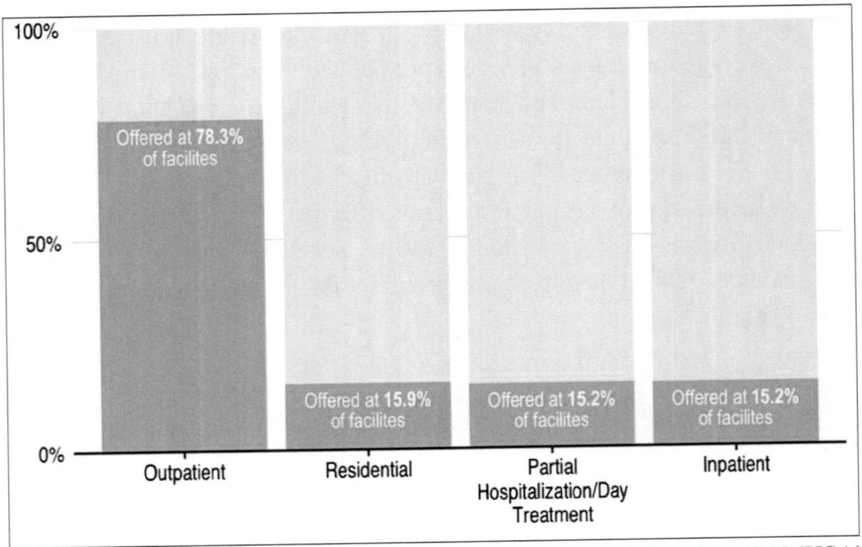

Source: Substance Abuse and Mental Health Services Administration (SAMHSA), National Mental Health Services Survey (N-MHSS): 2018, Data on Mental Health Treatment Facilities, Rockville, MD, 2019, available at https://www.samhsa.gov/data/sites/default/files/cbhsq-reports/NMHSS-2018.pdf

Notes: Outpatient mental health facilities provide only outpatient mental health services to ambulatory clients (i.e., <3 hours daily), residential treatment centers provide treatment in residential care settings, partial hospitalization/day treatment facilities provide partial day services to ambulatory clients (i.e., >3 hours daily), and inpatient facilities are hospitals that primarily provide 24-hour inpatient care to persons with mental illness. See the source cited above for more information.

Figure 2. Mental Health Service Settings in the United States, 2018. Percentage of Mental Health Treatment Facilities that Offer Certain Treatment Formats.

Experts and other stakeholders debate whether to add more psychiatric beds to meet demand or enhance community-based care to reduce demand for psychiatric beds by preventing mental health crises.[83] While lawmakers have pursued both paths, current federal policies primarily support community-based outpatient care, with states responsible for most inpatient psychiatric care.[84] SAMHSA has noted that the core structural elements of an optimal

[83] See CRS In Focus IF10870, Psychiatric Institutionalization and Deinstitutionalization.

[84] For example, the Medicaid Institutions for Mental Disease (IMD) rule limits the use of Medicaid payment for psychiatric inpatient care in hospitals for much of the adult population; see CRS In Focus IF10222, Medicaid's Institutions for Mental Disease (IMD) Exclusion for more information. Also, federal statute prohibits use of Mental Health Block Grant (MHBG) funds for inpatient services in any setting; see CRS Report R46426,

crisis response system include a regional call center, crisis mobile response teams, and crisis receiving and stabilization facilities with inpatient capacities or referral options.[85] Crisis response programs that train law enforcement officers to respond to people with mental health needs—or partner officers with a mental health provider—may only be as effective as the community mental health services available to individuals in need after crisis response triage occurs. The role of the federal government in psychiatric inpatient care remains up for debate: some believe more federal resources are necessary to promote adequate care while others believe this is the responsibility of the states, citing increased costs to the federal government, among other reasons.[86]

Identifying Available Bedspace in Treatment Facilities

In addition to an inadequate number of beds, identifying available beds in mental health treatment facilities can also be a challenge. The mental health treatment system is largely a patchwork of independently operated public and private facilities that rely primarily on limited informal communication networks. Some states have begun to create psychiatric bed registries or bed tracking systems as tools for providers, patients, and caregivers to identify open hospital beds more efficiently.[87] In 2016, Section 9007 of the 21st Century Cures Act (P.L. 114-255) required the HHS Secretary to award competitive grants to states to, among other things, develop and maintain a database of beds at inpatient behavioral health treatment facilities. In 2019, SAMHSA announced a pilot initiative to help select states establish or expand

---

Substance Abuse and Mental Health Services Administration (SAMHSA): Overview of the Agency and Major Programs for more information. Other public policies also play a role, such as regulations related to implementation of the Supreme Court's 1999 decision in Olmstead v. L.C.; see CRS In Focus IF10870, Psychiatric Institutionalization and Deinstitutionalization for more information.

[85] SAMHSA, *National Guidelines for Behavioral Health Crisis Care*, Best Practice Toolkit, Rockville, MD, 2020.

[86] See, for example, U.S. Government Accountability Office (GAO), *Medicaid: States Fund Services for Adults in Institutions for Mental Diseases Using a Variety of Strategies*, GAO-17-652, September 8, 2017, https://www.gao.gov/ products/gao-17-652; Jennifer Mathis, "Medicaid's Institutions for Mental Diseases (IMD) Exclusion Rule: A Policy Debate—Argument to Retain the IMD Rule," *Psychiatric Services*, vol. 70, no. 1 (January 1, 2019), pp. 4-6; and Aaron Glickman and Dominic Sisti, "Medicaid's Institutions for Mental Diseases (IMD) Exclusion Rule: A Policy Debate— Argument to Repeal the IMD Rule," *Psychiatric Services*, vol. 70, no. 1 (January 1, 2019), pp. 7-10.

[87] Laurel Fuller, Tami Mark, and Shilpi Misra et al., *Inpatient Bed Tracking: State Responses to Need for Inpatient Care*, HHS, Office of the Assistant Secretary for Planning and Evaluation (ASPE), Final Report, Washington, DC, August 2019, https://aspe.hhs.gov/ sites/default/files/migrated_legacy_files//190716/IPBedTrack.pdf.

psychiatric crisis bed registry programs.[88] A study by HHS's Office of the Assistant Secretary for Planning and Evaluation found that while state bed registries experience significant challenges—such as the reluctance of hospitals to update information frequently enough to be useful—states report that the registries can be helpful in locating open beds and identifying the need for additional psychiatric beds.[89]

Expanding Capacity for Mental Health Services

For law enforcement agencies to effectively divert certain people with mental health conditions from the criminal justice system, most jurisdictions would need to increase the capacity of their community mental health services. An effective crisis response system requires access to a spectrum of available services across a continuum of providers. Trained law enforcement officers may be able to effectively respond to certain situations involving persons experiencing a mental health crisis, but officers may be limited in their response without access to adequate follow-up care for those persons. Without mental health receiving facilities, individuals with further mental health needs are more likely to end up in emergency departments or jails. Increasing acute inpatient beds or establishing psychiatric crisis stabilization centers, for example, may improve outcomes for individuals in crisis, reduce the burden on health care or justice facilities, and reduce overall costs.[90]

Mental health services have historically been the responsibility of states. The federal government, primarily through Medicaid and discretionary grants administered by HHS, provides financial support to states for mental health treatment. Both Medicaid and discretionary grant programs have limits on funding inpatient mental health care. For example, SAMHSA's Community Mental Health Services Block Grant (MHBG) is the largest federal grant provided to states for mental health services. Each state may distribute MHBG funds to provide community mental health services and has flexibility in the use of funds within the framework of a state plan and federal requirements. The authorization for MHBG prohibits the use of block grant funds "to provide inpatient services."[91] Similarly, Medicaid, the single largest payer of mental

---

[88] SAMHSA, "Crisis Bed Registries to Assist People with Urgent Mental Health Needs," press release, January 24, 2019, https://www.samhsa.gov/newsroom/press-announcements/201901240130 (hereinafter, "SAMHSA, 'Crisis Bed Registries to Assist People with Urgent Mental Health Needs'").

[89] SAMHSA, "Crisis Bed Registries to Assist People with Urgent Mental Health Needs."

[90] Wells and Schafer, "Officer Perceptions of Police Responses to Persons with a Mental Illness."

[91] Public Health Service Act (PHSA) §1916 (42 U.S.C. §300x-5).

health treatment services in the United States,[92] has a long-standing policy that prohibits the federal government from providing federal Medicaid funds to states for services rendered to patients in health care facilities (of more than 16 beds) that primarily provide treatment for mental health disorders. Known as the IMD exclusion, this policy prevents the federal government from providing federal Medicaid funds to states for any service delivered to individuals aged 21 through 64 in an "institution for mental diseases (IMD)."[93] States can provide Medicaid coverage for services rendered in facilities that do not meet the definition of an IMD, such as facilities with 16 or fewer beds and facilities that are not primarily engaged in providing care to individuals with mental diseases.[94] Options to enhance mental health crisis response and treatment services could involve Congress amending the MHBG authorization or changing Medicaid rules to expand support for crisis response services and psychiatric inpatient care.[95] Tradeoffs to this approach, however, would include higher costs for inpatient care incurred by the federal government.[96]

Congress has recently increased federal support for crisis response programs. For example, Congress included a set-aside for "evidence-based crisis systems" in the FY2021 and FY2022 annual appropriations for the MHBG.97 Similarly, the American Rescue Plan Act of 2021 (ARPA, P.L. 117-2) provided flexibilities related to Medicaid coverage of community-based mobile crisis intervention services and appropriated $15 million for

---

92 Medicaid.gov, Centers for Medicare and Medicaid Services, *Behavioral Health Services*, Baltimore, MD, https://www.medicaid.gov/medicaid/benefits/behavioral-health-services/index.html.

93 The term *institution for mental diseases* means a "hospital, nursing facility, or other institution of more than 16 beds, that is primarily engaged in providing diagnosis, treatment, or care of persons with mental diseases, including medical attention, nursing care, and related services" (SSA §1905(i)).

94 States may also request waivers to receive federal Medicaid funds for services provided to individuals who are patients in IMDs or make monthly payments to managed care organizations for enrollees aged 21 through 64 who are patients in an IMD under Medicaid managed care coverage. For more information, see CRS In Focus IF10222, *Medicaid's Institutions for Mental Disease (IMD) Exclusion*.

95 Of note, the MHBG represents a small percentage of state spending on behavioral health activities. The MHBG funds an average of 1% of the expenses for state mental health agencies. See SAMHSA, *Funding and Characteristics of Single State Agencies*, 2017.

96 See, for example, U.S. Government Accountability Office (GAO), *Medicaid: States Fund Services for Adults in Institutions for Mental Disease Using a Variety of Strategies*, GAO-17-652, August 2017, https://www.gao.gov/assets/ gao-17-652.pdf.

97 Rep. Rosa DeLauro, "Explanatory Statement Submitted by Ms. DeLauro, Chair of the House Committee on Appropriations, Regarding the House Amendment to the Senate Amendment to H.R. 2471, Consolidated Appropriations Act, 2022," Proceedings and Debates of the 117th Congress, Second Session, *Congressional Record*, vol. 168, part No. 42, Book IV (March 9, 2022), pp. H2477-H3215.

these efforts.[98] Other options for Congress to enhance crisis response systems could include direct funding for these activities or further flexibilities for use of existing funds. Congress made use of both of these approaches when it appropriated $340 million for emergency substance use or mental health needs in COVID-19 supplemental appropriations measures, for instance.[99] Some states are using ARPA funds to bolster the continuum of mental health services as well. Massachusetts, for example, used $31 million of ARPA funds to support inpatient psychiatric acute facilities.[100]

California's Psychiatric Health Facilities

To create receiving facilities for individuals experiencing a mental health crisis—other than jails or emergency departments—California established alternative nonhospital 24-hour acute treatment facilities beginning in the 1980s. This strategy was designed to meet the need for inpatient services while also controlling costs.[101] California's psychiatric health facilities (PHFs) provide short-term mental health treatment to individuals in crisis or those with acute mental health needs. Similar to other short-term residential settings, psychiatric acute care facilities, or crisis stabilization units, PHFs provide short-term mental health treatment in less medically intensive, nonhospital settings.[102] PHF services utilize an interdisciplinary team that includes psychiatry, clinical psychology, psychiatric nursing, and social work personnel who provide crisis services, medication management, psychotherapy and other counseling, rehabilitation, drug administration, and pharmacy and basic support services, among others.[103] Initial estimates suggested that PHFs were associated with reduced costs

98 For more information, see CRS Report R46777, American Rescue Plan Act of 2021 (P.L. 117-2): Private Health Insurance, Medicaid, CHIP, and Medicare Provisions.

99 For more information, see CRS Report R46711, U.S. Public Health Service: COVID-19 Supplemental Appropriations in the 116th Congress.

100 National Academy for State Health Policy, How States Are Spending American Rescue Plan Funds, October 8, 2021, https://www.nashp.org/how-states-are-spending-american-rescue-plan-state-fiscal-recovery-funds/.

101 Sally Moltzen, Howard Gurevitz, and Maurice Rappaport et al., "The Psychiatric Health Facility: An Alternative for Acute Inpatient Treatment in Nonhospital Setting," *Hospital and Community Psychiatry*, vol. 37, no. 11 (November 1986) (hereinafter, "Moltzen et al., 'The Psychiatric Health Facility'").

102 HHS, ASPE, Office of Disability, Aging, and Long-Term Care Policy, *Inpatient Bed Tracking: State Responses to Need for Inpatient Care*, Washington, DC, August 2019, https://aspe.hhs.gov/sites/default/files/migrated_legacy_files// 190716/IPBedTrack.pdf.

103 California State Department of Health Care Services, *Psychiatric Health Facilities*, May 4, 2021, https://www.dhcs.ca.gov/psychiatric-health-facilities.

compared to emergency department or other acute hospital admissions.[104] As of 2021, California had over 20 PHFs in operation throughout the state.

Preventing Mental Illness and Mental Health Crises

Some experts have argued that an emphasis on psychiatric service expansion would be an insufficient way to address mental health crisis response, and would perpetuate an already inadequate "standard, reactive psychiatric consultation model."[105] A more upstream approach to addressing mental health crises would invest in prevention interventions prior to the onset of a mental health condition. Some proponents of this model note that prevention efforts, and more targeted programming, are more efficient uses of finite criminal justice and mental health resources.[106] An upstream approach to preventing mental health crises could focus efforts on economic initiatives,[107] education and school-based programs,[108] interventions addressing social determinants of mental health,[109] community development,[110] or medical care earlier in life (i.e., prenatal care, early childhood interventions).[111] Given the dearth of mental health providers, generating enough treatment services might

---

[104] Moltzen et al., "The Psychiatric Health Facility."

[105] Mara Laderman, Amrita Dasgupta, and Robin Henderson et al., "Tackling the Mental Health Crisis in Emergency Departments: Look Upstream for Solutions," *Health Affairs Blog*, January 26, 2018, https://www.healthaffairs.org/do/ 10.1377/forefront.20180123.222 48/full/.

[106] Jennifer D. Wood and Laura Beierschmitt, "Beyond Police Crisis Intervention: Moving 'Upstream' to Manage Cases and Places of Behavioral Health Vulnerability,' *Psychiatry*, vol. 37, no. 5 (September-October 2014), pp. 439- 447.

[107] Anna Macintyre, Daniel Ferris, and Briana Concalves et al., "What has Economics Got to Do with It? The Impact of Socioeconomic Factors on Mental Health and the Case for Collective Action," *Palgrave Communications*, vol. 4, article no. 10 (2018).

[108] Amanda Sanchez, Danielle Cornacchio, and Bridget Poznanski et al., "The Effectiveness of School-Based Mental Health Services for Elementary-Aged Children: A Meta-Analysis," *Child & Adolescent Psychiatry*, vol. 57, no. 3 (March 2018), pp. 153-165.

[109] Deidre M. Anglin, Sandro Galea, and Peter Bachman, "Going Upstream to Advance Psychosis Prevention and Improve Public Health," *JAMA Psychiatry*, vol. 77, no. 7 (April 1, 2020).

[110] Laura Choi, *Moving Upstream to Promote Mental Health: The Role of Community Development*, Center for Behavioral Health Statistics and Quality, 2018, https://www.frbsf.org/community-development/wp-content/uploads/ sites/3/moving-upstream-choi-mental-health-and-community-development-cdir-13-1.pdf.

[111] Celso Arango, Covadongo Diaz-Caneja, and Patrick McGorry et al., "Preventive Strategies for Mental Health," *The Lancet Psychiatry*, vol. 5, no. 7 (July 2018), pp. 591-604.

not be feasible, suggesting an opportunity for investments in prevention.[112] Additionally, outcome research on law enforcement crisis response models is nascent. If future research suggests ineffectiveness, resources to address mental illness and mental health crises may be better used elsewhere.

Training for Law Enforcement Personnel

Jurisdictions that want to establish a specialized response for individuals experiencing a mental health crises face potential challenges with developing that capacity, including finding the time and resources necessary to provide initial and then ongoing training for selected officers. For example, the CIT model requires 40 hours of training for law enforcement officers to be certified. The core elements of the model state that 20%-25% of patrol officers be CIT-certified to fully implement a CIT program.[113] For smaller law enforcement agencies, extended training sessions and continuing education can pose significant burdens. Data from the Bureau of Justice Statistics indicates that three-quarters of police departments in 2016 employed 24 or fewer officers and about half employed 9 or fewer officers.[114] In addition to staffing challenges, the cost of travel, per diem, and training might not be easily accommodated given limited budgetary resources. The Council of State Governments Justice Center and International Association of Directors of Law Enforcement Standards and Training noted that "for law enforcement agencies, there is also a concern with how to meet minimum deployment needs while officers are in training and how to cover any associated overtime costs, particularly for specialized training courses."[115]

In addition to training law enforcement officers to provide specialized responses to people with mental illness, there is also a need to train civilian

---

112 Corey L. M. Keyes, Satvinder S. Dhingra, and Eduardo J. Simoes, "Change in Level of Positive Mental Health as a Predictor of Future Risk of Mental Illness," *American Journal of Public Health*, vol. 100, no. 12 (2010), pp. 2366- 2371.

113 Randoph Dupont, Sam Cochran, and Sarah Pillsbury, *Crisis Intervention Team Core Elements*, University of Memphis, Memphis, TN, September 2007, p. 10, http://cit.memphis.edu/CoreElements.pdf.

114 Shelley S. Hyland and Elizabeth Davis, *Local Police Departments, 2016: Personnel*, DOJ, Office of Justice Programs, Bureau of Justice Statistics, NCJ 252835, Washington, DC, October 2019, p. 3.

115 Martha Plotkin and Talia Peckerman, *The Variability in Law Enforcement State Standards: A 42 State Survey on Mental Health and Crisis De-Escalation Training*, Council of State Governments Justice Center, New York, NY, January 2017, p. 7 (hereinafter, "Plotkin and Peckerman, 42 State Survey on Mental Health and Crisis De-Escalation Training").

staff at 911 call centers to appropriately navigate mental health emergencies. Call center operators are frequently the first point of contact for people who are suffering a mental health crisis. The 911 system is decentralized, with over 5,000 call centers across the country, each with their own standards regarding training, how calls are handled, dispatch protocols, and data management and reporting systems.[116] A "key insight" presented in a Pew study of call center capacity to handle mental health emergencies was that about two-thirds of respondents reported that their call center operators have not received any specialized mental health crisis training.[117] Even though the findings of this study cannot be generalized to all call centers, due to a small sample size and low response rate, it does reveal some potentially important insights. Barriers to accessing training included high staff turnover, staffing shortfalls resulting from the amount of time that a call taker is unavailable while he or she is in training and lack of funding or staff for backfilling call center shifts, budgetary constraints preventing staff from going to training that requires travel, and lack of awareness that training is available.[118] Given the lack of widespread specialized training in some jurisdictions, having access to mental health professionals who could assist call center operators with handling calls involving people with mental illness could be a valuable resource, though it may be prohibitively costly and cumbersome for some areas and centers, and lead to increased response times if additional mental health screening questions are added to 911 scripts.[119] Federal agencies involved in the transition to the new three-digit 988 Suicide & Crisis Lifeline have expressed ambitions to situate that crisis hotline in the center of a robust crisis response system.[120] However, building such a system would require substantial effort and considerable resources, and few areas are currently well positioned to establish this network.

---

[116] Pew Charitable Trusts, *New Research Suggests 911 Call Centers Lack Resources to Handle Behavioral Health Crises*, online issue brief, October 26, 2021, https://www.pewtrusts.org/en/research-and-analysis/issue-briefs/2021/10/ new-research-suggests-911-call-centers-lack-resources-to-handle-behavioral-health-crises (hereinafter, "Pew, 911 Call Centers Lack Resources").

[117] Pew noted that the results of the survey are not representative of call centers nationally (Pew sent their questionnaire to 233 call centers, only 37 responded), but it asserts that the results provide "key insights" into the mental health crisis system resources of 911 call centers. Pew, 911 Call Centers Lack Resources.

[118] Pew, 911 Call Centers Lack Resources.

[119] Jonathan Levinson, "Dying on hold: How new software is creating a logjam at Portland's 911," Oregon Public Broadcasting News, May 6, 2022, https://www.opb.org/article/2022/05/06/portland-911-calls-hold-times-multnomah-county-emergency-response-system-issues/.

[120] SAMHSA, *988 Appropriations Report*, Rockville, MD, December 2021.

Supporting Co-Responder and Mobile Crisis Teams

While CIT is the most widely used model, anecdotal evidence suggests that more jurisdictions are adopting CRTs and MRTs in order to improve their response to people with mental illness. As discussed previously, CRTs and MCTs employ mental health professionals in some capacity, while CITs consist entirely of law enforcement officers, albeit specially trained officers.

Policymakers might consider whether the federal government could support jurisdictions that want to start new or expand the capacity of existing CRTs or MCTs.

A key question might be whether funds under DOJ's Justice and Mental Health Collaboration and JAG programs could be used to support CRTs and MCTs. The authorization for the Justice and Mental Health Collaboration program specifically authorizes funds to be used for CIT programs, though the authorization states that the "appropriate use" of funds also includes "law enforcement diversion" (34 U.S.C. §10651(a)(4)(B)). The authorization for the program defines diversion as "the appropriate use of effective mental health treatment alternatives to juvenile justice or criminal justice system institutional placements for preliminarily qualified offenders" (34 U.S.C. §10651(a)(4)(A)). In addition, the authorization for the JAG program allows funds to be used for "mental health programs and related law enforcement and corrections programs, including behavioral programs and crisis intervention teams" (34 U.S.C. §10152(a)(1)(H)).

Congress might consider whether to amend the authorizations for the Justice and Mental Health Collaboration and JAG programs to make it explicit that funds under both programs can be used for CRTs and MCTs. However, some might question whether MCTs should be funded with grants from DOJ, which largely focus on law enforcement-based programs and responses. Supporters of MCTs argue that law enforcement does not need to be or should not be involved in responding to calls for service that involve people with mental health problems who are not engaging in violent behavior. There also might be a question about whether supporting MCTs through grants from DOJ, a prominent law enforcement agency, could harm their legitimacy in communities that want to separate responses to people with mental health problems from law enforcement. Policymakers might consider whether MCTs should be supported through grants from SAMHSA rather than DOJ.

Other questions regarding financial support for crisis response services surround the shared commitment between federal, state, and local governments and the private sector. If the responsibility for mental health emergency response shifts from law enforcement to health services, then it may be prudent to utilize the existing systems of health care financing—such as private health insurance and public programs like Medicaid and Medicare—rather than annual discretionary funding and competitive grants to fund such a system. A substantial share of behavioral health costs have historically been borne by states—an anomalous arrangement relative to other health conditions. Congress may consider options to incorporate payment for crisis response services into mainstream health care financing systems, and determine the appropriate balance between mandatory and discretionary funding streams.

Data Collection

Policymakers might consider whether there is a need for a requirement for DOJ to collect and report data on a broader range of contacts between law enforcement officers and people in mental health crises. DOJ currently collects data on some interactions between law enforcement officers and people experiencing mental health crises through its National Incident Based Reporting System (NIBRS) and its Use-of Force Data Collection program, but the data collected through these systems are limited, and in the case of the Use-of-Force Data Collection program, the data are hampered by limited participation on the part of law enforcement agencies. More complete data (e.g., collecting data on the situation surrounding the contact between the police and a person in a mental health crisis and the outcome of that interaction) could aid federal, state, and local policymakers with decisions about how to respond to people with mental illness. For example, policymakers could examine whether people in mental health crises in cities with CRTs or MCTs are less likely to be arrested or injured while they are experiencing a mental health crisis.

A potential mandate for DOJ to collect and report data on a wider variety of law enforcement interactions with people experiencing mental health emergencies does not mean that state and local law enforcement agencies will participate in a data collection program absent an incentive, and even then, that the incentive would be enough to induce law enforcement agencies to submit the required data.[121] Potential incentives could include making

---

[121] For a more in-depth discussion of the issues involved with crafting incentives for law enforcement agencies to submit data on their activities to the federal government, see CRS

participation a condition of accessing grant funds from DOJ, requiring states to collect and report data from their law enforcement agencies or face reduced funding under the JAG program, giving preferential consideration for competitive grants to law enforcement agencies who can demonstrate that they submit the required data, or awarding bonus allocations under the JAG program to states that participate in the data collection program.

Increasing the Capabilities of 911 Call Centers

A Pew study of 911 call centers suggested that these centers might require additional resources to increase their capacity to respond to mental health-related calls.[122] Many of the call centers that responded to the survey reported that their operators did not have training on how to handle mental health-related calls and lacked access to mental health professionals to aid in handling these calls.

To address these issues, policymakers may consider whether to authorize funding for research on how to improve 911 response to mental health calls, and to identify options and best practices that could be shared with 911 centers.[123] Policymakers may choose to authorize funding that would support hiring of mental health professionals to handle mental health-related 911 calls or to assist 911 call takers with those calls. While Congress has established programs to fund certain positions (e.g., police, firefighters), traditionally it has not funded 911 positions (state and local governments typically fund these). Further, it does not typically fund positions in perpetuity. For example, for the Department of Homeland Security Staffing for Adequate Firefighter Emergency Response (SAFER) program, federal funding is limited to three years, with localities assuming a higher percentage of the salaries each year. Policymakers may consider supporting the development of and providing

Report R46443, *Programs to Collect Data on Law Enforcement Activities: Overview and Issues*.

122 Pew, 911 Call Centers Lack Resources.

123 The National 911 Program office in the National Highway Traffic Safety Administration at the U.S. Department of Transportation used this approach to improve survivor rates for those experiencing heart attacks. Based on research from the National Academies, the National 911 Program office created "CPR Lifelinks"—a national initiative to train 911 call takers to help others administer CPR before professional help arrives.

funding for training programs, including train-the-trainer programs and other training to assist 911 operators responding to mental health calls.[124]

Call centers have also reported several logistical issues preventing effective response, such as inconsistencies in software used to manage 911 calls. These technological barriers prevent centers from collecting consistent data on the number of mental health-related calls they receive and the outcomes of these calls. Policymakers may consider authorizing funding to help upgrade local 911 systems to assist them in collecting data on the number of, responses to, and outcomes of mental health related calls. If Congress were to authorize a grant program to assist jurisdictions with data collection, policymakers may also consider the merits of requiring a federal agency to coordinate with industry stakeholders or lead a public-private effort to develop data collection standards for 911 call centers regarding mental health-related calls (and require any jurisdiction that receives funding to report data based on these standards). A challenge with this approach is that only 911 centers that have standardized software and receive grant funding would likely report, meaning that any collected data would be incomplete. Even if funding is not tied to implementing data collection standards, requiring a federal agency to encourage such standards, even as advisory guidance, might help promote more consistent data on mental health-related calls.

A final issue for consideration is coordination between 911 call centers and 988 calling services. Currently, the two systems are separate.[125] Industry stakeholders have encouraged greater planning, coordination, and shared protocols between 911 and 988 systems and have called for increased definition of roles, responsibilities, and procedures for managing and referring calls between the two systems.

Promoting Consistency in Law and Policies

States have a range of laws and policies regarding the training law enforcement officers receive on how to respond to people with mental

---

[124] The National 911 Program Office lists several (non-governmental) organizations that provide training for 911 call takers including the 911 Training Institute, which offers training for managing calls from those experiencing a mental health crisis, available at https://www.911training.net/.

[125] In some areas, the 911 and 988 systems may have formal relationships, but the infrastructure and routing systems remain separate.

illness.[126] States also have varying laws regarding what actions law enforcement officers can take when they encounter someone experiencing a mental health crisis, such as who can initiate a temporary hold so someone can be evaluated by a mental health professional or whether officers can issue a citation in lieu of an arrest, thereby diverting someone experiencing a mental health crisis from potential incarceration.[127]

Policymakers might consider whether the federal government should take any steps to promote more consistency in these laws and policies among states. One possible step might be for Congress to require DOJ to publish recommended standards regarding the type and amount of academy and in-service training law enforcement officers should receive. Policymakers might consider whether to authorize a new grant program to help support efforts to provide more academy-based and in-service mental health training to law enforcement officers for state or local governments that agree to meet the requirements of the recommended training standards. Federal agencies such as DOJ and HHS could issue model laws that states could adopt to improve how people with mental illness interact with the criminal justice and mental health systems. Due to the federalized system of government in the United States, it is unlikely that Congress could directly require states to adopt any recommended changes to their laws or policies, so Congress might consider providing an incentive for states to do so.[128] Policymakers might also consider whether to make adoption of any proposed changes to policies regarding mental health training for law enforcement officers or actions law enforcement officers can take when they encounter a person with mental illness a condition of receiving federal funding.

---

[126] For an overview of mental health and de-escalation training provided to law enforcement officers, see Plotkin and Peckerman, 42 State Survey on Mental Health and Crisis De-Escalation Training.

[127] For an overview of state laws that might affect law enforcement officers' ability to respond to people experiencing a mental health crisis, see Lars Trautman and Jonathan Haggarty, *Statewide Policies Relating to Pre-Arrest Diversion and Crisis Response*, R Street Policy Study #187, November 2019. The R Street Institute is described as a "nonprofit, nonpartisan, public policy research organization that promotes center-right solutions to public policy problems." MacArthur Foundation, R Street Institute, https://www.macfound.org/grantee/r-street-institute-10097751/.

[128] For a review of federalism and congressional influence over state and local law enforcement policy, see CRS Report R43904, *Public Trust and Law Enforcement—A Discussion for Policymakers*.

Supporting Research on Crisis Response Models

There is a dearth of high-quality research on the effectiveness of MCTs and CRTs, and to some extent CITs (though studies on CITs are more numerous than studies on the other two approaches). Concerns about how law enforcement officers handle calls for service involving people with mental health problems have led many jurisdictions to consider alternatives to traditional law enforcement responses.[129] This might provide an opportunity for the federal government to support more research on MCTs and CRTs. Policymakers could consider authorizing a new grant program that would help jurisdictions either start MCTs or CRTs or expand them beyond the pilot stage with the condition that jurisdictions evaluate their programs and make the results available to the granting agency. Congress could also provide funding for evaluation research on MCTs and CRTs through the National Institute of Justice (NIJ) or the National Institutes of Health (NIH).

Appendix. Examples of Mobile Crisis Teams

Members of Congress who want to learn more about responses to people in a mental health crisis that do not involve law enforcement might be interested in which jurisdictions have MCTs. While there is no comprehensive accounting of cities that utilize MCTs, this appendix provides examples of cities that are using them on either a permanent or pilot basis.

Albuquerque, NM

In September 2021, Albuquerque launched the Albuquerque Community Safety Department (ACS) to respond to emergency nonmedical calls that are not believed to involve violence or the threat of violence.[130] Unlike some of the other pilot programs highlighted below, ACS is now a cabinet-level city department, acting as a third public safety agency alongside the Albuquerque

---

[129] David A. Graham, "The Stumbling Block to One of the Most Promising Police Reforms," *The Atlantic*, February 22, 2022.

[130] Colleen Heild, "ABQ's Community Safety Department Launches Patrols," *Albuquerque Journal*, September 11, 2021.

police and fire departments.[131] 911 dispatchers route calls for disturbances, issues involving mental health or homelessness, possible suicides, welfare checks, and other calls believed to be nonviolent and nonmedical to ACS.[132] ACS responses to 911 calls for service are in lieu of a response from firefighters, EMTs, or law enforcement, preserving these first responders for other emergency calls.[133] ACS has several different types of responders. MCT clinicians are dispatched in joint responses with law enforcement and respond exclusively to ACS' 911 calls. Behavioral Health Responders (BHR) and Community Responders (CR) resemble traditional MCTs, and are dispatched in teams of two to respond to nonviolent 911 calls and tickets created by the city's nonemergency request line, 311.[134] Street Outreach and Resource Coordinators (SO) respond to 311 tickets, and do not respond to 911 dispatches. BHR, CR, and SO teams may also proactively aid individuals in need, resulting in a self-dispatch.[135] As of July 2022, the department has received nearly 14,000 calls for service from 911 dispatch, 311 tickets, and self-dispatch, and estimates that over 7,000 calls have been diverted from the Albuquerque Police Department to ACS. The majority of calls for service are taken by BHR teams, which are also the largest group of ACS responders.[136]

Denver, CO

The Supported Team Assistance Response (STAR) Program is a collaborative effort between the Caring for Denver Foundation, Denver Police Department, WellPower (Mental Health Center of Denver), Denver Health Paramedic Division, Denver 911, and other organizations offering community supports and resources. 911 dispatchers redirect certain calls related to individuals experiencing problems with mental health, poverty, homelessness, and/or

---

[131] City of Albuquerque, *Albuquerque Community Safety Department FY2022 Organizational Plan*, Albuquerque Community Safety Department, December 2021, p. 9 (hereinafter, "Albuquerque Community Safety Department FY2022 Organizational Plan").

[132] "Albuquerque Community Safety Department FY2022 Organizational Plan," p. 24.

[133] City of Albuquerque Mayor Tim Keller, "Albuquerque Community Safety Responders Hit the Street," press release, October 13, 2021.

[134] 311 is a specialized phone number supported by many cities in the United States that provides access to nonemergency municipal services and is intended to divert calls from 911.

[135] "Albuquerque Community Safety Department FY2022 Organizational Plan," p. 17-23.

[136] City of Albuquerque, *Albuquerque Community Safety Monthly Informational Report: July 2022,* Albuquerque Community Safety Department.

substance abuse issues to STAR.[137] A STAR mobile crisis response team (e.g., a social worker and paramedic) can provide medical assessment, crisis intervention, de-escalation, transportation, and connections to community resources.[138] STAR only responds to incidents in which there is no evidence of criminal activity or violence, weapons, threats, injuries, or serious medical needs. The STAR pilot program operated from June 1 to November 30, 2020. During the pilot phase, STAR operated one van staffed with a paramedic and a clinician that offered services from 10:00 a.m. to 6:00 p.m. on weekdays in high-demand neighborhoods. An evaluation of the STAR pilot found that the program reduced reports of less serious crimes in covered neighborhoods by 34% overall, and it found evidence of reduced crime levels outside of STAR operating hours.[139] Denver continued to operate STAR after the pilot phase and the program has secured additional funding to expand service. STAR currently operates from 6:00 a.m. to 10:00 p.m., and is in the process of trying to secure several new vans and expand service citywide.[140]

Anchorage, AK

The municipality of Anchorage launched an MCT program in the summer of 2021. MCT teams comprised of a mental health clinician and a paramedic from the Anchorage Fire Department (AFD) respond to 911 or 311 calls involving a mental health crisis that are believed not to involve a weapon, an active suicide attempt, or any other threat of violence toward the patient or responders. The program is housed in AFD, and initially received calls exclusively through the fire department's dispatch center. Police dispatchers have since been trained on how to use and dispatch MCTs, increasing dispatch volume for the teams. 911 callers may request an MCT response, and

137 STAR Program Evaluation; Li Cohen, "Health Care Workers Replaced Denver Cops in Handling Hundreds of Mental Health and Substance Abuse Cases—And Officials Say it Saved Lives," *CBS News*, February 6, 2021; David Sachs, "In the First Six Months of Health Care Professionals Replacing Police Officers, No One They Encountered was Arrested," *Denverite*, February 2, 2021.

138 City of Denver, "Support Team Assisted Response (STAR) Program," https://www.denvergov.org/Government/Agencies-Departments-Offices/Agencies-Departments-Offices-Directory/Public-Health-Environment/Community- Behavioral-Health/Behavioral-Health-Strategies/Support-Team-Assisted-Response-STAR-Program (hereinafter, "Support Team Assisted Response (STAR) Program").

139 Thomas S. Dee and Jaymes Pyne, "A community response approach to mental health and substance abuse crises reduced crime," *Science Advances*, vol. 8, no. 23 (June 8, 2022).

140 "Support Team Assisted Response (STAR) Program."

dispatchers screen and connect appropriate requests. The MCT program currently operates from 10:00 a.m. to 8:00 p.m., seven days a week, and responds to calls citywide.

However, in May 2022 the city assembly approved additional funding for the program with the intent to expand service to 24 hours a day.[141]

Olympia, WA

The Crisis Response Unit (CRU) in Olympia, WA, was started in 2019 as a unit within the Olympia Police Department and is staffed by six behavioral health specialists who work in pairs. The Olympia Police Department works with the Thurston County 911 Communications Center to identify calls where CRU might be an appropriate response. However, rather than dispatching CRU directly to calls based on certain criteria, the 911 call center shares all potentially eligible calls over the police radio frequency and CRU decides whether to respond. Alternatively, police officers can refer the call to CRU if they determine that a non-law enforcement based response would be better and the threat to first responders is minimal. CRU also provides a secondary response at the request of the first responding police officer. As CRU has become more established, some callers have started asking for CRU to respond. In addition to responding to calls for service, CRU also does proactive outreach to develop trust with the community, such as having a presence at the city-sanctioned encampment for people who are homeless.[142] With increased funding, Olympia expanded CRU operations to 24 hours a day, seven days a week. As of 2021, the program was working on hiring additional crisis response specialists and medical staff.[143]

---

141 Municipality of Anchorage, Anchorage Fire Department, "What is the Mobile Crisis Team (MCT)?," https://www.muni.org/Departments/Fire/Pages/Mobile-Crisis-Team.aspx; Tess Williams, "A new team of Anchorage first responders focuses on mental health crises. Officials say it frees up hospital beds and public safety resources," *Anchorage Daily News*, November 6, 2021; and Wesley Early, "Anchorage's Mobile Crisis Team hopes funding to operate 24/7 will expand ability to address mental health crises," *Alaska Public Media*, August 15, 2022.

142 Jackson Beck, Melissa Reuland, and Leah Pope, *Case Study: CRU and Familiar Faces*, Vera Institute of Justice, November 2020, https://www.vera.org/behavioral-health-crisis-alternatives/cru-and-familiar-faces.

143 Elizabeth Fleming, "Staffing Community Responder Programs: Q&A with the Olympia (WA) Crisis Response Unit," The Council of State Governments Justice Center, October 7, 2021, https://csgjusticecenter.org/2021/10/07/staffing-community-responder-programs-qa-with-the-olympia-wa-crisis-response-unit/.

Stockton, CA

In July 2022, the Stockton City Council approved the pilot of the Care Link Response Program. The program is to create a behavioral health first responder system to divert mental health crises calls to 911 that are believed to be nonviolent from the city's police and fire departments. Created by a partnership between the city and a local nonprofit, Community Medical Centers, the pilot program is to begin in late 2022 with one team, comprised of a licensed mental health clinician, an outreach worker, and a case manager. Programs goals include decreasing recidivism, decreasing repeat callers on emergency lines, increasing community trust, decreasing costs related to emergency calls, decreasing fears of calling the police, and diverting people from the criminal justice system.[144]

Austin, TX

The Expanded Mobile Crisis Outreach Team (EMCOT) in Austin, TX, is staffed with mental health providers from Integral Health, the mental health authority for Travis County (the county in which Austin is located). EMCOT started in 2013 and EMTs and law enforcement agencies in Travis County can request EMCOT assistance with calls through the county's 911 call center.

EMCOT connects people with treatment appropriate for psychiatric crises with the intent of diverting people from emergency rooms or jail.[145] The city increased the budget for EMCOT in 2020 with the intention of increasing staffing, thereby allowing all mental health-related 911 calls that do not involve a threat to public safety to be diverted to EMCOT. (EMCOT is not involved in cases where there is evidence that a crime has been committed, a weapon is present, someone is in need of medical assistance due to use of drugs or alcohol, someone is at risk of hurting themselves or someone else, or someone's life or property are under threat.) Law enforcement officers still have to be involved in some mental health calls because under Texas law only law enforcement officers can initiate an involuntary commitment of someone

---

[144] Gabriel Porras, "Stockton City Council approves pilot program to send crisis intervention team to some police calls," *ABC 10 News (Stockton)*, July 28, 2022.

[145] Jennifer Kendall, "Crisis Counselors Responding to More Mental Health Calls in Austin," *Fox 7 (Austin) News*, November 2, 2020.

at risk of harming himself/herself or others.[146] The increased funding allowed for EMCOT mental health clinicians to be added to local 911 call centers. All callers now have the option to choose from police, fire, EMS, or mental health services when they begin a 911 call. If callers request mental health services, the 911 call taker screens the call to try to ensure that police, EMS, or fire department responses are not needed, and then transfers the caller to an onsite health clinician for additional screening.[147] EMCOT services are currently available 24 hours a day, seven days a week.[148]

New York, NY

New York City piloted an MCT program in three police precincts in Harlem starting in February 2021.[149] The program, called the Behavioral Health Emergency Assistance Response Division (B- HEARD), has since been expanded to include additional areas of Harlem, Washington Heights, Inwood, and parts of the South Bronx, with plans to expand to central Brooklyn and eastern Queens in New York City's FY2023. Under the program, teams comprised of two paramedics from the fire department's Emergency Medical Services and one mental health professional from NYC Health + Hospitals respond to mental health emergencies. Teams respond to 911 calls involving a range of behavioral health issues, such as suicide attempts, substance use, and serious mental illness. However, if the subject is known to be armed or presents a danger, a police officer responds with or in place of the B-HEARD

---

[146] Ryan Thorton, "Integral Care Set to Address Most Mental Health Emergency Calls Without Involving APD," *Austin Chronicle*, August 18, 2020; and Integral Care, *Expanded Mobile Crisis Outreach Team*, https://www.austintexas.gov/ edims/document.cfm?id=302634.

[147] Amanda Ruiz, "Austin 911 adds fourth option for mental health services," *Fox 7 (Austin) News*, February 10, 2021; and The Council of State Governments Justice Center, "Integral Care's Expanded Mobile Crisis Outreach Team – Austin, TX," https://integralcare.org/ program/mobile-crisis-outreach-team-mcot/.

[148] Integral Care, "Mobile Crisis Outreach Team (MCOT)," https://integralcare.org/ program/ mobile-crisis-outreach- team-mcot/

[149] Associated Press, "Mental Health Workers to Take the Lead in Some NYC 911 Calls," November 10, 2020; City of New York, "New York City Announces New Mental Health Teams to Respond to Mental Health Crises," press release, November 10, 2020; and Lauren Cook, Nicole Johnson, and the Associated Press, "Social Workers, EMS—Not NYPD—to Respond to Non-Violent Mental Health Calls Citywide," *Pix 11 (New York) News*, updated April 30, 2021.

team. B-HEARD operates 16 hours a day, seven days a week.[150] Between January 1, 2022, and March 31, 2022, approximately 2,400 mental health calls to 911 were diverted to B-HEARD. Of those calls, 23% were routed to B-HEARD teams, and B-HEARD responded to 68% of calls routed to them. Of the calls routed to B-HEARD that B-HEARD was not able to respond to, it was typically because the B-HEARD teams were responding to another call or otherwise unavailable. Although most mental health calls in the B- HEARD operating area still receive a law enforcement response, of the calls that B-HEARD teams responded to, assisted individuals were more likely to accept help and less likely to be transported to a hospital than individuals assisted by traditional first responders.[151]

Portland, OR

Portland Street Response (PSR) launched in February 2021 as a pilot program that dispatches a paramedic, a mental health clinician, and, if necessary, one or more community health workers to 911 calls involving people who are homeless or have serious mental health issues. The paramedic and mental health clinician are dispatched first for mental health calls or when a wellness check is needed. Community health workers are dispatched if the individual expresses need for additional services such as shelter or housing.[152] PSR is dispatched only if the individual in crisis is believed to be in a publicly accessible space, not obstructing traffic, is nonviolent, does not have a weapon, and is not suicidal. PSR is coordinated through Portland Fire and Rescue because the program needs a connection to the current 911 system. Portland Fire and Rescue's Community Health Division focuses on preventive health care intervention, and the arrangement aligns with the intent to keep the program separate from the police department. The program was expanded citywide in March 2022. PRS currently operates 10 to 14 hours a day, seven days a week, but hopes by fall of 2022 to operate 24 hours a day with a staff

---

150 New York City Mayor's Office of Community Mental Health, "Re-Imagining New York City's Mental Health Emergency Response: FAQ," https://mentalhealth.cityofnewyork.us/b-heard.

151 New York City Mayor's Office of Community Mental Health, *B-HEARD: Transforming NYC's Response to Mental Health Emergencies, January-March 2022 (FY22 Q3)*, https://mentalhealth.cityofnewyork.us/wp-content/uploads/2022/06/FINAL-DATA-BRIEF-B-HEARD-FY22-Q3.pdf.

152 Nicole Hayden, "Portland Street Response Launches, Pairing Medics with Clinicians on Mental Health Calls," *The Oregonian*, February 17, 2021.

of 58 full-time employees.[153] An evaluation of the first year of the PSR pilot found that the calls responded to by PSR represented a 4% reduction in total calls that police would have traditionally responded to in the PSR operating area and service hours, despite PSR operating with a single team for two-thirds of the first year. The reduction in nonemergency calls was larger, representing a 27% decline in police responses to nonemergency welfare checks and unwanted persons calls,[154] and a 12.4% decline in fire department responses to behavioral health and illegal burn calls.[155]

San Francisco, CA

San Francisco launched its Street Crisis Response Team (SCRT) as a pilot program in November 2020.[156] The program is a joint effort between the San Francisco Fire Department and the San Francisco Department of Public Health, in collaboration with the Department of Emergency Management. SCRT started by exclusively serving the Tenderloin neighborhood, but it became a citywide 24-hour, seven days a week service by July 2021. Five teams are assigned to each respond to a specific neighborhood, and two teams provide overnight coverage and dispatch citywide as needed. SCRT teams are dispatched to 911 calls involving "mentally disturbed persons" experiencing behavioral health crises that are believed not to involve weapons or violence. Each team is staffed with a community paramedic, a behavioral health clinician, and a peer specialist. Teams are supported by the newly created Office of Coordinated Care, which staffs a special team of care coordinators that follows up with all SCRT contacts within 24 hours to help ensure connections to mental health care and substance use services.[157] In June 2022, Phase 2 of the SCRT program began with transitioning from police dispatch

---

153 City of Portland, "Portland Street Response Frequently Asked Questions," https://www .portland.gov/streetresponse/ psr-faq; and KATU 2 (Portland) News, "Portland Street Response sees surge in call volume with citywide expansion," June 22, 2022.

154 An unwanted persons call involves an individual refusing to leave a location when asked. City of Portland, "Police Dispatched Calls Dashboard," https://www.portland.gov/police/open-data/police-dispatched-calls.

155 Greg Townley and Emily Leickly, *Portland Street Response: Year One Evaluation*, Portland State University, April 2022.

156 City of San Francisco, Mayor's Office, "Mayor London Breed Announces Plan to Create Street Wellness Response Team To Expand Services For Those In Need," press release, May 10, 2021.

157 Harder+Company Community Research, *Street Crisis Response Team Pilot: Final Report*, May 2022.

to Emergency Medical Dispatch. This change further separates behavioral health crisis response from law enforcement, allows an EMS rather than a police response if SCRT is unable to respond to a call, and expands the range of calls for SCRT response. As of July 2022, SCRT has responded to 11,324 calls, with 5,508 client engagements on-scene.[158]

Minneapolis, MN

In December 2021, the City of Minneapolis launched the Behavioral Crisis Response (BCR) program to divert mental health crisis calls from law enforcement. The city contracted with Canopy Roots, a local private mental health services organization, to staff the BCR teams. Teams of mental health practitioners respond to mental health crisis calls to 911 in which there are believed to be no firearms involved and the person in need appears nonviolent. Two teams are available to respond citywide, 24 hours a day, Monday through Friday. If both BCR units are unavailable, then 911 dispatch sends a traditional police response to the mental health crisis call.[159] In the first six months of operation, BCR diverted an estimated 1,400 calls from the Minneapolis Police Department.[160]

Chicago, IL

The City of Chicago first launched its Crisis Assistance Response and Engagement (CARE) Program in September 2021 as a co-responder program with a Chicago Fire Department community paramedic, a Chicago Department of Public Health (CDPH) mental health practitioner, and a Chicago Police Department CIT officer on each team. CARE teams receive and respond to mental health crisis calls placed to 911 that are believed to be nonviolent. In May 2022, Mayor Lori E. Lightfoot announced that, with the approval of a new 911 routing and response protocol by the Illinois

---

158 City and County of San Francisco, Street Crisis Response Team (SCRT): July 2022 Update.

159 City of Minneapolis, "Behavioral crisis response," https://www.minneapolismn.gov/resident-services/public-safety/unarmed-public-safety/behavioral-crisis-response; and City of Minneapolis, "Behavioral health crisis," https://www.minneapolismn.gov/report-an-issue/behavioral-health-crisis.

160 CBS News Minnesota "Behavioral Crisis Response Team Diverted 1,400 Calls from MPD In The Last 3 Months," CBS News, May 4, 2022.

Department of Public Health, CARE teams of paramedics and mental health clinicians can respond to nonviolent mental health calls without involving police officers. As part of the CARE initiative, mental health professionals from CDPH are embedded in the 911 emergency communications center to provide support and mental health consultation to dispatchers. CARE teams operate in the Lakeview, Uptown, Auburn Gresham, Chatham, Chicago Lawn, Gage Park, West Elsdon, and West Lawn neighborhoods between 10:30 a.m. and 4:00 p.m., Monday through Friday.[161]

Baltimore, MD

In partnership with Baltimore Crisis Response, Inc. (BCRI), the City of Baltimore launched the Behavioral Health 9-1-1 Diversion Pilot Program in June 2021. The program diverts certain behavioral health related calls to 911 to the Here2Help hotline operated by BCRI. The mental health professionals staffing the BCRI line either resolve calls over the phone or dispatch a team of mental health clinicians to respond. MCTs are available 24 hours a day, seven days a week.

The city collects data on 911 calls and mental health related diversions and displays it on a frequently updated, interactive dashboard.[162] Currently, the program is only able to provide mobile crisis response for adults; however, the city has announced an upcoming expansion that will create youth-focused MCTs. The expansion is also expected to place mental health clinicians in the 911 call center to assist dispatchers with de-escalation and screening.[163]

Washington, DC

In May 2021, Mayor Muriel Bowser announced the pilot launch of a Mental Health Emergency Dispatch Program in Washington, DC. The program is a partnership between the Office of the Deputy Mayor for Public Safety and

---

161 City of Chicago, Office of the Mayor, "Mayor Lightfoot and the City of Chicago Announce Expansion of 911 Alternate Crisis Response and Engagement Program," press release, May 26, 2022; Chip Mitchell, "A glimpse inside mental health crisis response teams as Chicago creates versions without cops," *WBEZ Chicago*, April 6, 2022.

162 City of Baltimore, Mayor's Office, "Behavioral Health 9-1-1 Diversion," https://mayor.baltimorecity.gov/ behavioral-health-and-consent-decree/9-1-1-diversion.

163 Kevin Kinally, "Baltimore City Expanding Behavioral Health 9-1-1 Diversion Program," *Conduit Street*, July 1, 2022.

Justice, the Office of the Deputy Mayor for Health and Human Services, the Office of the City Administrator, the Office of Unified Communications, and the Department of Behavioral Health (DBH). The pilot builds on city resources by dispatching existing Community Response Teams from DBH to mental health crisis calls received by 911 that are not believed to involve drug use, alcohol use, or any perceived threat to patient or responder safety.[164] The mental health response program also complements the city's existing Right Care, Right Now program, which triages nonemergency medical calls received by 911 to registered nurses who advise on treatment options or dispatch resources.[165] In November 2021, the city announced additional pilot phases of the Mental Health Emergency Dispatch Program. The second and third pilot phases aim to increase the number of available responders, increase service hours from 12 hours a day to 24 hours a day, and allow teams to respond to a wider range of calls, including those involving substance use. In phase one of the pilot, teams responded to an estimated 2% of all behavioral health calls placed to 911. By phase three, the program hopes to respond to one-third of all behavioral health calls.[166]

---

[164] Rachel Weiner, "D.C. to divert some mental health calls away from police," *The Washington Post*, May 17, 2021; City of Washington, DC, Office of Unified Communications (OUC), "DBH and OUC Mental Health Emergency Dispatch Program," https://ouc.dc.gov/page/dbh-and-ouc-mental-health-emergency-dispatch-program; and Sarah Holder, "D.C. Extends Program Diverting Mental Health Calls From Police," *Bloomberg CityLab*, November 12, 2021, (hereinafter, "Holder, 'D.C. Extends Program Diverting Mental Health Calls From Police'").

[165] City of Washington, DC, Fire and EMS Department, "Frequently Asked Questions Right Care, Right Now," https://fems.dc.gov/page/frequently-asked-questions-right-care-right-now.

[166] Holder, "D.C. Extends Program Diverting Mental Health Calls From Police."

Chapter 11

Congress and Law Enforcement Reform: Constitutional Authority*

Whitney K. Novak

Incidents involving the use of force by law enforcement, such as the 2020 death of George Floyd and the 2023 death of Tyre Nichols, have generated heightened interest in the issue of reforming the policing practices of state and local law enforcement. As discussed in another Legal Sidebar, several existing federal laws seek to prevent and redress constitutional violations by state and local authorities. Congress is constitutionally limited in its ability to legislate on matters related to state and local law enforcement— limits that may inform any new laws Congress seeks to enact on this evolving issue. This Legal Sidebar begins with an overview of Congress's authority to enact legislation and the limits on those powers. It then discusses in more detail two of Congress's enumerated constitutional powers that may be most relevant to federal legislation on matters relating to state and local law enforcement.

Limits to Congressional Authority

The Constitution establishes a "system of dual sovereignty between the States and the Federal Government." Under the Tenth Amendment, "[t]he powers not delegated to the United States by the Constitution, nor prohibited by it to the States, are reserved to the States respectively, or to the people." The Supreme

* This is an edited, reformatted and augmented version of Congressional Research Service Publication No. LSB10487, updated February 15, 2023.

In: The Future of Law Enforcement
Editor: Mohamed Swift
ISBN: 979-8-89530-863-9

Court has recognized that there are certain subjects that are largely of local concern where states "historically have been sovereign," such as issues related to the family, crime, and education. In contrast, Congress may only enact legislation under a specific power enumerated in the Constitution, and it cannot use its power to intrude impermissibly on the sovereign powers of the states.

Because of these principles, the Supreme Court has recognized various limitations on Congress's power to legislate in areas that fall within a state's purview, observing that congressional power is "subject to outer limits," and that Congress must take care not to "effectually obliterate the distinction between what is national and what is local." For example, although Congress has invoked its power to regulate interstate and foreign commerce to legislate on a wide range of economic and social activities, the Court has limited its reach when the legislation seeks to regulate purely local, non-economic activities. Additionally, under the anti-commandeering doctrine, Congress is prohibited from directing states or localities to regulate the activities of private parties on behalf of the federal government.

Although these principles constrain Congress's power, Congress can sometimes rely on its enumerated powers to regulate in areas of state and local concern. The spending power and Section 5 of the Fourteenth Amendment are two of the most relevant authorities used by Congress to address state and local law enforcement issues.

Spending Power

The Spending Clause empowers Congress to "lay and collect Taxes, Duties, Imposts, and Excises, to pay the Debts and provide for the common Defence and general Welfare of the United States." The Supreme Court has held that incident to the spending power, Congress may further its policy objectives by attaching conditions on the receipt of federal funds. These conditions often involve compliance with statutory or administrative directives and can apply to any entity receiving federal funds, including states and localities. In *South Dakota v. Dole*, for example, the Supreme Court upheld as a valid exercise of Congress's spending power a statute that conditioned the grant of federal highway funds to any state upon that state prohibiting the legal purchase or possession of alcohol by individuals less than 21 years old.

There are, however, several limitations on Congress's authority to attach conditions to federal funds. First, a funding condition must be "in pursuit of the general welfare." However, courts generally afford Congress substantial deference in determining what expenditures are "intended to serve general public purposes." Second, if Congress intends to place conditions on federal funds, it must do so "unambiguously" so that states can knowingly choose whether or not to accept the funds. Third, conditions on federal funding must be related or "germane" to "the federal interest in particular national projects or programs." Fourth, other constitutional provisions may bar the conditions placed on the grant of federal funds. For instance, Congress may not condition a monetary grant on "discriminatory state action or the infliction of cruel and unusual punishment." Relatedly, conditions on federal funding are unconstitutional when they become coercive to the point that "pressure turns into compulsion" or commandeering. For example, in *National Federation of Independent Business (NFIB) v. Sebelius*, the Supreme Court held that a provision in the Affordable Care Act that withheld all Medicaid grants from any state that refused to accept expanded Medicaid funding was unconstitutionally coercive because it threatened to terminate "significant independent grants" that were already provided to the states.

Courts have rarely used these spending power limitations to invalidate conditions placed on the receipt of federal funds. *NFIB* remains the only instance in the modern era of the Supreme Court invalidating an exercise of the congressional spending power. Post-*NFIB* Spending Clause challenges have largely been unsuccessful in the lower courts.

Congress has used its spending power to enact legislation to influence the activities of state and local law enforcement. Federal regulation of state and local law enforcement primarily comes in the form of grant programs that provide money to local governments and police forces. For example, the Community Oriented Policing Services (COPS) program authorizes the Department of Justice to distribute grants to support community policing. Recipients can use these grants for hiring officers, procuring equipment, or establishing partnerships between local law enforcement agencies and local school districts. Additionally, the Edward Byrne Memorial Justice Assistance Grant (Byrne JAG) program provides federal financial support for state and local criminal justice programs. Funding for these grant programs is subject to various conditions that may further federal interests in regulating law enforcement activities. For instance, grants under the COPS program prohibit the grantee from subjecting any person to discrimination on the basis of race, color, or national origin (among other protected classes) in connection with any programs or activities funded in whole or in part with federal funds. Funds under the JAG program are conditioned on, among other things, compliance with the Death in Custody Reporting Act, which requires states to report information regarding the deaths of individuals in law enforcement custody.

Section 5 of the Fourteenth Amendment

The Fourteenth Amendment, in relevant part, provides that no state shall "deprive any person of life, liberty, or property, without due process of law" or "deny to any person within its jurisdiction the equal protection of the laws." The Supreme Court has interpreted the substantive component of the Due Process Clause as incorporating against state actors nearly all the rights found in the Bill of Rights, including those that pertain to criminal procedure and regulate the conduct of the police. In turn, Section 5 of the Fourteenth Amendment grants Congress the power to enforce the Amendment through "appropriate legislation." Section 5's "positive grant of legislative power" authorizes Congress to both deter and remedy constitutional violations; and in doing so, Congress may prohibit otherwise constitutional conduct that intrudes into "legislative spheres of autonomy previously reserved to the States." The Section 5 enforcement power (and the parallel enforcement powers found in the Thirteenth and Fifteenth Amendments) has been used to, for example, ban the use of literacy tests in state and national elections and abolish "all badges and incidents of slavery" by banning racial discrimination in the acquisition of real and personal property. Congress has also used its Section 5 power to provide remedies for the deprivation of constitutional rights. For example, 42 U.S.C. § 1983 (Section 1983) provides a private cause of action for individuals claiming that their constitutional rights were violated by state actors acting pursuant to state law. And 18 U.S.C. § 242 (Section 242)—also passed using the Section 5 power—imposes criminal liability on state actors who deprive individuals of their constitutional rights.

While Congress's Section 5 enforcement power is broad, it is not unlimited. Section 5 allows Congress to enforce constitutional rights directly through laws like Section 1983 and Section 242, however, the power does not allow Congress to supplement those rights through "prophylactic" legislation that regulates state and local matters without evidence of a history and pattern of past constitutional violations by the state.

According to the Supreme Court, when Congress exercises its Section 5 authority, its response must be congruent and proportional to a demonstrated harm. Congress may justify the need for Section 5 legislation by establishing a legislative record that shows "evidence ... of a constitutional wrong." For example, in holding that Congress exceeded its Section 5 authority in enacting the Religious Freedom Restoration Act (RFRA)—which, in relevant part, supplanted normal First Amendment standards to impose a heightened standard of review for state government actions that substantially burdened a person's religious exercise—the Supreme Court determined that Congress had failed to establish a widespread pattern of religious discrimination by the states. As a result, RFRA could not be justified as a remedial measure designed to prevent unconstitutional conduct and was outside of Congress's power over the states. As a result, the Court struck down the law in so far as it applied to the states.

As a consequence of this case law, the scope of Congress's Section 5 power hinges in part on the scope of the constitutional right that a given law aims to protect. With respect to regulating state and local police forces, one constitutional right that may be particularly relevant to Congress's use of its Section 5 power is the Fourth Amendment, which prohibits unreasonable searches and seizures by the government. The Fourth Amendment applies to many situations involving law enforcement including when police stop an individual on the street for questioning, when police conduct traffic stops, or when police make an arrest.

Police violate the Fourth Amendment, for example, if they use excessive force during an investigatory stop or arrest. According to the Supreme Court, the force used by law enforcement during an investigatory stop or arrest violates the Constitution when it is unreasonable considering the facts and circumstances of the case. This analysis requires a careful balancing of "the nature and quality of the intrusion on the individual's Fourth Amendment interests against the importance of the governmental interests alleged to justify the intrusion." For example, the Supreme Court has held that police use of deadly force against a fleeing suspect who poses no immediate safety threat is unreasonable in violation of the Fourth Amendment. Determining whether an act of force is excessive in violation of the Constitution, however, requires a fact-specific analysis—a certain act may be reasonable under some facts while in a different case, it may amount to excessive force. For example, some courts have ruled that police use of a chokehold is objectively unreasonable when used against individuals who are already under restraint and not a danger to others. In other circumstances, courts have upheld police use of a chokehold as reasonable when an individual was unrestrained and continued to pose a threat of serious harm.

Considerations for Congress

Although Congress is limited in its ability to regulate local policing, the Constitution does provide authority for some congressional reform and oversight of state and local law enforcement. Legislators proposed various avenues for reform and oversight of federal, state, and local law enforcement prior to the high-profile events surrounding the death of George Floyd, and events since May 2020 have prompted additional proposals to address police reforms. As discussed in another Legal Sidebar, several bills were introduced on the issue in the 116th and 117th Congresses, including comprehensive police reform proposals such as the George Floyd Justice in Policing Act and the JUSTICE Act. Multiple provisions of these bills would have placed conditions on the receipt of federal funds pursuant to Congress's spending power or utilized Congress's Section 5 authority to amend laws such as Section 242. The limitations on Congress's constitutional authority to regulate state and local police forces may be a consideration when evaluating these and other reforms.

Chapter 12

Congress and Police Reform: Recent Proposals*

Joanna R. Lampe

In May and June 2020, protests erupted nationwide after the publication of video footage of a Minneapolis police officer pressing his knee into the neck of George Floyd, causing his death. That incident and others like it sparked heightened interest in Congress's ability to implement reforms of state and local law enforcement. More recently, the January 2023 death of Tyre Nichols after a beating by Memphis police officers prompted renewed calls for law enforcement reform. A companion to this Legal Sidebar provides an overview of existing federal authorities intended to prevent and redress constitutional violations by state and local public safety officials. This Sidebar presents selected recent proposals related to federal regulation of federal, state, and local law enforcement, including an overview of two comprehensive law enforcement reform bills from the 117th Congress, the George Floyd Justice in Policing Act of 2021 and the Just and Unifying Solutions To Invigorate Communities Everywhere Act of 2021 (JUSTICE Act).

Proposals for Law Enforcement Reform in Congress

Before the high-profile events of May and June 2020, commentators and legislators had suggested various avenues for congressional reform and

---

* This is an edited, reformatted and augmented version of Congressional Research Service Publication No. LSB10914, updated February 7, 2023.

In: The Future of Law Enforcement
Editor: Mohamed Swift
ISBN: 979-8-89530-863-9

oversight of federal, state, and local law enforcement. Events since May 2020 have prompted additional proposals, including bills that would target specific issues and comprehensive proposals that would alter federal regulation of law enforcement on many fronts.

Qualified Immunity

One topic that has generated significant debate in recent years is the doctrine of qualified immunity, which limits the liability of federal law enforcement officers in suits under *Bivens v. Six Unknown Federal Narcotics Agents* and state and local law enforcement officers in suits under 42 U.S.C. § 1983 (Section 1983). A May 2020 report by Reuters found that "since 2005, the [federal appellate] courts have shown an increasing tendency to grant immunity in excessive force cases." Critics of qualified immunity assert that the flexibility the Supreme Court provided to courts in *Pearson v. Callahan* improperly hinders Section 1983 claims. That decision allows courts in some cases to consider only whether a defendant violated clearly established law, without reaching the question of whether the defendant violated the plaintiff's rights. Critics therefore assert that not only is it difficult for plaintiffs to overcome a claim of qualified immunity, but such cases will also not clearly establish law that could govern future Section 1983 cases.

Some commentators assert that the current doctrine of qualified immunity fails to protect law enforcement officers from suit. Others defend the doctrine or favor limited judicial reforms, seeking to preserve police officers' ability to make split-second decisions about the use of force, for example, while requiring courts to take seriously the constitutional questions that plaintiffs raise.

Qualified immunity arises from the Supreme Court's interpretation of Section 1983. Thus, either the Court or Congress could modify the doctrine, and some legal scholars have called on both branches to address the issue. The Court has considered multiple petitions for certiorari raising challenges to qualified immunity, and Justice Thomas and Justice Sotomayor have both expressed concerns about the doctrine.

On the legislative side, the Ending Qualified Immunity Act, introduced in June 2020 and reintroduced during the 117th Congress, would have "remove[d] the defense of qualified immunity." Another proposal from the 116th Congress that sought to remove barriers to Section 1983 liability was the Reforming Qualified Immunity Act, which would have changed the burden of proof in Section 1983 cases in plaintiffs' favor and would have made it easier to establish liability against municipalities and local governments. A proposal from the 117th Congress entitled the Constitutional Accountability Act would have rendered federal, state, and local governments civilly liable for constitutional violations by law enforcement officers in their employment, "without regard to whether such employee or contractor would be immune from liability, and without regard to whether the employee or contractor was acting pursuant to a policy or custom" of the employer. The Accountability for Federal Law Enforcement Act would have imposed similar liability on the federal government only.

In contrast to proposals that would limit qualified immunity, other recent legislation sought to maintain or expand the doctrine. The Qualified Immunity Act of 2021 would have amended Section 1983 "to codify the defense of qualified immunity." The Local Law Enforcement Protection Act of 2021 would have required states that receive certain federal funds to have in place laws that "provide robust qualified immunity to law enforcement officers."

Criminal Liability

While changes to the doctrine of qualified immunity could alter civil liability for law enforcement officers, other recent proposals aimed to expand criminal liability for civil rights violations by officers under 18 U.S.C. § 241 (Section 241) and 18 U.S.C. § 242 (Section 242). For example, the Eric Garner Excessive Use of Force Prevention Act of 2021 would have amended Section 242 to provide explicitly that "the application of any pressure to the throat or windpipe which may prevent or hinder breathing or reduce intake of air is a punishment" that may not be imposed on a racially disparate basis. The Police Accountability Act of 2020, introduced during the 116th Congress, would have provided a federal criminal penalty for assault or homicide committed by certain state or local law enforcement officers.

Some commentators also advocate removing the specific intent requirement for Sections 241 and 242 that the Supreme Court announced in Screws v. United States and United States v. Guest.

Limitations on Transfer of Military-Grade Equipment

Under a federal program known as the 1033 Program, the federal government transfers certain excess military equipment to state and local law enforcement agencies. Some commentators contend that this equipment contributes to militarization of police forces without increasing public safety and increases the risk of incidents of excessive force. The 1033 Program is authorized by statute, so Congress has the power to alter or discontinue the program. In 2021, Congress enacted the William M. (Mac) Thornberry National Defense Authorization Act for Fiscal Year 2021 which, among other things, prohibited transfer through the 1033 Program of bayonets, grenades, weaponized tracked combat vehicles, and weaponized drones. In February 2022, some Members of Congress urged President Biden to limit the program further. President Biden's May 2022 executive order related to law enforcement reform directed relevant federal agencies to limit certain transfers under the 1033 Program to the extent authorized by law. One proposal introduced in the 116th and 117th Congresses, the Stop Militarizing Law Enforcement Act, would have imposed statutory limitations and reporting requirements on the 1033 Program.

Grants and Conditions on Federal Funds

Numerous recent proposals would have invoked the Spending Clause in an effort to regulate state and local law enforcement activities. Some proposals would have funded voluntary state and local measures, such as use-of-force and bias awareness training or body cameras. Other proposals would have required states to enact certain policies in exchange for federal grants. For instance, the Police Training and Independent Review Act of 2021 would have funded training on cultural diversity and de-escalation tactics while requiring participating states to "enact laws requiring the independent investigation and prosecution of the use of deadly force by law enforcement officers." The Preventing Tragedies Between Police and Communities Act of 2021 would have obliged recipients of funds under the Edward Byrne Memorial Justice Assistance Grant (Byrne JAG) Program to mandate training on ways to reduce the use of force. The Police Exercising Absolute Care With Everyone Act of 2022 (PEACE Act) would have required Byrne JAG grantees to enact laws limiting the use of lethal and less-than-lethal force by law enforcement. The Next Step Act of 2019 would have, among other things, directed Byrne JAG grant recipients to submit reports to the Attorney General on officers' use of force.

Comprehensive Reform Efforts

On June 8, 2020, Members of the 116th Congress, led by the Congressional Black Caucus, presented the Justice in Policing Act of 2020. Later renamed the George Floyd Justice in Policing Act, the bill passed the House in 2020 and 2021. On June 17, 2020, Senate Republicans unveiled the JUSTICE Act of 2020. Both proposals sought to reform multiple facets of federal, state, and local law enforcement, and each of them included some proposals discussed above that had also been introduced separately. An earlier Legal Sidebar compared 2020 versions of the two proposals in detail. Both bills were reintroduced with limited changes in 2021 during the 117th Congress. This section summarizes key provisions of the two 2021 bills.

George Floyd Justice in Policing Act of 2021

The Justice in Policing Act as passed by the House in the 117th Congress included the following provisions:

- *Section 101* of the bill would have amended Section 242 to change the mental state required for conviction from "willfully" to "knowingly or recklessly." It would also have removed the possibility of a death sentence for violating Section 242.
- *Section 102* would have limited qualified immunity for state and local law enforcement officers in suits under Section 1983 and for federal law enforcement officers "in any action under any source of law," providing that it is not a defense to liability if an officer believed in good faith that his or her conduct was lawful or that the rights the officer allegedly infringed were not clearly established.
- *Sections 103 and 104* sought to enhance investigations into incidents involving law enforcement uses of force or a pattern or practice of law enforcement misconduct by, among things, granting subpoena power to the Department of Justice (DOJ) under 34 U.S.C. § 12601

and authorizing state attorneys general to bring suit based on violations of that provision.

- Multiple provisions of the Act sought to facilitate federal data collection related to police reform. For instance, Section 118 and Title II, Subtitle B, of the Act would have required federal funding recipients to report incidents involving uses of force by law enforcement, and Section 201 would have created a federal law enforcement misconduct registry.
- Section 362 would have banned no-knock warrants in drug cases at the federal level. The section would also have conditioned certain federal funding upon states and localities prohibiting the use of no-knock warrants in similar drug cases.
- Section 363 would have required states and municipalities that receive certain federal funding to enact laws banning the use of chokeholds by law enforcement officers.
- Section 364, the PEACE Act, would have allowed federal law enforcement officers to use deadly force only as a last resort to prevent imminent death or serious bodily injury when certain conditions are met and imposed limits on the use of "less lethal" force. This provision would also have conditioned federal grants on state and local law enforcement agencies' establishing the same use-of-force standard.
- Section 365, the Stop Militarizing Law Enforcement Act, would have limited the transfer of certain military-grade equipment to state and local law enforcement.
- Title III, Subtitle A of the Act sought to prevent and remedy racial profiling by law enforcement, including by authorizing civil suits by DOJ and affected individuals. The title would have established various programs and policies to help eliminate racial profiling, such as by funding training programs for state and local police.
- Title III, Subtitle C would have required certain federal law enforcement officers to use body cameras and funded expanded use of body cameras by state and local officers.
- Title VI, the Closing the Law Enforcement Consent Loophole Act of 2021, would have imposed criminal liability when a person "acting under color of law, knowingly engages in a sexual act" with a person in federal custody and would have authorized grants to states, municipalities, and Indian tribes that enact similar laws.

JUSTICE Act of 2021

The version of the JUSTICE Act introduced in the House in the 117th Congress included the following provisions:

- Section 101 of the bill, the George Floyd and Walter Scott Notification Act, and Section 102, the Breonna Taylor Notification Act, would respectively have required recipients of certain federal funding to report to the federal government information related to incidents involving law enforcement uses of force and no-knock warrants.
- Section 105 would have required recipients of certain federal funding to develop law enforcement agency policies "prohibit[ing] the use of chokeholds except when deadly force is authorized." This section would also have required the Attorney General to develop such a policy at the federal level.
- Section 106 would have created a new criminal offense of "knowingly and willfully falsify[ing] a report ... in furtherance of the deprivation of any rights, privileges, or immunities secured or protected by the Constitution or laws of the United States where death or serious bodily injury ... occurs." The penalty for violating this provision would have been a fine and/or imprisonment for up to 20 years.
- Title II of the bill would have provided grants to covered government agencies to support the use of body-worn cameras by law enforcement officers.
- Title III would have required law enforcement agencies that receive certain federal funding to retain various disciplinary records and to search the records of prior employers before hiring a law enforcement officer.
- Title IV, the Justice for Victims of Lynching Act, would have created a new criminal prohibition on lynching, defined as conspiracy to violate certain federal hate crime laws.
- Title V would have directed the Attorney General to develop training on alternatives to use of force, de-escalation tactics, responding to behavioral health crises, and duty to intervene when another officer uses excessive force.

- Titles VI and VIII would have established a temporary National Criminal Justice Commission and required the commission to create best practices and conduct certain studies related to law enforcement oversight.
- Title VII would have provided for development of an educational curriculum for law enforcement personnel or candidates on the history of racism in the United States.
- Title IX, the Closing the Law Enforcement Consent Loophole Act, would have imposed criminal liability for sexual acts with persons in federal custody as discussed above.

Chapter 13

Congress and Police Reform: Current Law*

Joanna R. Lampe

In May and June 2020, protests erupted nationwide after the publication of video footage of a Minneapolis police officer pressing his knee into the neck of George Floyd, causing his death. That incident and others like it sparked heightened interest in Congress's ability to implement reforms of state and local law enforcement. More recently, the January 2023 death of Tyre Nichols after a beating by Memphis police officers prompted renewed calls for law enforcement reform. This Legal Sidebar provides an overview of existing federal authorities intended to prevent and redress constitutional violations by state and local public safety officials. A companion Sidebar presents selected recent proposals related to federal regulation of federal, state, and local law enforcement.

Federal Regulation of State and Local Law Enforcement

As another Legal Sidebar outlines in greater detail, congressional power to regulate state and local law enforcement is not without limits. The Constitution grants the federal government only certain authorities, with the Tenth Amendment reserving all other powers for the states. The regulation of state and municipal law enforcement is an area that the Constitution generally entrusts to the states. However, Congress possesses some authority to legislate on that subject, primarily through statutes designed to enforce the protections

* This is an edited, reformatted and augmented version of Congressional Research Service Publication No. LSB10486, updated February 7, 2023.

In: The Future of Law Enforcement
Editor: Mohamed Swift
ISBN: 979-8-89530-863-9

of the Fourteenth Amendment and legislation requiring states to take specified action in exchange for federal funds disbursed under the Spending Clause.

Existing federal remedies for constitutional violations by state and local law enforcement include civil and criminal enforcement by the U.S. Department of Justice (DOJ) and private suits by individuals deprived of their rights by someone acting "under color of" state law. In addition, the federal government encourages states to enact certain policies related to law enforcement by placing conditions on federal funding. Federal agencies also independently investigate and gather data on law enforcement activities.

Federal Criminal Law

A provision of the federal criminal code, 18 U.S.C. § 242 (Section 242), makes it a crime for (among other things) a person acting "under color of any law, statute, ordinance, regulation, or custom" to "willfully subject[ ] any person ... to the deprivation of any rights, privileges, or immunities secured or protected by the Constitution or laws of the United States[.]" As another Legal Sidebar discusses further, Section 242 also prohibits a person acting under color of law from subjecting any person to "different punishments, pains, or penalties, on account of such person being an alien, or by reason of his color, or race, than are prescribed for the punishment of citizens[.]" A simple violation of the statute is punishable by a fine and/or up to a year in prison, and the penalties increase if the violation leads to bodily injury or death. A related provision, 18 U.S.C. § 241 (Section 241), makes it a crime for "two or more persons [to] conspire to injure, oppress, threaten, or intimidate any person ... in the free exercise or enjoyment of any right or privilege secured to him by the Constitution or laws of the United States[.]" Violations of Section 241 are punishable by up to 10 years in prison—or more if certain aggravating factors are present.

The Supreme Court has held that "officers of the State ... performing official duties," including public safety officials, act "under color of ... law" for purposes of Section 242. As DOJ has explained, law enforcement officers may violate Section 242 through "excessive force, sexual assault, intentional false arrests, theft, or the intentional fabrication of evidence resulting in a loss of liberty to another." DOJ enforces Sections 241 and 242 by bringing criminal charges against officers accused of violating those statutes. People who believe their rights have been infringed may report such violations to DOJ, but Sections 241 and 242 do not authorize suits by individuals. If DOJ elects to pursue criminal charges under Section 241 or 242, it faces a high standard of proof. Under the cases *Screws v. United States* and *United States v. Guest*, the prosecution must prove the defendant had "a specific intent to deprive a person of a federal right made definite by decision or other rule of law." *Specific intent* means that the defendant must not intend only to, for example, assault a victim but must also intend to violate a federal right by doing so. This results in what some view as a significant hurdle to bringing Section 241 and 242 claims.

DOJ brought charges under Section 242 against the officers involved in the deaths of George Floyd and Breonna Taylor. The officers involved in Mr. Floyd's killing pled guilty or were convicted by a jury. As of February 2023, charges against the officers involved in Ms. Taylor's death remain pending.

DOJ Civil Enforcement

Another section of the U.S. Code, 34 U.S.C. § 12601 (Section 12601, formerly codified at 42 U.S.C.§ 14141) renders it "unlawful for any governmental authority, or any agent thereof, ... to engage in a pattern or practice of conduct by law enforcement officers or by officials ... that deprives persons of rights, privileges, or immunities secured or protected by the Constitution or laws of the United States." Another CRS Legal Sidebar discusses this statute in more detail. According to DOJ, potential violations of the provision include "excessive force, discriminatory harassment, false arrests, coercive sexual conduct, and unlawful stops, searches or arrests." DOJ enforces the provision by filing civil complaints against allegedly offending law enforcement agencies. The statute does not create a private right for individuals harmed by violations to sue. Moreover, because the law applies only to a "pattern or practice of conduct," it cannot remedy isolated instances of misconduct. Finally, the statute does not provide for monetary penalties. If DOJ successfully sues under the provision, it may "obtain appropriate equitable and declaratory relief to eliminate the pattern or practice."

Private Civil Rights Litigation

Federal law also allows individuals to seek civil redress for violations of their legal rights. The applicable statute, 42 U.S.C. § 1983 (Section 1983), provides in relevant part:

> Every person who, under color of any statute, ordinance, regulation, custom, or usage, of any State. . . subjects, or causes to be subjected, any citizen of the United States or other person within the jurisdiction thereof to the deprivation of any rights, privileges, or immunities secured by the Constitution and laws, shall be liable to the party injured[.]

Unlike the other statutory provisions discussed above, Section 1983 creates a private right of action, meaning that anyone suffering a covered deprivation of rights may sue the persons responsible. Moreover, unlike Sections 241 and 242, courts have interpreted Section 1983 not to contain a specific intent requirement, making it easier for plaintiffs to prove violations of the statute. A prevailing Section 1983 plaintiff may be entitled to injunctive relief, attorney's fees, and/or money damages. Recovery may include both compensatory damages (designed to compensate the plaintiff for the legal injury) and punitive damages (designed to punish the defendant and deter future misconduct).

Similar to Section 242, Section 1983 applies to persons acting "under color of" state law. State and local public safety officers generally act under color of state law for purposes of Section 1983. However, based on concerns that frequent litigation could interfere with the work of law enforcement officers, the courts have created a significant limitation on liability: Under Section 1983, law enforcement officers benefit from qualified immunity from suit. The Supreme Court announced the modern qualified immunity test in Harlow v. Fitzgerald, holding that "government officials performing discretionary functions, generally are shielded from liability for civil damages" if they do not "violate clearly established statutory or constitutional rights of which a reasonable person would have known."

The Supreme Court has explained that qualified immunity is "an immunity from suit rather than a mere defense to liability; and like an absolute immunity, it is effectively lost if a case is erroneously permitted to go to trial." As a result, courts generally consider qualified immunity early in a Section 1983 case, and if the court finds that a defendant is not entitled to qualified immunity, the defendant is entitled to an immediate interlocutory appeal. A court evaluating a claim of qualified immunity considers two questions: (1) whether, viewed in the light most favorable to the plaintiff, "the facts alleged show the officer's conduct violated a constitutional right;" and (2) "whether the law clearly established that the officer's conduct was unlawful in the circumstances of the case." While that two-step analysis was once considered mandatory, in the 2009 case Pearson v. Callahan, the Supreme Court held that judges could "exercise their sound discretion in deciding which of the two prongs of the qualified immunity analysis should be addressed first." In a series of recent cases involving police use of force, the Supreme Court has reversed lower court denials of qualified immunity, stating that "clearly established law" must not be defined at a high level of generality and instead needs to be particularized to the facts of the case. This can create a high bar for plaintiffs.

The Supreme Court articulated another limitation on Section 1983 suits in Monell v. Department of Social Services. In that case, the Court held that a municipality is a "person" subject to suit under Section 1983. However, the Court further held that a local government cannot be sued "for an injury inflicted solely by its employees or agents" under the theory of respondeat superior (the legal doctrine that an employer may be liable to suit for wrongful acts of its employees). Rather, under Monell, a Section 1983 plaintiff must show that an injury stems from a "policy or custom" of the municipality. This requires a showing that "through its deliberate conduct, the municipality was the 'moving force' behind the injury alleged," and that the municipality acted with "deliberate indifference to the risk that a violation of a particular constitutional or statutory right will follow." This exacting standard has led one commentator to assert that municipal liability "is practically a dead letter." Plaintiffs may still sue individual officers under Section 1983, subject to the limitation of qualified immunity, but they may be less likely to recover significant damages or induce change in a municipality's practices.

Grant Conditions and Federal Oversight

The federal government provides financial support to state and local law enforcement in the form of grants, and may require states to enact certain policies to qualify for such funding. As one example, the Edward Byrne Memorial Justice Assistance Grant (Byrne JAG) Program provides federal support for state and local criminal justice programs. Among other conditions, states that receive Byrne JAG funding must certify compliance with the Death in Custody Reporting Act (DCRA). Enacted in 2014, the DCRA requires states to report to the Attorney General certain information regarding the deaths of individuals in the custody of law enforcement agencies. Byrne JAG grants have also been used to train officers on use of force and de-escalation of conflict. In addition to guiding state and local law enforcement policy through grant funding, federal government agencies independently collect data related to the use of force by state and local law enforcement.

Executive Orders

On June 16, 2020, President Donald Trump issued an Executive Order on Safe Policing for Safe Communities. Among other things, the 2020 executive order directed the Attorney General to establish best practices for law enforcement agencies; certify independent credentialing bodies that could assess agencies' policies in areas such as use of force, de-escalation, and identifying officers who may require intervention; and condition federal grants on compliance with those standards.

In addition, the 2020 executive order directed the Attorney General to create a database to track and publish data related to instances of excessive use of force by law enforcement, requiring law enforcement agencies that receive discretionary grant funding to submit information to the database. (Recent court rulings, however, have expressed skepticism of the executive branch's ability to unilaterally change conditions related to federal grants.) The executive order also required the Attorney General to develop and propose legislation to improve law enforcement practices and build community engagement, and to identify and develop opportunities to train law enforcement officers with respect to encounters with individuals suffering from impaired mental health, homelessness, and addiction.

On May 25, 2022, President Joe Biden issued an Executive Order on Advancing Effective, Accountable Policing and Criminal Justice Practices to Enhance Public Trust and Public Safety. Among other things, the 2022 executive order directed the Attorney General to take steps to enhance DOJ's enforcement of Section 242 and Section 12601. It sought to improve law enforcement recruitment, hiring, promotion, and retention practices at all levels. It also provided for the establishment of a National Law Enforcement Accountability Database; expanded collection of various criminal justice statistics; and sought to limit the transfer of military equipment to state, local, and tribal law enforcement.

The 2022 executive order imposed numerous requirements on federal law enforcement. It directed the Attorney General to ensure timely investigations into federal law enforcement uses of deadly force and deaths in federal custody. It also directed federal law enforcement agencies to ban the use of chokeholds and carotid restraints "except where the use of deadly force is authorized by law," limited the use of no-knock entries, required the use of body cameras in appropriate circumstances, called for clear guidance on use-of-force standards, and required anti-bias training for federal law enforcement officers.

Chapter 14

Regulating Federal Law Enforcement: Considerations for Congress*

Whitney K. Novak

Incidents involving the use of force by law enforcement, such as the 2020 death of George Floyd and the 2023 death of Tyre Nichols, have raised questions regarding Congress's authority to regulate law enforcement officers. While federalism principles limit the extent to which Congress may pass laws directly affecting state and local police officers, Congress has broader authority to regulate federal law enforcement officers and agencies such as the Federal Bureau of Investigation (FBI), the Drug Enforcement Administration (DEA), or Customs and Border Protection (CBP). This Sidebar explores the existing criminal, administrative, and civil remedies that impose liability on federal law enforcement officers for claims of excessive use of force, including those brought under the Bivens doctrine and the Federal Tort Claims Act (FTCA). It then concludes by discussing considerations for Congress regarding further regulation of federal law enforcement officers.

Current Law Regulating Federal Law Enforcement

Existing federal laws provide a number of criminal, administrative, and civil remedies to hold law enforcement officers and agencies accountable for misconduct.

---

* This is an edited, reformatted and augmented version of Congressional Research Service Publication No. LSB10500, updated February 23, 2023.

In: The Future of Law Enforcement
Editor: Mohamed Swift
ISBN: 979-8-89530-863-9

Federal Criminal Law

One way to regulate the behavior of federal law enforcement officers is through criminal law. The chief criminal law regulating federal, state, and local law enforcement officers is 18 U.S.C. § 242 (Section 242)—described in more depth in this Sidebar. In relevant part, that statute makes it a crime for a person "acting under the color of law" to deprive someone of their constitutionally protected rights. According to the U.S. Department of Justice (DOJ), under the color of law means that an individual is acting "using power given to him or her by a governmental agency," and it is irrelevant whether the actor is "exceeding his or her rightful power." The Supreme Court has explained that to successfully prosecute an alleged offender—such as a police officer—under Section 242, DOJ must show that the defendant had "a specific intent to deprive a person of a federal right made definite by decision or other rule of law." According to DOJ, which enforces Section 242, examples of misconduct prosecuted under the statute include "excessive force, sexual assault, intentional false arrests, theft, or the intentional fabrication of evidence resulting in a loss of liberty to another." Section 242 has been used in recent years to investigate Border Patrol agents, U.S. Park Police, and FBI agents. Violations of Section 242 are punishable by fine and/or up to a year in prison or, if certain aggravating factors are present, up to life in prison or death.

Administrative Remedies

Beyond criminal law, other federal guidelines and statutes provide more limited methods of remedying misconduct by federal law enforcement within the confines of a given agency. Agencies' internal policies may address how federal law enforcement agents conduct themselves in specific situations, including provisions on when the use of force is appropriate. For example, the Attorney General's Guidelines for Domestic FBI Operations instruct that "acts of violence" are not authorized unless FBI agents are engaging in the lawful use of force, such as in incidents of self-defense or "otherwise in the lawful discharge of their duties." Federal law enforcement agencies, similar to other federal agencies, have various legal avenues to address employees whose conduct departs from established norms, such as through censures, reprimands, suspensions, demotions, and removals.

Beyond the ordinary employee discipline process, federal law enforcement agencies may have other, more general processes to examine civil rights violations by federal agents. For example, Section 1001 of the USA PATRIOT Act directs the Office of the Inspector General (OIG) of DOJ to "review information and receive complaints alleging abuses of civil rights and civil liberties" by DOJ employees, including employees of the FBI; the DEA; the Federal Bureau of Prisons (BOP); the Bureau of Alcohol, Tobacco, Firearms, and Explosives; and the U.S. Marshals Service. DOJ has relied on this congressional directive to investigate allegations of civil rights violations against "ethnic and religious groups who would be vulnerable to abuse due to a possible backlash from the terrorist attacks of September 11, 2001." Under Section 1001, for example, the OIG has investigated allegations that BOP employees tortured a prisoner because of his Muslim religion. Pursuant to statutes like Section 1001 and more general authorities, inspectors general have sometimes investigated allegations of excessive use of force by federal law enforcement agents and reported findings to the DOJ Civil Rights Division for possible prosecution or other administrative misconduct.

Civil Remedies Under *Bivens* and the FTCA

Beyond criminal and administrative remedies that the government may use to address excessive use of force, some limited civil remedies also exist for individuals to seek redress against federal law enforcement officials for misconduct.

Bivens Claims

42 U.S.C. § 1983 (Section 1983), as discussed in more detail in this Legal Sidebar, is a federal law designed to prevent and redress constitutional violations, such as the right to be free from excessive force under the Fourth Amendment, by *state and local* government actors. No federal statute provides an equivalent cause of action against federal officials. Instead, the Supreme Court has recognized an implied cause of action, similar to the Section 1983 remedy, for individuals seeking money damages against individual federal law enforcement officers in certain circumstances.

In its 1971 decision *Bivens v. Six Unknown Named Agents of Federal Bureau of Narcotics*, the Supreme Court established that in limited circumstances, "victims of a constitutional violation by a federal agent have a right to recover damages against the official in federal court despite the absence of any statute conferring such a right." In *Bivens*, the plaintiff filed a claim against a group of federal narcotics agents after they conducted what he alleged to be an unconstitutional search of his home. The Court, in holding that the plaintiff could pursue money damages for his Fourth Amendment claim, reasoned that when federally protected rights have been "invaded," a plaintiff is entitled to a remedy—whether that remedy is statutorily or judicially created. Thus, the Court held that the Constitution implicitly includes a private cause of action for individuals seeking money damages for Fourth Amendment violations.

The Court recognized an implied remedy for constitutional violations committed by federal actors in two other circumstances following *Bivens*. In a 1979 case, *Davis v. Passman*, the Court held that an administrative assistant who sued a Congressman for gender discrimination could pursue a claim under the equal protection principles embodied in the Fifth Amendment's Due Process Clause. One year later, in *Carlson v. Green*, the Court extended a *Bivens* remedy to a federal prisoner's estate against the director of BOP for allegedly failing to provide adequate medical treatment in violation of the Eighth Amendment.

The Supreme Court has not recognized a new implied cause of action under *Bivens* in more than 30 years.

For example, the Court declined to extend a *Bivens* remedy in a First Amendment suit against a federal employer, in several Eighth Amendment cases brought against private prison officials under contract with BOP, and in a Fifth Amendment case for federal government interference with a landowner's property rights. The Court continued its trend of limiting *Bivens* remedies in its 2017 decision *Ziglar v. Abassi*. In declining to extend the doctrine, the Court noted that since *Bivens* was decided, the Court had "adopted a far more cautious course" in allowing recovery under judicially created causes of action, recognizing that it is a "significant step under separation-of-powers principles for a court to determine that it has the authority ... to create and enforce a cause of action for damages against federal officials in order to remedy a constitutional violation." As a result, further expansion of the *Bivens* doctrine, according to the Court, is now considered a "disfavored judicial activity."

The *Abassi* Court provided a two-part test used to determine whether a *Bivens* remedy is available. First, the Court looks at whether the case presents a "new context"—that is, whether the case differs meaningfully from the three cases where a *Bivens* remedy has been established. Second, if the case does present a new context, the Court considers whether there are "special factors" counseling against creating a remedy. If any such factors are present, then the *Bivens* approach of an implied remedy is inappropriate.

Central to this analysis, according to the Court, are separation-of-powers principles, and the Court has declined to extend *Bivens* remedies in cases implicating issues more appropriate for the other branches, such as federal fiscal policy or international relations. The Court has most recently declined to extend a *Bivens* remedy in the 2020 case *Hernandez v. Mesa* and the 2022 case *Egbert v. Boule*.

Despite these limitations on the *Bivens* doctrine, the Court has emphasized that *Bivens* itself is "well- settled law," and it continues to allow for claims against federal actors for money damages in the three limited contexts the Court has already recognized, including those against federal law enforcement officers for violations of the Fourth Amendment—such as claims alleging excessive use of force.

Nonetheless, even if a federal court allows a plaintiff to pursue a *Bivens* remedy for an alleged constitutional violation by a federal official, qualified immunity—discussed in more depth in this Sidebar—may shield that federal official from liability.

The FTCA

The FTCA also provides a remedy for the wrongful acts of federal officials, including federal law enforcement. Subject to various exceptions, limitations, and prerequisites, the FTCA—enacted in 1946— allows plaintiffs to sue the United States for money damages for certain types of state law torts committed by its employees. The FTCA acts as a waiver of federal sovereign immunity in limited cases involving tortious acts—such as negligence—committed by federal employees within the scope of their employment. In contrast to a *Bivens* claim, which is brought against the individual official, an action brought pursuant to the FTCA is one against the United States. The FTCA does not allow such a suit until the plaintiff first exhausts administrative remedies in the relevant federal agency.

Generally, plaintiffs may not recover for intentional torts, such as assault or battery, committed by federal employees. However, in 1974—in response to a series of no-knock drug enforcement raids by federal law enforcement agents on private homes—Congress amended the FTCA to allow for claims of intentional torts of assault, battery, false imprisonment, false arrest, abuse of process, and malicious prosecution committed by certain federal law enforcement officers. The amendment applies to "investigative or law enforcement officer[s]," which is defined as "any officer of the United States who is empowered by law to (1) execute searches, (2) seize evidence, or (3) make arrests for violations of Federal law."

Congress enacted the 1974 FTCA amendment nearly three years after the Supreme Court's *Bivens* decision. In 1980, the Court clarified that the 1974 amendment to the FTCA did not preempt a *Bivens* claim, meaning that the judicially created *Bivens* remedies were still available to plaintiffs who could also bring FTCA claims. In reaching its decision, the Court emphasized that Congress had expressed its intent that the FTCA and *Bivens* actions be "parallel, complementary causes of action." The Court also highlighted four factors that suggested that the *Bivens* remedy is more "effective" than the FTCA and therefore a *Bivens* claim should coexist with claims brought under the FTCA: (1) the *Bivens* remedy serves a "deterrent purpose" because it seeks damages against individual officers; (2) a court may award punitive damages in a *Bivens* suit, while 28 U.S.C. § 2674 generally prohibits courts from awarding punitive damages against the United States in FTCA cases; (3) a plaintiff cannot opt for a jury trial in an FTCA action; and (4) an action under the FTCA exists only if the state in which the alleged misconduct occurred has a law prohibiting the conduct.

In 1988, Congress passed the Westfall Act to substitute the United States as the defendant in FTCA claims to "protect Federal employees from personal liability for common law torts committed within the scope of their employment." Congress did not extend the Westfall Act's protections for individual federal employees who commit *constitutional violations*, thus effectively preserving the *Bivens* remedy.

Therefore, FTCA claims against the United States for certain intentional torts committed by federal law enforcement may remain available alongside the limited *Bivens* actions available against individual federal law enforcement officials. Some courts, however, have interpreted provisions of the FTCA to preclude recovery under both the FTCA and a *Bivens* action. Thus, in some jurisdictions, plaintiffs must choose whether to proceed under the FTCA or *Bivens*.

Considerations for Congress

As Congress continues to explore police reform proposals, one consideration has been whether existing law adequately regulates federal law enforcement. Police reform bills introduced in the 116th and 117th Congresses included several proposed reforms that would have regulated how federal officers operate in the field. The JUSTICE Acts of 2020 and of 2021, for example, included provisions that would have directed the Attorney General to develop a policy banning the use of chokeholds by federal law enforcement agents except in situations involving deadly force. The Justice in Policing Acts of 2020 and 2021 (JIPA) would have banned no-knock warrants in drug cases at the federal level and would have required federal law enforcement officers to use deadly force only as a last resort when necessary to prevent death or serious bodily injury. (A more detailed overview of the provisions in these bills can be found in this Sidebar.)

These and other proposals would have more broadly restructured existing criminal and administrative remedies regulating federal law enforcement officers. Provisions in both the JUSTICE Act and the JIPA sought to create or amend existing criminal liability for police, including federal officers. For example, Section 106 of the JUSTICE Acts of 2020 and 2021 would have created a new criminal offense for "knowingly and willfully falsify[ing] a report" that involved a law enforcement officer's violation of an individual's constitutional rights. Section 101 of the JIPA of 2020 and 2021 would have amended the mental state required for a conviction under Section 242, changing it from "willfully" to "knowingly or recklessly." Other bills would have imposed additional *administrative* oversight of federal law enforcement agencies. Legislation introduced in the 116th Congress, such as H.R. 2203 and S. 2691, and in the 117th Congress, such as H.R. 3557, would have established a position within the Department of Homeland Security that would have addressed complaints related to the CBP and Immigration and Customs Enforcement and required training on the use of force and civil rights violations.

Legislation introduced in the 116th and 117th Congresses would also have reformed *civil* liability for law enforcement. Many of these efforts focused on Section 1983, which would have had no effect on federal law enforcement. For example, H.R. 7085/S. 4142, the Ending Qualified Immunity Act, and S. 4036, the Reforming Qualified Immunity Act (introduced in the 116th Congress), would have abolished or curtailed qualified immunity under Section 1983. (The Ending Qualified Immunity Act was reintroduced in the

House and the Senate in the 117th Congress). Because Section 1983 applies only to state and local officials, these proposals would not have applied to federal law enforcement in *Bivens* actions. The JIPA, however, would also have abrogated the qualified immunity defense in "any action under any source of law against" federal investigative or law enforcement officers, as defined in 28 U.S.C. § 2680(h). This provision would have appeared to eliminate the availability of qualified immunity in *Bivens* actions.

With regard to *Bivens* actions generally, although the Supreme Court has recognized an implied cause of action for Fourth Amendment violations committed by federal law enforcement, as discussed above, the Court has expressed disfavor with extending the *Bivens* doctrine to new contexts. According to some commentators, this judicial restraint in extending *Bivens* leaves individuals without a civil damages remedy against many federal actors who may have violated their constitutional rights. The Court's caution in this area, however, is explicitly intended to allow Congress to consider remedies for such violations, and the Court has continued to emphasize that point in recent cases. Congress, therefore, could choose to create a Section-1983-type action for claims against federal officials. In creating a new statutory cause of action, Congress could establish its parameters, including which federal officials would be liable, what federal rights would be protected, and whether officials are entitled to qualified immunity. For example, Congress could make all federal officials liable for violations of all constitutional rights—much as Section 1983 does for state and local officials—or could limit the remedy to cases involving federal law enforcement officials who commit certain Fourth Amendment violations, such as excessive use of force.

If Congress chose to create a cause of action specifically for money damages against federal officials, it could also decide whether to make the individual actor liable, as in Section 1983, or whether the action would be against the United States, as in the FTCA. Members of Congress have in the past proposed legislation to allow recovery against the United States for constitutional violations committed by federal employees. Exposing the United States or federal employees to liability may present other policy considerations such as increased costs to the federal government in paying for judgments and additional burdens on the federal agencies in defending such lawsuits.

Index

A

artificial intelligence, 2, 10, 55

B

bias, 56, 138, 145, 204, 215
Border Patrol, 3, 28, 218
border security, 15
budget cuts, 104, 112, 142
budgetary resources, 176
bullying, 65, 95
Bureau of Alcohol, Tobacco, Firearms, and Explosives, 7, 18, 23, 64, 219
Bureau of Indian Affairs (BIA), 109
Bureau of Justice Assistance (BJA), 10, 13, 14, 30, 31, 39, 46, 47, 60, 61, 65, 66, 77, 118, 129, 134
Bureau of Justice Statistics (BJS), 3, 60, 116, 131

C

civil liberties, 3, 10, 11, 18, 19, 22, 23, 25, 27, 57, 219
civil rights, 10, 11, 18, 22, 23, 27, 57, 68, 203, 219, 223
communication, 17, 19, 33, 35, 36, 37, 52, 126, 171
Communications Act, 41
Communications Decency Act, 42
constitution, 22, 88, 195, 199, 200, 207, 209, 210, 211, 212, 220
counterterrorism, 27
criminal behavior, 121, 126, 150
criminal investigations, 3, 6, 27
criminal justice system, 2, 7, 10, 57, 60, 70, 105, 106, 144, 149, 153, 154, 161, 163, 164, 165, 166, 172, 178, 187
crisis management, 149, 157, 159
critical infrastructure, 92, 93, 96
Customs and Border Protection, 14, 18, 28, 217
cybersecurity, 25

D

deprivation, 58, 198, 207, 210, 212
detention, vii, 168
deterrence, 121, 123
discrimination, 57, 197, 198, 199, 220
domestic violence, 8, 84
Drug Enforcement Administration (DEA), 6, 18, 23, 26, 112, 138, 143, 217
drug trafficking, 6

E

education, 31, 61, 62, 65, 66, 67, 70, 159, 164, 175, 176, 196
E-Government Act, 15
e-learning, 79
electronic communications, 50, 51, 52
electronic surveillance, 12, 29, 50
encryption, 42, 49, 51, 52, 53
ethnic minority, 106
ethnicity, 9
exploitation, 41, 42, 50

F

Federal Bureau of Investigation (FBI), 2, 4, 6, 7, 8, 9, 10, 18, 23, 26, 28, 29, 40, 43, 44, 45, 82, 86, 91, 217, 218, 219
federal law, 2, 4, 5, 6, 9, 11, 12, 14, 15, 17, 18, 19, 20, 21, 22, 24, 25, 28, 29, 30, 33, 37, 39, 41, 47, 57, 58, 85, 93, 135, 195, 202, 205, 206, 214, 217, 218, 219, 221, 222, 223, 224
federalism, 182, 217
Fifth Amendment, 220
financial support, 172, 178, 197, 213
First Amendment, 18, 22, 27, 28, 34, 43, 199, 220
fiscal policy, 221
Fourteenth Amendment, 196, 198, 210
Fourth Amendment, 199, 219, 220, 221, 224

H

homeland security, 9, 71, 96, 108
homelessness, 144, 184, 214

I

Immigration and Customs Enforcement (ICE), 18, 27, 223
information technology, 15, 25

J

juvenile justice, 60, 66, 163, 164, 166, 178

M

mental disorder, 67, 149
mental illness, 66, 109, 110, 148, 149, 150, 151, 158, 161, 162, 166, 168, 170, 176, 178, 179, 182, 188
mentoring, 86, 110, 111
methamphetamine, 60, 73, 110, 112, 117, 138, 142, 143
militarization, 204

N

National Center for Missing and Exploited Children, 41
National Crime Information Center, 7, 8, 9
National Defense Authorization Act, 204

P

perpetrators, 151
platform, 22, 34, 35, 38, 39, 40, 41, 42, 52
police, 1, 3, 4, 5, 6, 13, 19, 37, 39, 56, 59, 60, 63, 72, 81, 82, 83, 85, 94, 95, 97, 104, 105, 106, 115, 116, 121, 123, 125, 126, 128, 129, 130, 131, 132, 133, 134, 136, 141, 144, 145, 147, 148, 149, 150, 152, 153, 154, 156, 157, 158, 159, 161, 162, 164, 167, 176, 179, 180, 184, 186, 187, 188, 189, 190, 191, 192, 193, 197, 198, 199, 200, 201, 202, 204, 206, 209, 213, 217, 218, 223
policy, 9, 10, 11, 12, 13, 15, 18, 24, 25, 26, 27, 29, 46, 47, 48, 57, 66, 86, 122, 129, 135, 158, 159, 173, 182, 196, 203, 207, 213, 221, 223, 224
policy problems, 182
poor relationships, 125
population, 69, 91, 119, 150, 151, 170
positive interactions, 36, 130
prevention, 5, 36, 59, 60, 61, 65, 75, 77, 79, 82, 105, 129, 132, 134, 141, 175
principles, 38, 131, 196, 217, 220, 221
prisoners, 72
prisons, 165
private information, 40
problem-solving, 36, 105, 128, 129, 130, 132
procedural justice, 128
procurement, 25, 26, 59, 60
programming, 111, 166, 175
property crimes, 121
property rights, 220
Prosecutorial Remedies and Other Tools to End the Exploitation of Children Today (PROTECT) Act, 108

protection, 11, 15, 22, 25, 198, 220
Public Health Service Act, 172
public safety, vii, 7, 18, 19, 28, 35, 43, 44, 46, 53, 64, 66, 82, 85, 99, 104, 106, 119, 120, 121, 123, 128, 129, 130, 159, 163, 164, 183, 186, 187, 201, 204, 209, 210, 212

R

race, 9, 27, 56, 197, 210
racial equity, 67
racism, 208
recession, 112, 142
recidivism, 66, 67, 187
recognition, 4, 19, 29, 56, 57, 58
recruiting, 57, 103, 111, 124
reform(s), 45, 77, 124, 126, 127, 128, 135, 138, 143, 144, 145, 147, 195, 200, 201, 202, 204, 205, 206, 209, 223
regulations, 22, 23, 24, 25, 27, 46, 52, 171
religion, 9, 27, 219
resolution, 78, 79, 105
restrictions, 19, 30, 34, 38, 39, 45
restructuring, 112, 142
rights, 2, 10, 11, 18, 22, 23, 27, 43, 57, 58, 68, 198, 202, 203, 205, 207, 210, 211, 212, 218, 219, 220, 223, 224
risk(s), 11, 15, 25, 30, 43, 56, 57, 84, 97, 149, 164, 187, 204, 213
rules, 11, 23, 24, 34, 38, 42, 130, 173

S

safety, vii, 7, 8, 18, 19, 21, 22, 27, 28, 35, 41, 42, 43, 44, 46, 53, 57, 59, 60, 64, 66, 79, 82, 83, 84, 85, 95, 96, 98, 99, 104, 106, 119, 120, 121, 123, 128, 129, 130, 156, 158, 159, 163, 164, 168, 183, 186, 187, 191, 193, 199, 201, 204, 209, 210, 212
saving lives, 83
secret service, 94
security, 5, 9, 10, 12, 13, 14, 18, 23, 25, 26, 28, 43, 44, 50, 53, 56, 57, 71, 72, 76, 82, 83, 92, 93, 94, 95, 96, 97, 98, 108, 117, 164
security threats, 44
service provider, 40, 41, 42, 50, 51, 53, 129
social problems, 144
software, 5, 52, 53, 56, 177, 181
solidarity, 83
solution, 86, 94
specialists, 156, 158, 186
spending, 111, 112, 113, 142, 173, 174, 196, 197, 200
state laws, 19, 182
statistics, 214
statutes, 11, 209, 210, 218, 219
statutory provisions, 212
structure, 101, 102, 103, 104, 108, 117, 118
subpoena, 34, 40, 52, 53, 205
substance abuse, 66, 109, 164, 185
Substance Abuse and Mental Health Services Administration (SAMHSA), 148, 160, 170, 171
substance use, 67, 164, 168, 174, 188, 190, 193
substance use disorders, 67, 164
suicidal ideation, 151
suicide, 75, 79, 95, 160, 164, 185, 188
suicide attempts, 188
support services, 51, 63, 165, 174
surveillance, 12, 26, 27, 28, 29, 50
suspensions, 218

T

tactics, 128, 204, 207
target, 59, 87, 97, 202
Task Force, 36, 37, 45, 72, 126, 132, 138
teams, 62, 65, 105, 133, 148, 153, 157, 158, 159, 165, 171, 178, 184, 185, 188, 190, 191, 192, 193
techniques, 34, 39, 123, 128, 141
telecommunications, 50, 51, 52
tension(s), 13, 42, 51
territorial, 23, 24, 25, 31, 58, 62, 63, 68, 69, 71, 72, 74, 75, 77, 82, 96

terrorism, 8, 79, 93
terrorist attack(s), 97, 219
terrorist organization, 44
theft, 3, 210, 218
threatening behavior, 94, 95
threats, 44, 61, 92, 93, 94, 95, 96, 98, 126, 151, 185
trafficking, 6, 56, 72
training, 11, 23, 24, 26, 56, 57, 58, 59, 60, 62, 65, 70, 71, 74, 76, 77, 78, 79, 85, 88, 91, 93, 95, 96, 102, 105, 109, 110, 113, 117, 124, 127, 137, 141, 143, 145, 148, 149, 150, 151, 154, 155, 156, 158, 159, 161, 163, 164, 165, 166, 167, 176, 180, 181, 182, 204, 206, 207, 215, 223
training programs, 63, 181, 206
transport, 72, 98, 157
Tribal Law and Order Act, 109
tribal police, 6

U

unreasonable searches, 199
USA PATRIOT Act, 219
user data, 34, 43

V

variables, 122
variations, 156
vehicles, 1, 2, 4, 5, 7, 8, 10, 11, 31, 157, 204
victims, 8, 21, 56, 69, 151, 220
videos, 1, 4, 29, 38
violence, 8, 44, 59, 65, 75, 76, 77, 78, 79, 82, 83, 84, 85, 126, 135, 150, 151, 183, 185, 190, 218
violent behavior, 178
violent crime, 60, 61, 62, 64, 69, 70, 71, 77, 82, 122, 133, 134, 145, 151

W

war, 88, 98, 163
weapons, 19, 27, 56, 82, 83, 95, 105, 158, 185, 190
weapons of mass destruction, 27
wiretaps, 12, 29, 52
witnesses, 36, 81, 82
workers, 63, 66, 159, 160, 189
workforce, 84, 125
working conditions, 87